SHATTERING EUROPE'S DEFENSE CONSENSUS

Pergamon Titles of Related Interest

Schelling & Halperin STRATEGY AND ARMS CONTROL
Tsipis & Janeway REVIEW OF MILITARY RESEARCH AND
DEVELOPMENT 1984

Related Journals*

DEFENSE ANALYSIS

***Free specimen copies available upon request.**

SHATTERING EUROPE'S DEFENSE CONSENSUS

The Antinuclear Protest Movement and the Future of NATO

Edited by James E. Dougherty and Robert L. Pfaltzgraff, Jr.

PERGAMON-BRASSEY'S
International Defense Publishers

Washington New York Oxford London Toronto Sydney Frankfurt

Pergamon Press Offices:

U.S.A.   Pergamon-Brassey's International Defense Publishers,
                       1340 Old Chain Bridge Road, McLean, Virginia, 22101, U.S.A.

                       Pergamon Press Inc., Maxwell House, Fairview Park,
                       Elmsford, New York 10523, U.S.A.

U.K.   Pergamon Press Ltd., Headington Hill Hall,
                       Oxford OX3 0BW, England

CANADA   Pergamon Press Canada Ltd., Suite 104, 150 Consumers Road,
                       Willowdale, Ontario M2J 1P9, Canada

AUSTRALIA   Pergamon Press (Aust.) Pty. Ltd., P.O. Box 544,
                       Potts Point, NSW 2011, Australia

FEDERAL REPUBLIC   Pergamon Press GmbH, Hammerweg 6,
OF GERMANY   D-6242 Kronberg-Taunus, Federal Republic of Germany

Library of Congress Cataloging in Publication Data
Main entry under title:

Shattering Europe's defense consensus.

    Includes bibliographies.
    1. North Atlantic Treaty Organization--Addresses,
essays, lectures. 2. Antinuclear movement--Europe--
Addresses, essays, lectures. 3. Europe--Military
policy--Addresses, essays, lectures. 4. Nuclear
weapons--Europe--Addresses, essays, lectures.
5. Intermediate-range ballistic missiles--Addresses,
essays, lectures. 6. Cruise missiles--Addresses,
essays, lectures. I. Dougherty, James E.
II. Pfaltzgraff, Robert L.
UA646.3.S436   1985   355'.0335'73   85-12013
ISBN 0-08-032770-2

Contents

Chapter 1

Strategy, Politics, and Ethical Feelings: A Perspective of the Protest Movement

James E. Dougherty

The fifteen months during which Yuri Andropov served as head of the Soviet Communist party and government—from November 1982 to February 1984—were dominated by a titanic propaganda effort on the part of Moscow to prevent NATO from carrying out the "two-track decision" which it had taken at Brussels in December 1979. According to that decision, taken unanimously, the members of the Atlantic Alliance agreed to modernize NATO's European nuclear capabilities on schedule by deploying 108 Pershing-2 missiles in West Germany and 464 ground-launched cruise missiles (GLCMs) in five West European countries—160 in Britain, 112 in Italy, 96 in the Federal Republic, and 48 each in Belgium and the Netherlands—while the United States was negotiating the European nuclear missile balance with the USSR.

The Soviet leadership was determined to assert for itself a monopoly of the right to modernize Eurostrategic nuclear forces. The Soviet political warfare machine rolled into high gear to convince the Europeans and the world that the European military balance, which Soviet spokesmen proclaimed to be in existence a decade earlier, was being strengthened by the deployment of more than 240 SS-20s (each with three nuclear warheads), whereas NATO's new comparable intermediate-range missiles, the first ever to be deployed on European soil, would upset both the European and the central strategic balance. Andropov virtually staked his political career on the effort to exercise an effective Soviet veto over a NATO decision, and he counted heavily on the West European antinuclear protest movement to accomplish his purposes. This book deals with that movement and attempts to show why Andropov almost succeeded in his aim before NATO demonstrated that it could do what it had to do for its own defense late in 1983, a few months before Andropov's death.

The antinuclear protest movement in Western Europe began in earnest during the period 1977–1978. It came to birth with a public victory in the Netherlands over an issue which, from a political standpoint, had been badly managed by U.S. policy makers—the projected deployment of the enhanced radiation warhead (ERW, or the misnamed "neutron bomb") as a means of strengthening NATO deterrence and defense capabilities in Europe. The merits of the military case for ERW deployment within the NATO area are not directly relevant to the purposes of this study. The fact is that the Carter administration was made to look diplomatically inept. As a result of poor planning and inadequate preparation on the part of U.S. officials, the European leftists and other critics of the United States and its military policies were handed an unexpected propaganda windfall—the notion of the perfect "capitalist weapon" that kills people, but leaves property intact. With the memory of the Vietnam War fading, the militant protesters against U.S. involvement in that conflict had nowhere to go. Their organization was on the verge of collapse. Suddenly, the Interchurch Peace Council of the Netherlands (IKV) was amazed to find itself able to collect more than a million signatures—almost ten percent of the Dutch population—expressing opposition to the storage of "neutron bombs" on European soil. Quickened as if by a shot of adrenalin, the moribund antiwar movement gained a new lease on life.

It would be not only misleading but grossly distorting to suggest that the contemporary peace movement in Western Europe is comprised largely of "hippie" war resisters, pacifists, social dropouts, and alienated intellectuals who figured so visibly more than a decade ago in Amsterdam, Stockholm, Copenhagen, and some German cities. To be sure, many of the organizers of the spectacular demonstrations, which attracted hundreds of thousands of participants in several NATO capitals during the fall of 1981, were activists who had acquired their crowd-manipulation skills in those years of national trauma for the United States. But even during the earlier period, the countercultural cadres enjoyed some measure of political success because they managed to win support from large numbers of middle-class voters who were not given to militant activism. It is even more true now to say that the antinuclear peace movement, which emerged in the late 1970s and early 1980s — specifically, the campaign against NATO missile modernization — is led largely by ideologically committed, militant, self-righteous, intolerant countercultural cadres (to be described more fully later) but depends on people who by no stretch of the imagination fit into the cadre stereotype for its political significance. The numbers are supplied by church groups (clergy, nuns, and laity), women's groups, labor organizations, environmentalists, peace societies (some headed by former military officers), political parties, scientific groups, businesspeople, university professors, journalists, writers, physicians, students, civil servants, and other "respectable" elements from a wide spectrum of socio-economic backgrounds. Indeed, it may well be that the active cadres have now been swollen by the addition of people who were part of the age cohort of the anti-Vietnam generation but who never became involved at the time and who later wanted to "catch up" on that exciting "socializing experience" they missed earlier, if not to allay vague, residual feelings of incompletion, non-fulfillment or guilt after having earlier let down the "vanguard" of their generation.* In short, participation in the peace-through-appeasement movement today can furnish at least a partially satisfying psychological sense not only of being personally redeemed but also of becoming a part of the process of salvation for a society under increasing assault from without and self-incrimination from within because of its collective and institutional sins. The one-sided antinuclear protest, which began in Western Europe — one-sided because it is for all practical purposes aimed only at the United States and NATO — received so much attention from the media that it quickly took on a transatlantic character and contributed to the rapid growth of the campaign for a nuclear freeze in this country.

At this point, a few caveats are in order. It has become fashionable for commentators to speak of a West European "peace movement," a term which contains at least two seriously misleading implications. *First*, it implies that those who are seriously concerned about peace have come together in one great, broadening stream while those who have not yet joined are indifferent to the problem of maintaining peace, and that those who disagree with the movement, as well as its goals and methods, are actually opposed to peace and in favor of nuclear war. *Second*, it implies that the "peace movement" is a single, homogeneous sociological-political entity, with all the participants marching together in one display of solidarity. Both implications reflect fundamental distortions of reality that leading figures in the movement find to their advantage to perpetuate as a means of exaggerating their own political strength and which the mass media, with

---

*The author is grateful to his colleague, Charles M. Perry, for contributing this insight.

their penchant for simplistic stereotypes, find convenient to accept and propagate, insofar as they assume that the "masses" would become confused by the subtle distinctions that mark accurate reporting.

The peace movement has no monopoly either on peace or on moral virtue. In fact, one can adduce no historical evidence in support of the hypothesis that peace movements or political pacifist organizations have ever prevented a war. We can, however, cite one significant instance in modern times when pacifist and anti-defense sentiment in France, Britain, and the Low Countries contributed to a climate of defeatism, unilateral disarmament for economic motives, and appeasement which emboldened the fascist dictators to believe that they could safely indulge their aggressive appetites. Few writers have ever described the consequences of interwar pacifism as trenchantly as the eminent historian of nationalism, Hans Kohn:

> Pacifism—entirely legitimate as a religious pattern of life, as a witness through sacrifice and martyrdom, and, as such, a salt of the earth and a reminder of the verities—underwent a strange corruption. It began to cater to the egotism and understandable longing for peace of the people, promising them peace and happiness only if they would not declare their readiness for timely action. Thus pacifism, by helping to dull the understanding of the present situation and undermining the will to intelligent and timely resistance and the necessary preparations for it, objectively supported plans of aggression. By a supreme irony the pacifists thus helped the most antipacific force on earth. From this point it was only a slight step to a pacifism asserting that the totalitarians really meant peace, in a more or less veiled way accepting most of their pretexts and excuses, and finally justifying Hitler or Stalin and finding fault with their victims. The principle of nonresistance to evil is a great principle if men carry it out, listening only to the voice within themselves, and ready to bear all martyrdom for its sake. It becomes something entirely different if it is transferred to the political scene . . . not in absolute earnestness, but in an argument as to the time when a nation should defend itself, whether in an unchristian egotism only when its own frontiers are invaded, or wisely and courageously helping fellow victims of potential aggression. The principle of nonresistance to evil degenerated into a denial that evil exists, into an appeal to accept the evil and to condone injustice. Thus pacifism, instead of bearing witness to the verities, became in the universal crisis one of the elements which could be used and abused by the aggressor nations for the destruction of the verities.[1]

It is a basic premise of this study that mass movements of political pacifism seldom if ever strengthen genuine peace and actually may jeopardize the conditions necessary for a stable peace by introducing lopsided disturbances into an existing equilibrium, interfering with diplomatic negotiations that could otherwise solidify the balance and reduce international tensions, and tempting expansionist powers to press their fortune to its utmost limits, if not by intentionally going to war then by increasing political pressure upon other states to make concessions which curtail their freedom of action. In such a situation, the more dynamic and aggressive party may be induced to undertake imprudent risks which lead to unintended war. We must remember that decisions for war or peace in the contemporary world are made by bureaucratic governments, not by numbers of citizens, however large, who demonstrate for this or that position with regard to the deployment of weapons. It is also governments, *not* individuals, peace organizations, political parties, women's groups, universities, ecologists, or churches, which ultimately determine the policy choices to be made concerning the maintenance of effective deterrence and the combination of diplomatic and military strategies best calculated to produce satisfactory results from arms control negotiations. Antinuclear protest movements — a more accurate designation than "peace movement" (and the one we prefer to use in this text) — are not significant in themselves (just as public opinion polls are not) except insofar as they influence the outcome of elections in democratic parliamentary systems. As we shall see in the course of this study, antinuclear demonstrations and threats of civil disobedience or direct violent action by "extra-parliamentary" lovers of peace can often generate by a dialectical process an electoral effect the very opposite of the one sought. Demonstrators thrive on threatening incumbent governments with dire consequences unless all their irresponsible demands are fully and immediately met. But in the final analysis, it is the voters who select the power-wielding personnel who in turn determine the policies of the state.

There is no monolithic "peace movement" in Western Europe. Just as we cannot speak about "West Europeans" in general without distinguishing among nation-states, social stratifications, and vertical groupings (religious, linguistic, political party, occupational, professional, and so on), so it is essential to keep several distinctions in mind when dealing with the antinuclear protest, for this differs characteristically from Britain to Germany, from the Netherlands to Italy and France. Peace organizations, political parties, churches, trade unions, women's and ecologists' groups approach the issues of nuclear weapons within their unique frame of reference based on their interests, values, and ideologies. They emphasize different themes, strategies, tactics, goals, and rationales according to their respective outlooks.

Some protesters are nuclear pacifists; others, absolute pacifists, opposed to all military programs. Some insist that they favor the retention of NATO, which enjoys popular support throughout Western Europe; others despise NATO because it depends upon a strategy of extended nuclear deterrence and demand a dissolution of the two alliances, beginning with NATO if necessary, so that Europe can become "neutral" in the rivalry of the superpowers. Some antinuclearists want disarmament, but only if it is negotiated on a multilateral, equitable basis with adequate safeguards; others call for unilateral disarmament by their own governments regardless of what others do. Some appear to be sincere in their condemnation of all nuclear weapons; others who believe (and openly declare) that the United States represents a greater threat than the Soviet Union work primarily to get rid of American weapons. Component groups within the movement often clash sharply over ideological issues and political tactics (e.g., passive, nonviolent resistance or violent and terroristic actions). The antinuclear movement frequently appears to be a house divided. But even its internal divisions and arguments impart to it a certain dynamic ability to sustain a high level of interest and excitement in the intervals between large-scale demonstrations and dramatic "direct actions." Within recent years, all of the groups that flow into the antinuclear movement, regardless of their squabbles, have managed to coalesce successfully in the common cause of opposing the deployment of U.S. cruise and Pershing-2 missiles. Now that four NATO countries—Britain, the Federal German Republic, Italy, and Belgium—have firmly committed themselves to proceed with deployment, the coalition has undergone strains and shown signs of disintegrating, as we shall see.

The antinuclear protest movement is not a totally new phenomenon in Western Europe. During the mid-1950s, the West German Social Democratic Party (SPD), highly skeptical of Adenauer's policy of joining the Atlantic Alliance, supported the "Gottingen Appeal" in 1957 and the *Kampf dem Atomtod* ("The Struggle against Atomic Death"), which brought hundreds of thousands into the streets for several days in 1958 against the decision to arm the *Bundeswehr* with nuclear-capable delivery systems.[2] In the early 1960s, Britain's Labour Left joined in the Aldermaston marches as part of the Campaign for Nuclear Disarmament (CND), which was aimed at the British independent deterrent. Neither of those campaigns was virulently anti-American, or even as anti-American as Gaullism, which was certainly not antinuclear. Concerning the earlier protest movements and the contrast between them and the later one, *The Economist* editorialized as follows:

> In the past—in the 1950s, and again in the 1960s—the ban-the-bomb movement gathered support for a time but then saw its support trickle away when people had time to consider the matter coolly. The case for rejecting nuclear weapons was, on calm reflection, itself rejected. But this time the necessary coolness is in shorter supply, because people are more frightened. They are frightened because Russia has grown militarily stronger in the past dozen years, and seems to be willing to use its new strength to get its way in the world: the risk of war, it seems, has grown.

The fear is understandable but it is a bad reason for turning anti-nuclear. If the argument against throwing away nuclear weapons is that these things are the only way of avoiding either a war with Russia or a capitulation to Russian demands, then the growth in Russian power does not weaken the pro-nuclear argument; it strengthens it. . . . Revulsion at what the use of nuclear weapons would do to others, and fear about what it would do to oneself, are legitimate emotions; but they do not lead to clear thinking. . . . By the test of common sense, the arguments of those who want to abandon nuclear weapons do not stand up to examination.[3]

It is important at the outset to pose this question: To what extent is the antinuclear protest movement the result of a heightened sense of morality within the West and to what extent is it a product of fear—fear that nuclear war is becoming more likely than it was in the past, not because of U.S. strategic policies (on which the protestors publicly blame it, for the most part) but more so because of a vague and seldom, if ever, articulated perception by the Western antinuclearists that both the objective military balance (nuclear and conventional) and the political will to employ military power in support of foreign policy (a combination which Soviet strategists call the "world correlation of forces") has shifted to the Soviet Union? In this connection, it is interesting to note that when the United States began deploying tactical nuclear weapons in Western Europe in the late 1950s, the first NATO country to welcome them on its territory was the Netherlands.[4] The Dutch then believed that the presence of such weapons would strengthen deterrence against any Soviet attack, particularly since the United States at that time enjoyed unquestioned nuclear superiority.

More than a decade ago, when the assumption became widespread that the two superpowers were entering upon an era of strategic parity, European analysts began to worry seriously about the regional military imbalance in Europe, where the Soviet Union had always held a quantitative conventional edge (especially in armor) and was correcting its nuclear deficiency by deploying nuclear weapons of longer range than most of those in the NATO inventory. During the latter 1970s, increasing numbers of defense analysts in the West expressed concern over the long-term trends at both the strategic (or inter-continental) level and the Eurostrategic (or regional) level. The United States over the course of two decades had moved from a clear margin of nuclear superiority toward parity and perhaps something less, while the Soviet Union had moved from nuclear inferiority toward parity and seemed bent on achieving superiority. Not a single knowledgeable observer in the 70s suggested that the curves were moving in the other direction. So long as the U.S. strategic nuclear deterrent, based on the McNamara Doctrine of Mutual Assured Destruction, was thought to be credible and effective, only a handful of writers in the

West criticized it on moral grounds. But the number of morally sensitive consciences multiplied rapidly once the massive Soviet military build-up had led to a significant erosion of Western deterrence credibility.

Years ago, de Gaulle had often expressed skepticism over the degree to which the West Europeans could rely for their defense upon the willingness of the United States to place its own cities at risk. All through the era of de Gaulle, most Europeans retained confidence in the success of the U.S. deterrent policy. The French president, however, turned out to be something of a prophet, for as the West Europeans listened to increasingly ominous reports in the 1970s about the deployment of heavy Soviet strategic missiles (SS-17s, SS-18s, and SS-19s) and Soviet preparations for the deployment of intermediate-range missiles that could target Western Europe (SS-20s), their apprehensiveness rose, particularly when they heard American strategists and policy makers say that the U.S. nuclear arsenal could no longer deter the full range of threats posed by the Soviet Union, with its recently acquired capabilities. If the United States no longer possessed an assured capability of destroying all the targets necessary to inflict an unacceptable amount of damage in retaliation and had to think seriously about modifying its strategic doctrine in the direction of "selective counterforce targeting" and "limited nuclear options," as well as the option to "launch on warning/assessment," many in Western Europe lost confidence in the effectiveness of deterrence and felt that nuclear war was becoming less unthinkable and therefore more likely to occur. Moreover, the Europeans took it for granted that if nuclear war could be limited, it would probably be limited to Europe while the territory of the two superpowers would be spared. At that point, strategic analysis began to be displaced by moral theology and by mounting fears for biological survival.

Fear of the expanding Soviet military power base, then, is probably the major fundamental cause of the West European antinuclear protest movement, but it is by no means the only significant factor contributing to the present climate of opinion in that region. At least six additional explanatory factors, related to the fundamental cause and to each other, can be cited:

Resurgent Nationalism

It is no longer the case, as it was historically, that the conservative right holds a virtual monopoly on nationalist sentiment. The left was traditionally thought to be internationalist in outlook and weak in patriotic feeling, although it often proved adept at appealing to nationalist emotions in its propaganda. Within recent years, political observers have spoken increasingly of a "new nationalism of the left" which is much more anti-Western than anti-Communist. The rise of this particular brand of nationalism has weakened the earlier sense of Atlantic Alliance solidarity, as well as of

European unity, although it pays lip service to the latter as a preferred alternative to the former.

Revival of Socialist Pacifism

From the beginning, Marxist socialism was ideologically pacifist in the sense that it was unwilling to participate in wars between capitalist bourgeois states. World War I turned out to be a scandal for the socialists, because it demonstrated that the Nation was a more powerful sociological entity than the Class. Whereas orthodox socialists expected that a future war would solidify the international proletariat in an uprising against the capitalist oppressors, 1914 saw British and French capitalists and workers march off and fight German capitalists and workers. The socialists reverted to pacifism in the interwar years and, as we have seen, contributed to the onset of another war in which they had to bear arms. Following World War II and throughout the postwar period, the left wings of socialist parties have reaffirmed their pacifist and anti-military convictions from time to time, but when social democratic-labor parties have formed governments or participated in governing coalitions a majority of their parliamentary members have acted responsibly in defense matters. This is true of Mitterand's Socialist Party in France, Craxi's in Italy, and Gonzalez's in Spain. In Northern Europe, however, where the electoral fortunes of democratic socialist-labor parties have declined since 1979 (e.g., in Britain, Belgium, the Netherlands, and West Germany) the influence of the pacifist left has expanded considerably (further compounding the parties' electoral problems, as well as the defense decision-making problems of incumbent nonsocialist governments).

The Sense of Powerlessness

For a long time, and increasingly since the energy crisis began a decade ago, many people in Western Europe have felt that they are suspended aimlessly and unstably between two superpowers which oscillate from tense Cold War rivalry to fragile detente in a protracted conflict. They complain of being almost helpless in their dependence upon external forces and events (for example, in the Middle East) over which they appear to have little or no control and which threaten world peace or their assured access to economically vital oil. The resulting widespread frustration activates a somewhat aggressive determination to reassert mastery over their own destinies. Among some on the nationalist left and right, this can involve the adoption of a negative, critical stance toward the one superpower whose policies they have a hope of affecting—the United States. When they oppose U.S. and NATO policies, they receive positive reinforcement in the form of commendation and support from the other superpower to the east.

They can then experience satisfaction that by drifting toward neutralism they are making a genuine contribution to peace and independence for Europe, reducing their worst fears—namely, that a superpower nuclear exchange would be confined to the European region.

A Rising Tide Against Military Defense

This general syndrome has a number of components. After two world wars in this century, all intelligent Europeans share the conviction that modern war is futile and absurd—it is the most stupid way imaginable to settle international disputes. The older generation, however, recognizes the persistence of a very real danger of aggression or political intimidation posed by a type of totalitarian, fanatical ideology which has been expurgated from the West. The older generation, dreading another war on the basis of its own experience, has always shown a strong preference for nuclear deterrence over conventional defense preparations. Knowledgeable defense elites in Western Europe have been concerned about proposals by former U.S. policy makers that NATO adopt a formal "no first use of nuclear weapons" pledge.[5] They are convinced that the problem in Europe is to deter not only nuclear war but also *any* war waged with modern hi-tech conventional weapons, such as precision-guided munitions (PGMs), both because such a conventional war would be quite horrible in its results and because it might escalate to the nuclear level despite advance declarations and pledges to the contrary. NATO political and military leaders are also convinced that conventional deterrence is much less effective than nuclear deterrence, as history has shown, and much more costly.[6]

The strategy of deterrence, of course, although it has been effective now for nearly four decades, is both subtle and complex, politically and psychologically. It is not readily grasped by the masses, and it is easier to ridicule than to defend. It is particularly vulnerable to "bumper sticker" attacks by propagandists who seek to make the public equate nuclear deterrence with nuclear war. Such slogans as "Nuclear war is bad for your health" are irrelevant to the realities of deterrence, but they are clever nonetheless, and corrosive of the West's political will to continue paying the cost required for the maintenance of a deterrent adequate for political self-confidence.

The antinuclear tide in Europe (and in the United States) reflects the tendency of a younger generation that has never known war to ignore the requirements of military security, as if responsible governments were free to assign these a much lower priority in national budgeting. This goes, of course, with the distaste of an idealistic yet sybaritic youth in affluent Western societies for the inconveniences, discomforts, and hardships of military service (and the consequent unpopularity of conscription). There was a time when genuine conscientious objection to war or military service demanded authentic inner spiritual conviction and a good deal of personal courage. That is no longer the case. It is now fashionable for the "educated" to hold the military in disdain and to demonstrate their altruism not by being willing to perform military service either to avert war by deterring it or to lay down their lives, if necessary, to defend the values cherished by their countrymen, but rather by occasionally taking to the streets by the scores of thousands to undermine, if possible, the deterrence policies to which the NATO governments are collectively and unanimously committed. One can scarcely help wondering whether heroic sanctity, which throughout history has been confined to the chosen few, has in these latter days become thoroughly democratized.

The Economics of the Protest Movement: Butter over Guns

The increasing costs of modern sophisticated weapons technology have undoubtedly (despite beneficial "spin-offs") placed a burden upon Western economies. Military expenditures contribute to employment, the gross national product, and technological growth. They also contribute to inflation and deficits. In all the Western economies, they have generated a sharpening debate over the issue "guns versus butter" — between allegedly constructive social welfare programs and allegedly wasteful military expenditures. The last decade has witnessed a growing tendency on the part of many journalists and politicians in democratic countries to blame nearly all economic problems on the military portion of the budget. Thus sizeable segments of the public have been conditioned to regard defense programs with skepticism or outright hostility.

The Mobilization and Coalescence Around the Nuclear Weapons Issue

As noted earlier, the countercultural cadres of the antinuclear protest movement are not numerous. They have been remarkably successful, however, in eliciting organized support from areas of society not traditionally involved on a sustained basis in public political action. They have managed to mobilize the resentments and frustrations against the existing system of the more extreme members of several groups and to channel them against Western policies of nuclear deterrence. Many women, for example, have been persuaded that defense policies of male-dominated governments threaten world peace and the lives of their children. Those who are concerned about the quality of the environment have a natural and easily exploitable aversion to weapons which, if ever used, would produce radioactive contamination. Squatters, alienated youth, social drop-outs, and others who harbor deep-seated antagonisms toward all authority are always ready to demonstrate their feelings. Most important of all in providing numerical strength to the movement are the churches — Catholic and Protestant.

Concerning the developing role of the churches, a further word is in order. Throughout the modern nation-state era from the seventeenth century to the twentieth century, the Catholic and Protestant churches may have occasionally disagreed with Western governments — especially those controlled by Liberal Republican parties — over such issues as the use of public funds for religious schools and the historic privileges of religious institutions, but they did not part company with governments on questions of war and peace, which were considered the province of the state. The orthodox Christian churches prayed for and preached peace, but they did not try to tell governments how to conduct their foreign and defense policies. They left the policy decisions on war and peace to political rulers, and when war came they ministered to the spiritual needs of their people but refrained from interfering in the political realm, especially after the separation of church and state, or religion and politics, came to be looked upon increasingly as an advantage to both institutions. Precisely because of this tendency toward the mutual nonintervention by the spiritual and temporal authorities in each other's realms, liberal Western governments (particularly in Britain and the United States) were able to tolerate the pacifism and conscientious objection of the relatively small and politically less significant "peace churches" — Quakers, Mennonites, and Brethren.

The larger Christian churches traditionally upheld the "just war theory" or some equivalent of it, generally rejected doctrinal pacifism, and supported the defense policies of governments according to political theories based upon the theologies of St. Paul, St. Augustine, St. Thomas Aquinas, Martin Luther, John Calvin, and such modern American writers as John Courtney Murray and Reinhold Niebuhr. There was an upsurge of pacifism among intellectuals in the orthodox Christian churches of the West following World War I. Catholic and Protestant moralists began to question whether, in view of modern weapons technology, war could any longer be considered justifiable. Nevertheless, the war against Nazism was widely regarded by Western Christians as a "just war." The advent of nuclear weapons in 1945, however, gave rise to new problems for the Christian conscience. Even before World War II, the Protestant theologian Paul Tillich had written about the "dialectical relationship between the Gospel and the State," postulating a tension between conflicting aspects of political authority as "divinely appointed" and as "demonic."[7]

After World War II, the World Council of Churches and Protestant theologians took the lead in questioning nuclear defense policies, and Catholic thinkers in Britain, Germany, and the United States began to follow suit in the early 1960s. Pope Pius XII as early as 1954 had condemned strategies aimed at the wholesale obliteration of urban centers with nuclear weapons, but he did not condemn nuclear weapons per se. Pope John XXIII, who said there was no reason to doubt that the nuclear powers wanted to prevent rather than wage war, called for reciprocal nuclear disarmament with safeguards. The Second Vatican Council reiterated those Papal teachings and stopped short of condemning the possession of nuclear weapons for deterrent purposes.[8] Since the late 1950s, however, Protestant and Catholic clergymen — few at first but in growing numbers during recent years on both sides of the Atlantic — have preached an antimilitarist and antinuclear message that has become, for all practical purposes, a constant and one-sided criticism of the defense policies of Western governments. Until a few years ago, both the leadership and the rank-and-file membership of the largest Christian churches were content to abjure nuclear warfare while tolerating a successful nuclear deterrence policy. But that has begun to change, as substantial minorities among clergy and laity have embraced nuclear pacifism, if not pacifism of a more general and absolute brand.[9]

The present study is designed to describe the major political, philosophical, and religious thought trends underlying the antinuclear protest movement in Western Europe. After an initial general survey of the movement's idea base, attention will be focused upon the various elements that enter into the thinking of political parties, countercultural groups, "peace organizations," churches, and other social components that comprise the movement in five countries — Britain, West Germany, the Netherlands, Italy, and France. One can trace some common threads through all five. But the protest movement in each country has been shaped by factors that are the product of its own unique cultural and political history.

Some analysts would caution against attributing any profound or coherent ideological/philosophical basis to the West European peace movement. This movement, they say, is a purely contemporary political phenomenon that behaves according to the same laws of leadership, organization, motivation, conditioning stimuli, and crowd psychology as does any modern mass movement. In an era of highly developed communications technology, intelligent, hard-working organizers, and clever propagandists, any group with adequate financial resources and a carefully planned strategy can influence public opinion for any cause, so it is thought, no less than for a commercial product. To be sure, there is an analogy between commercial advertising and political salesmanship of a candidate or program. But to galvanize large numbers of people into public political activism takes more than it does to promote the purchase of automobiles, breakfast cereals, electrical appliances, and deodorants, for this type of advertising looks to simple economic transactions in which individuals will spend specific, limited amounts of money for tangible products designed to satisfy private needs for a finite time. Consumer choices require no decisions about values, no altruism, no political decision to support a public cause that transcends oneself, no commitment of time, effort, substance, and reputation.

For higher things, organizers of causes require an idea content to make their arguments persuasive. They cannot rely exclusively upon irrational forces — the herd instinct, peer group pressure, faddism, the desire for excitement, the urge to belong to a community engaged in what seems to be a worthwhile effort, etc. All these factors are important; organizers of popular movements are quite familiar with them. But by themselves they are not sufficient. The Europeans are, for the most part, a thoughtful people. Even when they are being asked to commit themselves to a political course of action which, in the eyes of their own government policy makers, is more emotional than rational, they still demand arguments that appeal to their reason — the reason of abstract, disembodied logic rather than the reason that derives from practical experience and goes by the name of political wisdom.

Those who organize and lead peace movements are fully cognizant of such a demand. They know how to formulate arguments, slogans, and symbols that will strike responsive chords in the minds as well as the hearts of the elites, the molders of opinion, the leaders who enjoy being able to influence a following of their own (i.e., intellectuals, teachers, journalistic pundits, and other dominant personality types). Western officials and analysts who are responsible for coping with the continuing challenge of winning the support of democratic publics for national security policies cannot and should not be expected to become acquainted with the complex history of modern European philosophy. This is not necessary. But it would not hurt and might help them to have at least a passing acquaintance with the major modern thought themes which appear to underlie the contemporary peace movement — themes with which the chief architects of the movement are bound to be familiar and which they must take into account if they wish their appeals, however simplistic they may seem to us, to be politically effective. Philosophy may strike many as irrelevant in the era of mass media conditioning.

We are often told that it is futile to try to identify coherent thought strands in a movement many of whose militant leaders do not appear to be well versed in philosophical theories. Yet it cannot be denied that many of today's activists were budding revolutionary theoreticians fifteen or twenty years ago, by day reading tracts written long before and by night arguing about how to apply them to a transforming critique of the society which nurtured them. Ideas do have consequences; if repeated often enough, they may even take on an appearance of conventional or popular truth. The media are only instruments for the transmission of ideas, however superficially they may be merchandised in the form of arresting slogans. Here we are concerned with the ideational background on which the peace movement draws, for this may contain at least some of the clues that policy makers need in order to understand the *elan vital* that infuses the antinuclear crusade and gives it the strength to recover from temporary reversals.

Moscow, having counted too heavily upon the antinuclear protest movement to disrupt NATO's "two-track" INF decision by putting popular pressure on the parliamentary governments of Western Europe, suffered a major setback. After the downing of a Korean airliner by the Soviet Union in late August shocked European opinion, the "hot autumn" forecast for 1983 turned out cooler than expected.[10] West Germany, Britain, Italy, and Belgium remained determined not to be intimidated away from the course which they had set for themselves; only the shaky coalition cabinet in the Netherlands vacillated.* With failure staring it in the face, the Soviet leadership, weakened by Andropov's illness, lashed out by suspending the INF negotiations in Geneva, undertaking the deployment of new medium-range missiles in East Germany and Czechoslovakia, threatening additional deployments of submarine-based missiles near U.S. coasts, and blaming the breakdown of arms control on NATO and the deterioration of East-West relations on the Reagan administration.

During late 1983 and early 1984 the West European peace movement appeared to some observers to be running out of political steam. The Eastern demonstrations were disappointing in their size and impact so far as their organizers were concerned. In West Germany, the antiparliamentary Greens, who had entered the Bundestag a year earlier on an environmentalist, antinuclear, anticapitalist, and anti-American platform, began to undergo internal division over strategy, tactics, and ideological stance, some leading figures disassociating themselves from the one-sided, anti-American tone of the Communist-sponsored Krefeld Appeal.[11] Meanwhile, the governments of the Federal Republic of Germany and the German Democratic Republic, anxious to make certain that the bitter East-West tensions over missile deployments not jeopardize their detente relationship carefully built up over more than a decade, intensified their political communications in a manner not to Moscow's liking. Whereas the Soviet Union had sought to wean West Germany away from NATO, the net result was at least a temporary East German tilt westward.[12]

It would be a mistake, however, to think that the European antinuclear movement has entered into an irreversible decline. People eventually become bored over any kind of campaign and tired of sustaining a high level of emotional interest in a particular issue of public policy. But if the issue is important — and the question of nuclear war certainly is — it will always be possible to return to it at a later time and to exploit it for the pur-

---

*See chapter 7. It should also be noted that the Danish Parliament voted on May 10, 1984, to cut off the country's share of payments for the NATO missile infrastructure. Denmark, however, is not due to receive any missiles. The Danish government, i.e., the executive, supports the deployment of NATO missiles.

pose of generating powerful political passions over it. If political parties can do this time and again over such bread-and-butter issues as inflation and unemployment, they can do it over the life-and-death issue of nuclear war. Both the Soviet Union and Western peace organizations can be expected to cooperate tacitly in the future in their effort to put the possibility of a nuclear holocaust at the center of all Western debates about military defense and deterrence policies. Only by doing that were the antinuclearists able, for the first time in 20 years in Britain, 25 years in West Germany and the entire postwar period in the Netherlands, to make national security a profoundly divisive subject in the internal politics of West European parliamentary democracies. All of these countries would correctly regard the fall of a government over a question of foreign or defense policy seriously destabilizing. Yet the antinuclear protest had that as its goal, and came closer to achieving it than had any earlier pacifist movement. Early in 1985, as the Soviet Union was prepared to return to arms negotiations in three different forums—strategic weapons, intermediate-range weapons and space defense—many West European protectors undoubtedly derived comfort from the thought that their five-year effort, far from being a failure, had affected the policies of Western political parties and governments. In their eyes, if East-West arms agreements are reached, it will be due to their acknowledgment of the popular yearning for peace, not because of the NATO INF deployments or Reagan's space defense initiative. Those programs will certainly be blamed if there is no progress, or very slow progress, at the negotiating tables.

As my co-editor will argue in the concluding essay, the West European social phenomenon, which is the focus of this book, has played a critically significant part in contributing to the breakdown of a once solid NATO consensus on deterrence and defense. The antinuclear ideology will help to shape the debate over Western security for years to come. To pronounce obsequies over the grave of the "peace movement" would be most premature. This being the case, it will be worth the while of anyone wishing to understand the evolving psychopolitical climate in Europe to ponder the idea base of that movement, as James Foley traces it for us in the following chapter.

NOTES

1. Hans Kohn, *The Age of Nationalism* (New York: Harper, 1962), p. 63.
2. Jeffrey Boutwell, "Politics and the Peace Movement in West Germany," *International Security* 7 (Spring 1983), esp. pp. 73-74.
3. "Let's not ban the bomb," Editorial, *The Economist*, August 2, 1981.
4. Joris J. C. Voorhoeve, *Peace, Profits and Principles: A Study of Dutch Foreign Policy* (The Hague: Martinus Nijhoff, 1979), p. 112.
5. For the transatlantic debate over "no first use," see McGeorge Bundy, George F. Kennan, Robert S. McNamara and Gerard Smith, "Nuclear Weapons and the Atlantic Alliance,"

Foreign Affairs, 60 (Spring 1982), 753-768 and Karl Kaiser, Georg Leber, Alois Mertes and Franz-Joseph Schulze, "Nuclear Weapons and the Preservation of Peace: A Response to an American Proposal for Renouncing the First Use of Nuclear Weapons," *Foreign Affairs*, 60 (Summer 1982), 1157-1170.

6. On the economic and political prospects for a NATO conventional deterrent, see Michael Getler, "Atom Arms Debates Overlook Key Fact: They're Cheap," *Washington Post*, October 29, 1983; Charles W. Corddry, "Non-Atom Arms Asked for NATO," *Baltimore Sun*, May 17, 1983; Fred Hiatt, "High-Tech Weapons Sharpen NATO Debate over Procurement," *Washington Post*, June 2, 1982; William Drozdiak, "NATO Allies Face Cost Dilemma," *ibid.*, September 25, 1983; Elizabeth Pond, "Can NATO Lessen Its Nuclear Tilt?" *Christian Science Monitor*, October 14, 1983; "Battlefield Atom Weapons Here to Stay," *Suddeutsche Zeitung*, October 25, 1983, trans. in *German Tribune*, November 6, 1983; Gary Yearkey, "NATO Expected to OK Plan for More 'Smart' Non-nuclear Arms," *Christian Science Monitor*, May 14, 1984; Roger Thurow, "NATO's Economic Bind Restricts Its Defense Options," *Wall Street Journal*, June 5, 1984; "Supreme Commander Pessimistic on Defense Buildup," *ibid.*, June 5, 1984. General Bernard W. Rogers, SACEUR, although strongly in favor of a NATO conventional build-up, is opposed to a no-first-use declaration, and wants NATO to develop by the end of the decade a conventional capability to defeat a nonnuclear attack "without necessarily resorting" to the use of nuclear weapons. "Greater Flexibility for NATO's Flexible Response," *Strategic Review*, 11 (Spring 1983), p. 13 and "Conventional Punch that Might Avert a Nuclear Knock-out," *Manchester Guardian*, October 2, 1983.

7. Paul Tillich, "The Gospel and the State," *Crozer Quarterly* (1938), reprinted in David Cooperman and E. V. Walter, eds., *Power and Civilization: Political Thought in the Twentieth Century* (New York: Thomas Y. Crowell, 1962), pp. 523-534.

8. See James E. Dougherty, "The Catholic Church, War and Nuclear Weapons," *Orbis*, 9 (Winter 1966), 878-892.

9. A voluminous literature on this subject has emerged in recent years. Much of it is cited in the author's book, *The Bishops and Nuclear Weapons: The Catholic Pastoral Letter on War and Peace* (Hamden, Conn.: Archon Books, 1984): Cf. also L. Bruce van Voorst, "The Churches and Nuclear Deterrence," *Foreign Affairs*, 61 (Spring 1983) and the references to Church activity in Chapters 3 through 6 in this volume.

10. Frederick Kempe, "Lukewarm West German Demonstrations Against Missiles Could Hinder Movement," *Wall Street Journal*, September 6, 1983; Mary McGrory, "Image of Andropov as a Shrewd Propagandist Has Dissolved," *Washington Post*, September 13, 1983; David K. Willis, "Britain's Antinuclear Protesters Fight On," *Christian Science Monitor*, September 13, 1983.

11. William Drozdiak, "West German Peace Movement Divides Over Nonviolent Tactics," *Washington Post*, September 20, 1983; Elizabeth Pond, "West German Peace Activists Start Losing Their Public — and MPs," *Christian Science Monitor*, February 17, 1984; James M. Markham, "Germany's Anti-Missile Movement Has Lost Its Thrust," *New York Times*, March 11, 1984.

12. See Elizabeth Pond, "Soviets Alarmed at East-West German Ties," *Christian Science Monitor*, August 1, 1984, and "For Now, NATO Can Sit Back and Watch Soviet–East German Spat," *Ibid.*, August 13; William Drozdiak, "East Germany Renews Call for Detente," *Washington Post*, August 11, 1984; "East Germans Defend Moves to Improve Ties with the West," *New York Times*, August 14, 1984; and "East German Leader Asks Return to Detente," *Ibid.*, August 19, 1984.

Chapter 2

The Idea Base of the Protest Movement

James B. Foley

The powerful peace and antinuclear movements that have swept across the nations of Western Europe since the mid-1970s have encountered remarkable success in no small measure because they have managed to elevate their cause to the level of philosophical principle. They have sounded themes that echo in the great philosophical, ideological, and political debates that have raged throughout the Western world for more than two centuries. By appealing to the deep-seated sentiments and ideological reflexes common to idealists everywhere in the West, especially among youth, the movement has succeeded in transforming a single issue into a referendum on the nature of Western civilization, with enormous consequences for the security of the NATO Alliance.

To be sure, the peace campaign was activated internationally by the decision of December 12, 1979, to modernize NATO's intermediate range nuclear forces, and has directed its energies principally with a view towards preventing the deployment of Western missiles and, to a lesser extent, towards removal of the Soviet SS-20s. In response, government leaders and analysts in the West have tended to focus their attention on the strategic/political rationale behind NATO's "two-track" INF decision of December 12, 1979, and its implications for both Western security and East–West arms negotiations. However, if we are to understand the difficulties NATO has encountered in attempting to rally public support for its nuclear diplomacy, attention must be paid to the ideological milieu from which antinuclear, antidefense and anti-American sentiments spring. To understand this milieu, one must examine some of the abiding traditions in Western thought contributing to the growth of such sentiments, and probe several of the basic themes that seem to infuse and animate the peace movement: the distrust of reason, science and technology; the reliance upon emotions and intuitive feelings for what is right and human; the hatred of capitalism, industrialism and liberal parliamentarianism; the sense of alienation and *Angst,* combined with a yearning for internal and social purification through a process of conversion and return to a simpler condition of nature. Many of these themes are deeply rooted in the major philosophical systems of thought that have pulsated through the intellectual history of modern Western civilization — Enlightenment rationalism, Liberalism, Romanticism, Marxism, and Existentialism. Some are traceable to older mythologies or religious beliefs, and thus can appeal to devout Christians, fanatical sun worshippers and those who readily hear "sermons in brooks and stones."

ENLIGHTENMENT RATIONALISM AND ITS ROMANTIC CRITICS

The 18th century movement of the *philosophes** known as the Enlightenment involved two revolutions: one in the human *power* potential to make of nature a servant to be exploited for the material improvement of society, and the other in the *expectation* that reason and science would lead to the emancipation of humankind from disease, ignorance, superstition, war, poverty, and from all oppressive political, religious, and social structures. Since then, there has been a persistent motif of utopianism in Western thought, of which some evidence can be found in virtually all movements of political protest designed to change reality by appeals to logic. One must always demonstrate the absurdity of that which is being opposed. The conviction that it is the function of reason to criticize, ridicule and tear down all obstacles to human emancipation, especially today the Western nuclear establishments, is a powerful factor in the contemporary "peace movement."

The Enlightenment, however, produced not only the revolt of reason but also a contradictory revolt against reason, and a long Romantic tradition in Western thinking hostile to the Enlightenment's legacy of scientific rationalism, technology and industrialism. The Romantics, more poetic than philosophical, extolled living in harmony with nature rather than exploiting and spoiling it for human material satisfaction. One can perhaps attribute much of the emotional appeal of the current protest movement to its ability to strike chords of discontent, vaguely defined yet profound misgivings over the value of Western-style modernization and industrialization, that

*The leading figures included Descartes, Spinoza, Locke, Voltaire, Newton, Kant and others. Rousseau was also a philosopher of the period, but much more of a romantic than a rationalist.

run deep through Western history. For antinulcear ideologues, the NATO force modernization decision of 1979 revealed merely the tip of the iceberg: For them, our current dilemma is but the fateful, inevitable outcome of the capitalist, industrial form of development the West has been pursuing for over two centuries. In fact, this is a theme quite prevalent among the movement's ideologists: the bankruptcy of the Enlightenment, the perversion of rationalism, and the inner logic by which capitalism, in their view, leads to exterminism, "the last stage of civilization."[1] Thus, what is at stake in this debate is not merely a question of NATO's security policy, but the very foundation of the West's liberal, capitalist and industrial system.

The indictment of industrialization in the name of lost or threatened values and life styles associated with the *ancien regime* and the pre-industrial order is echoed in the antimissile campaign. In particular, this critique stems from the psychological pain that societies undergo when experiencing a transition from a traditional to a modern, industrial society, and the unceasing transformation of the latter into ever more technologically sophisticated modes. We can readily see in the extreme example offered by the Third World just how painful and unsettling such transitions can be. The German historian, Karl Dietrich Bracher, conceives of the current European peace and protest movement as a classic case of this difficult cultural adaptation to technological change:

> The present fears, whether with or without foundation, are mainly due to a crisis in respect of confidence which confirms historical experience: experience of the "cultural lag," the fact that cultural scales of values tend to lag behind technical and civilisatory development. This is a constantly recurring difficulty in handling rapid progress, both from the technical and ecological and the intellectual and moral viewpoints.[2]

The United States, by way of contrast, underwent what was probably the most painless adaptation to the transformation wrought by the Industrial Revolution; because the founding of the new republic was almost coterminous with the emergence of the industrial order, the new did not have to engage in a tooth-and-nail struggle with the old to establish itself. The American continent, moreover, was so vast that its cities never became as overcrowded and slum-ridden in the 19th century as did many European cities; it was impossible to destroy all the forests, denude the earth or foul the atmosphere with the smoke of belching factory chimneys. Thus, the American people, while using nature to their advantage, continued to love it and to believe that they were living in perfect harmony with it. There was scarcely any necessity for a Romantic reaction against industrialization on this side of the Atlantic—at least nothing comparable to that which developed on the other side. The United States did not experience popular manifestations of dissatisfaction with the industrial system until the countercultural and environmentalist movements of the 1960s and 1970s, considerably more than a century later than the European Romantics had taken up the cudgels. When these movements finally blossomed in this country, they exhibited all the essential characteristics of their European forerunners: the longing for a pre-industrial order, a return to an agrarian emphasis on the simpler over the complex, the warmth of organic community (*Gemeinschaft*) over the cold, contractual relations of an individualistic, legal–commercial modern society (*Gesellschaft*).

Although the protest today focuses on nuclear weapons, it is against much more—Enlightenment rationalism, technology, industrialism, pollution of the biosphere, economic growth that prodigally consumes natural resources—nearly all that has passed for progress and development during the last two centuries. Indeed, the protesters appear to know more certainly what they are *against* than what they are *for*, and they are against what Western society has become. Nuclear weapons are a final, hyperbolic symbol of the threat that Western rationalist civilization poses to itself and to the whole planet. Since Soviet communism has merely aped the West in its emphasis on development, and developed nuclear weapons in defensive reaction, it does not share the blame with the West. There are, to be sure, humane values in the Western experience that the protest movement admires and wants to preserve. Indeed, the critique of the West is based on those values. The irony is that the protesters, by engaging in their one-sided indictment of the West, place in jeopardy the preservation of the very values they profess to cherish.

For the better part of two centuries, the Cultural Romantics have condemned modern society for its materialism and spiritual emptiness. Max Weber has called it a "disenchantment" with a world that had been secularized and shorn of mystery. For such Romantic poets as Wordsworth, man's newfound mastery over nature was experienced as a loss of nature as man's psychic home, a symbol of life and fertility. Science has transformed nature into a world of dead objects, to be subjected to control by human technology. Thus, the Romantic writers equated industrial civilization with death, and technology with murder—the murder of nature and the murder of humanistic society. They experienced modernization as profoundly alienating in psychological, aesthetic, and social terms.

On aesthetic grounds, the Romantics opposed capitalism not only for having blighted nature with its machines and factories, but also for having poisoned the moral climate of the West by pushing Western societies to a mad scramble for money. The Romantic critique was buttressed by the literary Realists: The novels of Balzac are replete with biting satire on the spirit of acquisitiveness that, in his view, was corrupting the morals and vulgarizing the taste of French society. This essentially aristocratic disdain for democratic culture we find echoed today on all sides of the political spectrum in Europe. Ironically, the Left itself often expresses this none-too-egalitarian scorn for certain features of the modern West such as consumerism, materialism, and acquisitiveness.

Finally, the Cultural Romanticists condemned modernization for its harmful effect on social unity and cohesiveness. In particular, they missed the certainty and the security offered by the *ancien regime* with its political authoritarianism and religious dogma. By contrast, the rise of secularism and the liberal state tended to destroy the organic unity of the traditional society. In place of the communal bonds and traditional virtues, the liberal, capitalist order championed the individual and urged him to fulfill himself in striving against his fellow man. The Romantics rejected this type of external, egoistic individualism in favor of what the Germans termed the "freedom of the inner man."[3] Of the German cultural pessimists, Fritz Stern writes:

> Theirs was a resentment of loneliness; their one desire was for a new faith, a new community of believers, a world with fixed standards and no doubts, a new national religion that would bind all Germans together. All this, liberalism denied. Hence, they hated liberalism, blamed it for making outcasts of them, for uprooting them from their imaginary past, and from their faith.[4]

Politically, the Cultural Romantic movement was essentially reactionary because it idealized the virtues of the premodern era and hoped to recover them by doing away with industrialism, capitalism, or both. Their political legacy includes the Luddites, who set out to smash industrial machinery, anarchists, utopian socialists, and such contemporary offerings as countercultural groups, urban terrorists, and environmentalists. All of these heirs to the Romantic tradition are united in their opposition (partial, if not total) to the rationalist ideology, industrial economy, and bureaucratic state of the modern era.

The Cultural Romanticists were unable to stem the inexorable advance of the forces of modernization in the 19th and 20th centuries, nor were they able to create a coherent ideology or a viable political alternative to capitalism and Marxism, both of which embraced wholeheartedly the industrial creed of productivity and progress. What they did bequeath to the future, however, was a pervasive feeling of dissatisfaction with life in industrial society among the cultural-artistic elite, the intelligentsia, and the youth of the West.

The effort to escape from the sordidness, boredom and meaninglessness of life in modern industrial, materialist, commercial, technological society has assumed many forms. Those who believe that "man does not live by bread alone" have sought through various avenues (from joining monastic orders to participating in tent-covered revival meetings) to return to the fundamental truths of the Gospel; some have tried with limited success to bridge the gap between the Christian message and what Niebuhr called "immoral society." From time to time, many people are willing to follow a charismatic leader who confidently proclaims a sense of purpose and a knowledge of how to reach the "Promised Land." Many have pursued their quest for a new mythology (to replace a lost faith) for the ideological certitude offered by various "isms," especially fascism and communism. Others, no less bent on escaping from the burdensome uncertainties, ambiguities and responsibilities of life in a liberal political order, look elsewhere for community, meaning, liberation or relief from boredom—in family; work; a plurality of professional, occupational, neighborhood and particular interest associations; utopian socialist living experiments; and so on. The adventurous minority oriented toward excitement, danger, the sense of hardship and comradeship demanded by the field campaign, and the readiness for heroic action and ultimate self-sacrifice for a cause divides into two groups: Those who feel loyal to and appreciative of their own political system enter its military service; those who despise the system gravitate toward the antisocial extremes of anarchism, guerrilla warfare against the incumbent regime, nihilism and terroristic violence against the status quo.

In Germany in 1914, the dissatisfied romantic spirit found its outlet in the widespread enthusiasm among German youth at the outbreak of war. The war seemed to offer them the very type of opportunity for romantic adventure and communal experience that the rational, industrial order had seemingly banished forever. In war, they hoped to find an escape from modernity, an escape from a life style that was both predictable and meaningless. In the 1930s, Hitler's irrational creed and promise of glory and adventure exercised a similar appeal for the postwar generation.

Today's German youth, animated by the same admixture of idealism and resentment that carried their predecessors into World War I and later into Hitler's arms, registers its alienation from modern industrial society by adhering to a movement combining an ideological indictment of the system they detest with a program for undermining its defense and security. They find great psychological satisfaction in belonging to the peace movement, for it allows them to project their alienation onto external objects that they have chosen to demonize—to wit, the threat of nuclear war, the Pentagon, the military-industrial complex and related Satanic works and pomps. This deft psychological stratagem is really a manner of self-deception, a means of escaping responsibility for facing the spiritual *Angst*, which is an unavoidable condition of living in the modern world.

The depth of the European conservative, Romantic reaction against capitalism, industrialization and political liberalism should not be underestimated. In Russia, for example, those forces were identified as the characteristic marks of the despised, alien West. Tolstoi and Dostoyevski regarded Western rationalism and materialism as mortal threats to the preservation of Russian cultural purity and values. From their almost medieval Christian standpoint, the West appeared as a decadent, predatory, blasphemous civilization. Interestingly, the extreme form of pacifism advocated by Tolstoi bears resemblance to the thought of some contemporary peace ideologists, based as it was on a "rejection of contemporary Western society, of which war and the state appeared to him (Tolstoi) essential aspects."[5]

As for Germany, there is a long history of the rejection of liberal parliamentary politics. Political liberalism suffered a major setback in the revolutionary year of 1848 when Frederick William IV of Prussia contemptuously refused the crown of a German federal empire offered by the Frankfurt Parliament under a moderately liberal constitution. Germany was finally united under the authoritarian auspices of Bismarck. The autocratic regime of Wilhelm II collapsed in 1918 and was succeeded by the Weimar Republic, in which the Germans' initial encounter with Western-style democracy proved to be an unmitigated disaster. Hitler rode to power on a wave of anti-Western, anti-liberal sentiment, promising to transcend the endless strife of party politics and to restore the vital communal virtues of a heroic German past. Not until 1945 was non-Prussian Germany transformed into a fully Westernized political economy, under circumstances that would later make it possible for critics of the liberal consumer society to characterize the process as "the Americanization of Germany" and to revive as part of the new "nationalism of the left" an old Cultural Romantic animus against trends deemed alien to the Germanic spirit.

The countercultural movement that swept across the United States and Western Europe in the 1960s provides ample evidence of the abiding influence of Romantic antimaterialist, antimodernist values. The antinuclear protest itself is a similar phenomenon in that it regards nuclear weapons as epitomizing the threat advanced industrialism poses towards the physical survival of the ecosystem and the human race. It argues that the form of modernization and development the West has pursued over the past few centuries suffers from a one-sided emphasis on power accumulation, domination of nature, and self-aggrandizement that will eventually end in destruction. What is ironic about all this, however, is that this basically leftist, i.e., "progressive," perspective is based on essentially reactionary premises, many of which it shares with the conservative cultural pessimists of the 19th century. As one observer has put it, "It is precisely the anti-enlightenment rhetoric in both theological and secularized forms that has nourished the growth of the West German peace movement."[6]

MARXISM

Marx's vision was fundamentally at odds with the Romantics' rejection of modern industrial society. On the contrary, Marx enthusiastically embraced the Enlightenment's commitment to the conquest of nature and the fullest development of man's productive capacities. In fact, the idea of the control, domination, and exploitation of nature by man is at the very heart of Marxist theory. Marx was totally unsentimental when it came to issues of industrialization, modernization, and technological growth. He had no patience for the utopian socialists of his day, nor would he probably have had much for the environmentalists and antinuclear activists of today.

Marx, however, owed to his Romantic heritage the notion that human beings are fundamentally natural creatures who express themselves in production. In the capitalist mode of production, where one group owns what another group produces, the product itself becomes the means of enslaving the producer. Hating what should be their means of creative self-expression, human beings become alienated from themselves, from their work, and from each other. Alienation is thus the result of a particular set of social relations. Marx further believed that human alienation would have to be *intensified*, not alleviated, before it could be definitely abolished. This, Marx held, was happening around him with the development of industrial-capitalist society. In creating an enormous, international class of dehumanized workers — the proletariat — capitalism had fashioned the very tool of its own destruction. Any efforts at improving the lot of the proletariat would only serve to perpetuate the capitalist system based on alienated labor, private property, and class divisions. For this reason, Marx categorically rejected all Revisionist attempts at piecemeal reforms aimed at softening the effects of industrial development, ameliorating the condition of the working classes through the ballot box, or turning the clock back to a pre-industrial order.

Because Marxism proclaimed itself to be both an explanation for and a solution to the problem of alienation in the modern world, it exercised a powerful magnetism on dispirited Western intellectuals who otherwise might have succumbed to romantic despair and escapism. With its claim to scientific certitude, to an understanding of the riddle of history, and to the ultimate meaning of human existence, Marxism offered itself as a substitute for the apparent loss of meaning due to scientific inroads against the Christian world view. Communism became the new creed, the only meaningful cause to live for in a secular age; and the proletariat was worshipped as the agent of universal salvation. The message was deceptively simple: the Golden Age would be recaptured not by a romantic return to the past, but by the socialization of the means of production.

However, the history of late 19th century capitalism failed to conform to

Marx's predictions. In particular, the proletariat seemed either unwilling or unable to assume its messianic role, and appeared rather more interested in emerging from its social and cultural ghetto and taking its place as a fully integrated component of bourgeois society. Marxist theorists in the West, such as Eduard Bernstein and Karl Kautsky in Germany, emphasized the gradual inevitability of democratic socialism as an objective and scientific fact, downplaying the need for a subjective, violent, revolutionary act of will.

Lenin reacted to these disappointing developments by revising Marx's view of the proletariat, although he did not abandon Marx's goals. In his view, the proletariat would never by itself be able to transcend the world view of the ruling class; left to its own devices, it would find satisfaction in mere trade unionism rather than a radical transformation of the capitalist system. Lenin's strategy was to replace the theory of the proletariat with a theory of the professional cadre party as the vanguard of the proletariat and the agent of universal salvation. The party, because of its unique access to the science of objective historical laws, would know how to bring about the Marxian promise of social unity. The party-ruled state, i.e., the Soviet Union, must repress individual freedom and subjectivity, maintain an unrelenting war against society for fear that it might develop autonomously and carry out a counterrevolution against rule by the omniscient party. Thus it took a totalitarian regime to achieve Marx's vision of a recovery of the totality and unity of the mythical Golden Age.

Marx cannot be exculpated for the manner in which his ideas have been implemented in the 20th century. Certain features of his thought, such as his denigration of political pluralism and reformism and his denial of the universal validity of ethics, helped pave the way for the rise of barbarity in the 20th century. In effect, the promise of an earthly paradise, of the end to all domination by governments and classes, is so appealing that it tends to overwhelm any procedural or ethical questions which might stand in its way. In the words of Walter Lippmann, "the inhuman means are justified by the superhuman end."[7] Marx's contempt for liberal, pluralistic democracy as practiced in the West parallels the very different rejection by the German Cultural Romantics of liberal politics; both contribute to the anti-parliamentary and extraparliamentary activities of radical antinuclearists in Western Europe today.

From our post-Stalinist perspective, it is perhaps difficult to conceive of the enthusiasm with which Western intellectuals admired the Soviet regime at its inception. The decadence of the West appeared to them to be definitive after the debacle of 1914–1918; now, suddenly, history was again invested with meaning. In the following years, mounting evidence that the revolution was being betrayed was ignored because, if true, it would have meant that there was no political solution to the problem of alienation, no substitute for lost religious faith. Many Western intellectuals have applied a double standard in comparing the Soviet Union and the Western democracies in the 20th century. As Raymond Aron so persuasively demonstrated in his classic, *The Opium of the Intellectuals* (1955), they refuse to make concrete comparisons of the two systems; although the capitalist democracies have largely achieved the economic goals of the Left, they remain indifferent to the philosophical concerns of Western intellectuals. The latter have thus continued to evaluate the democracies according to a utopian standard while remaining indulgent towards the Soviet Union because it maintains a verbal adherence to utopian goals.

There have been attempts in the 20th century to articulate a Western brand of Marxism, one that would retain a commitment to Western liberal institutions and values. Such was the attempt of the Frankfurt School in the 1930s, and of the French Existential Marxists in the 1950s. By and large, however, Marxism remains influential today as a *critique* of capitalism rather than as a solution in its own right to the problems of modernity. Most current writing on the subject of alienation, inspired more by Max Weber than by Karl Marx, portrays alienation as an inevitable product of the rational-industrial process, whether capitalist or socialist. Contemporary radical peace ideologists are both anticapitalist and anticommunist. They have a greater affinity with the tradition of Cultural Romanticism than with a Marxism whose unabashed commitment to industrial and military growth cannot be justified by a mythology of human liberation which, two thirds of a century after the Leninist Revolution, is no longer believable. Nevertheless, they continue to despise American capitalism more than Soviet Marxism.

THE EXISTENTIALIST CRITIQUE OF WESTERN RATIONALISM

Unlike Marxism, the Existentialist movement never produced a coherent political ideology. Existentialism is indeed radical, but it represents a purely philosophical rejection of the premises of the Enlightenment. The earliest Existentialists, Kierkegaard and Dostoyevski, criticized those premises from a Christian perspective. Man, they argued, is neither rational nor capable of perfectability, as the optimistic Enlightenment thinkers held. According to the Christian view, man ought humbly to acknowledge his limitations as a finite being tragically alienated from God. To hold that man is intrinsically good and that ultimate happiness and fulfillment can be achieved on earth is tantamount to blasphemy. Dostoyevski and Kierkegaard were fundamentally opposed on religious grounds to both the capitalist and socialist visions of society's future because neither one supplied the spiritual sustenance that human beings must have. Any attempt to create a perfectly rational society must lead to tyranny, to alienation and to psychological oppression. Any social order based essentially on economics would, regardless of its professed adherence to democracy, freedom, justice and human rights, prove to be implicitly or explicitly Godless and therefore antihuman. Humans would be treated as pawns in the service of abstract, rational schemes designed to promote the welfare of "the great anthill."

What is common to virtually all Existentialist thinkers, not only the earlier Christians but also such later atheists as Sartre and Camus, is the search for authentic existence in the face of an almost universal conspiracy by modern ideologists to deceive their followers into believing that they can escape from *Angst*—not a shallow cognitive dissonance arising from an awareness of the conflict of values, but a profound spiritual anguish at the core of human existence. Modern society, East and West, claims to be based on the assumption that earthly life is a good in itself, and that we should all aspire to the happiness that consists of such human goods as health and well-being, material prosperity, security in our temporal possessions, the enjoyment of family, friends and pleasures, and the freedom to fulfill ourselves in our work, in cultivating our minds and talents, advancing the arts and sciences, and serving other human beings in society. According to Existentialist thought, life has value only in light of a confrontation with the ultimate reality—death. Only out of that confrontation is authentic experience to be derived.

Both Dostoyevski and Nietzsche had forebodings of a coming age of catastrophic wars and upheavals. They sensed that the mastery of nature the Enlightenment had conferred upon Western society would produce the ultimate alienation of the producer from the product. From the Existentialist perspective, this is the meaning of our nuclear dilemma: The existence of huge nuclear weapons stockpiles shatters all the optimistic assumptions which were the Enlightenment's legacy to the West and reveals to us that our world is in fact irrational. Paradoxically, the revelation is a blessing, for it reopens the possibility of the reemergence of a tragic world view which is prerequisite to an authentic probing experience at the core of our spiritual being. Existentialism, in the words of William Barrett, is "the philosophy of the atomic age."[8]

Today, Existentialism—not as an intellectual body of philosophical thought, but as a popular "filtered down" outlook on life that goes unchallenged—exercises a pervasive influence on the thinking that infuses the antinuclear protest movement. It is perhaps more of a threat to Marxism and its implicit optimism than to capitalism, which is, after all, less an ideology than a "fact," as French philosopher Bernard-Henry Levy has argued. The Existentialist outlook helps to account for at least some of the nihilistic attitudes prevalent among European youth, for example, a lack of commitment to values worth defending, the morbid preoccupation with dying in a nuclear war, and perhaps even an unacknowledged desire to exchange the existential burden of "boring freedom" in bourgeois consumer society for the excitement of having to face death or communist domination after the breakdown of stable nuclear deterrence. Conversely, the peace movement itself could be subjected to an Existentialist critique, inasmuch as its followers are engaged in the futile quest for escape from *Angst* so that they may return to the pursuit of happiness and personal fulfillment. Existentialist philosophy does not regard *Angst* as something that can be avoided or projected onto some external object and thus safely conjured away.

After the failure of revolutionary utopian movements in the 1960s, and with the abatement of antiwar protests, the focus of the Left's attention shifted from the struggle between communism and capitalism to the antagonism between popular democracy and the bureaucratic state. The development marked a break with the tenets of orthodox Marxism because the Marxist commitment to rational, social control and industrial growth was fundamentally at odds with the neoromantic ideals of the countercultural movement. The movement's values and life styles were now perceived to be threatened by the expansionary bureaucratic state that gave priority to material over spiritual goods, to the economic standard of living over the quality of life. Both the capitalist and the communist state glorify science and technology. Both stand for the same domination of man over nature, and for gigantism, urbanization, and concentration of technocratic power. Both types of state, communist and capitalist, had become the enemy. Since the Western countercultural movement, however, was better acquainted with what it regarded as the evils of the capitalist state, it was more preoccupied with them than with the more remote and only dimly perceived evils of totalitarian communism.

The new discourse has owed much to two German philosophers, Herbert Marcuse and Jurgen Habermas. Both thinkers look upon the rationality leading to open-ended economic-technological growth as a perversion of the Enlightenment reason that was meant to liberate but not control man. In *One Dimensional Man*, Marcuse argued that technological rationality has become its own justification. Unlimited growth is presumed to be a good end in itself, and therefore beyond question. In *Toward a Rational Society*, Habermas agrees with Marcuse that economic expansion is never the result of a rational political discussion about ends. The debate always focuses on what we want in order to live, not on how we would like to live. This produces an essentially depoliticized society in which economic processes rather than political values determine the quality of life. Marcuse and Habermas would probably concede that the element of political-ideological control is more prominent in communist society. When they advocate introducing into Western society rational procedures for deciding what the proper goals of society ought to be, they probably have in mind either a proletarian dictatorship or a rule by an elite on behalf of the proletariat. It should be noted, however, that Habermas' popularity with the New Left is not overwhelming, because his decidedly unromantic faith in technology makes him suspect.

Since the incumbent bureaucratic elites are governed by a rationality that has produced the deadly logic of deterrence and the dangers of an unending nuclear armaments race, their power must be challenged by the counter-cultural and antinuclear movements. These newer movements have sought to place distance between themselves and the bureaucratic organizations of the traditional Left, historically concerned over the redistribution of wealth, but now so tied into existing power structures that they are incapable of promoting real social change. One of the main reasons why these movements are so disenchanted with existing bureaucracies is that the latter fail to show sufficient interest in ecological and public health issues in the face of industrial pollution threats. Nuclear weapons have been seized upon as the paradigmatic threat to the environment and to civilization, but many warriors in the "eco-peace" campaign do not see the abolition of nuclear weapons as their only objective. Indeed, since military power is an essential characteristic of the existing nation-state system, they insist that there is an indissoluble link between ending the nuclear danger and fundamentally transforming society. Mient-Jan Faber, a prominent leader of the Dutch antinuclear movement, has said: "The problem of nuclear weapons is only the start. We are really interested in much more: the construction of a completely different culture."[9]

It is possible, and certainly to be hoped, that with the passage of time the antinuclear movement will mature to the point of realizing that from 1977 to 1984 it was quite one-sided in its strident opposition to U.S. nuclear weapons in Western Europe, while offering only perfunctory criticism of Soviet nuclear weapons aimed westward or even rationalizing their presence as a defensive necessity. Some who were active in the movement have already begun to fault it for its excesses and its fundamental unfairness in this regard. Churches preaching peace through justice would do well to strive to be equitable in the judgments they pass on contemporary societies.

The antinuclear protest in Western Europe has already produced significant political effects, as other chapters in this volume describe in detail. It has generated huge demonstrations, affected the outcome of parliamentary elections (even if not decisively), complicated the life of governing coalitions and traditional political parties, and influenced to a considerable extent the evolution of public opinion in the Western democracies and strategic analysis within NATO. The antinuclear flareup in European capitals undoubtedly helped to ignite the prairie fire of nuclear freeze resolutions that swept through countless American communities in the early 1980s. It also led to a mounting demand for a NATO policy declaration of "no first use" of nuclear weapons, despite the fact that for more than three decades the Atlantic Alliance has depended heavily on the nuclear response option to compensate for Warsaw Pact conventional force superiority.

As we have seen, the concern of many and probably most of the antinuclear protesters pertains to the quality of human life in the age of an overwhelming technological power to destroy. The fear of nuclear weapons, and even more of nuclear war, is quite rational and healthy. In fact, the effectiveness of deterrence depends heavily upon the operations of such fear in the calculations of governments that possess nuclear weapons. The protesters cannot and should not be discouraged in their efforts to call attention to the dangers posed by the existence of nuclear weapons. But if their message is to have enduring validity for the human race, it must cease to be polemically anti-Western and lopsided in its political consequences. The leaders will have to realize that the dangers of nuclear weapons are political as well as military—perhaps more political than military, insofar as they lend themselves, in an atmosphere of artificially stimulated hysteria, to manipulation by those who would use the popular fears for purposes of intimidation. The Soviet Union has certainly used the West Europeans' antinuclear protest to gain unilateral political advantage in arms control negotiations, while insulating itself from comparable popular pressures to make concessions. A totalitarian system need not seriously worry about elections, political parties, churches, peace demonstrations, town meetings, parliamentary debates, or the mass media. Most of the impulses and institutions that can be exploited in the West to increase alienation from the government can be harnessed in support of whatever the Soviet leadership wishes to do. If the Western peace movement wants genuine rather than phoney peace, it will have to come to grips with this fundamental asymmetry between the two models of society. Otherwise, it may produce a kind of strategic instability whose consequences would be worse than a continuation of the present arms balancing policies of the NATO governments.

NOTES

1. E. P. Thompson, *Beyond the Cold War* (New York: Pantheon Books, 1982), p. 41.
2. Karl Dietrich Bracher, "Afraid of the Future?," in *Scala*, 4 (1982), p. 44.
3. Fritz Stern, *The Politics of Cultural Despair: A Study in the Rise of the Germanic Ideology* (Berkeley: University of California Press, 1961), p. xxix.
4. *Ibid.*, pp. xxii-xxiii.
5. Peter Brock, *Twentieth-Century Pacifism* (New York: Van Nostrand Reinhold Company, 1970), p. 4.
6. Russell Berman, "Opposition to Rearmament and West German Culture," in *Telos*, 51 (Spring 1982), p. 147.
7. Walter Lippmann, *The Public Philosophy* (Boston: Little, Brown and Company, 1955), p. 83.
8. William Barrett, *Irrational Man* (Garden City, NY: Doubleday Anchor Books, 1962), p. 65.
9. Frits Bolkestein, "Neutralism in Europe: The Dutch Qualm Disease," *The Economist* (June 5, 1982), p. 44.

Chapter 3

The British Antinuclear Movement: Precedents, Program, and Prospects

Thomas M. Cynkin

The British antinuclear movement is unique among the Western European "peace" movements, because it entails an expression of anti-American hostility from among the populace of one of America's oldest and closest allies. Americans have been concerned by increasing allied assertiveness and reluctance to provide uncritical support, and have resented the lack of concomitant European shouldering of responsibility. The blatant anti-Americanism manifested by some in the British protest movement, while overshadowed by Prime Minister Thatcher's staunch support of the United States, seems almost a caricature of these trends.

While the British antinuclear movement has demonstrated itself to be capable of attracting substantial media coverage, which tends to magnify its actual importance, it must be recognized that its support is limited to a narrow segment of the British people. Core proponents consist of alienated socialist elements and of Christian moralists, in accord with a legacy of British radical and religious dissent. Traditional British tolerance of such dissent, which is usually quite insulated, has allowed the movement to draw attention to itself and to the nuclear issue, and to have an impact on broader segments of society, particularly among the Labour left. However, as the protest movement's influence has increased, so too has critical scrutiny of its presumptions and platform, ultimately limiting its appeal, as

Mrs. Thatcher's landslide victory of June 1983 clearly indicated. The magnitude of that victory made it possible for the Conservative government to ride out the spirited minority protest against the deployment of cruise missiles that began in late 1983.

The British antinuclear movement is far more tightly knit and well-organized than most of its counterparts in other Western European countries. It is not difficult to discern and identify its component parts, primarily Christian pacifism and radical socialism, and to trace their origins; analyze their structure and perspectives; and examine and predict their present and future impact on the Labour Party in particular, and on British politics in general.

THE BRITISH ANTIWAR LEGACY:
CHRISTIAN PACIFISM AND
RADICAL SOCIALISM

Traditional strains of British antimilitary dissent have included both Christian pacifism, which had a moralistic basis, and radical socialism, which had a political foundation. Christian antiwar elements arose in the form of Quaker peace testimony during Cromwell's reign in the late 1650s, and were based upon an intuitive, personal witness against the ravages of warfare. By the 19th century, however, as the social structure of the Quaker movement evolved to include more affluent elements of society, a more formalistic frame of reference was derived, which involved the principles of moral protest against the killing and material destruction of warfare which seemed increasingly senseless. This led to a more evangelical-political approach, which found expression in domestic politics and even international relations. Thus, the later disciples of William Penn sought to promote international peace through the political structure without proselytizing unconditional Quaker pacifism. They could be said to represent a realistic political outreach from a core idealist position. The Church of England and other more traditional Christian denominations, Protestant and Catholic, were not pacifist.

By contrast, socialist antimilitarism had its roots in the organized labor movement of the 20th century. Substantial numbers of radical socialist pacifists were to be found only in the Independent Labour Party (ILP), which involved a utilitarian approach to antimilitarism and focused on the economic issues concerned. Central to the radical socialist position was a perception of mankind as transcending political boundaries and national (capitalist) governments. The waste and destruction of material resources through arms races and wars were perceived as nonutilitarian, if not futile.

Yet the competitive basis of capitalism was thought to be expressed internationally through armed conflict, and in order to foment imperialist rivalries, nationalism and militarism. Thus, war was perceived as a symptom of the ills of the economic-political system. Consequently, radical socialists perceived the issues of capitalism and warfare to be intertwined and inseparable, making necessary the parallel pursuit of a socialist order and the abolition of war. This was orthodox Marxist-Leninist theory.

The First World War served as the catalyst for 20th century British antiwar elements. Secular antimilitarism had previously found expression only in several antiquated organizations that emphasized the principles of international arbitration over those of military conflict. The president of the largest such group, the London Peace Society, had approved the declaration of war as a necessary response to aggression (and subsequently resigned). Meanwhile, even the Society of Friends, which since the late 17th century had served as the bastion of British religious pacifism, saw nearly a third of its members eligible for service enlist.

During the course of the First World War, however, there was an emergence of significant antiwar sentiment, largely manifested with a utilitarian socialist or moralistic Christian tenor. As pursuit of the war served to disassociate liberalism and antimilitarism, the political focus of antiwar sentiment shifted towards socialism. Meanwhile, the war helped to promote the emergence of small but vocal pacifist minorities in a number of Protestant churches. The Society of Friends came to serve as the center of religious objectors for religious rather than for political reasons.

Radical socialist and Christian pacifist sentiments were, by late 1914, allied in the No-Conscription Fellowship (NCF), an umbrella group whose membership reached almost 10,000. This forebear of the Campaign for Nuclear Disarmament (CND), which counted Bertrand Russell among its more prominent members, was notable for its efficiency. It lobbied Parliament, organized petitions, produced pamphlets, publicized NCF's activities in the press, and aided COs. While the group faded after World War I with the end of its *raison d'être*, conscription, the NCF served as an important precedent for organized radical antimilitary dissent in Britain. Pacifist sentiment never surfaces politically without an experienced, hard working cadre of organizers.

During the interwar years, antiwar sentiments gained legitimacy when in 1924, the first Labour Government took office. The ranks of the antiwar movement were swelled by several major strains of supporters: the radical left, including among others advocates of class warfare and apologists for the Soviet Union; more moderate internationalists, who supported the League of Nations sanction system; Christian pacifists; and youth who found in an antimilitarism, sometimes superficial, a means of rebellion not just against jingoism, but against the older generation as well. Thus the

Oxford Union resolution, passed in February 1933, ". . . that this House will in no circumstances fight for King and Country," had significant support beyond that of pure pacifists.[1]

The tragic events of the 1930s made the cost of antimilitarism increasingly clear. Hitler's rise to power in 1933 and the adumbration of further fascist aggression by Mussolini's assault on Abyssinia in 1935 discredited antimilitarism and drove most internationalists from the antiwar ranks. The erosion of the international situation had a crucial impact on the British Labour Party. Led by Ernest Bevin, moderate internationalist Labourites who supported collective security voted for sanctions against Italy at the October 1935 annual party conference. Furthermore, the Spanish Civil War, which represented an ultimately successful fascist attempt to extinguish leftist groups in a (Soviet-backed) democracy, alienated the radical left from the antiwar cause. Thus only unadulterated Christian pacifists remained active in the antiwar movement.

The potential radical socialist/Christian pacifist antiwar coalition remained dormant for more than a decade after World War II. It was rekindled in November 1957 when, in keeping with an increased British emphasis on nuclear deterrence in the aftermath of the Suez crisis, Britain detonated its first H-bomb. J. B. Priestley articulated a nascent British antinuclear sentiment and helped catalyze it:

> The British of these times . . . seem to be waiting for something . . . great and noble in its intention that would make them feel good again. And this might well be a declaration to the world that after a certain date one power able to engage in nuclear warfare will reject the evil thing forever.[2]

During the previous two years more than one hundred local Committees for the Abolition of Nuclear Weapons Tests had sprung up across Britain. The *New Statesman* convened a meeting, attended among others by Michael Foot, who was later to become leader of the Labour Party, and by Bertrand Russell, at which the Campaign for Nuclear Disarmament (CND) was formed.

CND was soon able to co-opt the varied strains of British antimilitary sentiment by focusing its program on efforts to "Ban the Bomb," rather than on more absolute disarmament measures which would have narrowed its appeal. Thus it was able to expand its support beyond religious and secular pacifists and to draw in many who simply felt a sense of alienation from Western society in general, and were critical of the existing British political system in particular. Thus, radical socialists among the Labour left and trade unions, together with many of the young, were mobilized in support of CND's antinuclearism. The Communist Party of Great Britain (CPGB) lent its support only after some hesitation owing to the philosophical implications of CND's platform for the Soviet Union.

CND's "respectable" middle-class composition led it to concentrate its activities on reforming the system from within. Hence, Michael Foot stated in 1958: "Only through the election of a Labour Government and the political pressure which we may exert afterwards can we succeed."[3] The CND surge captured the Labour Party in 1960 when the annual party conference voted to support unilateral nuclear disarmament by Britain. This has been described as a result of a temporary political rebellion within the party against the moderate Hugh Gaitskell's leadership rather than a manifestation of ideological conviction, as demonstrated by the fact that Gaitskell's decision to "fight, fight and fight again" against this position helped reverse it the following year.

CND's failure as a political lobbying force led to frustration and, ultimately, a split in the organization. Bertrand Russell, who summarized the radical antinuclear perspective in the phrase "better red than dead," resigned as president of CND, whose leadership opposed circumvention of the British political process, in order to lead a mass antinuclear civil disobedience campaign. While CND had gained significant support, mainly among the young, for its early mass demonstrations such as an annual Easter Aldermaston-to-London march, the actions of Russell's Committee of 100 divided the antinuclear movement. By 1962 the Committee adopted an increasingly social revolutionary platform that further limited its appeal. Moreover, the demonstrated success of deterrence in the Cuban missile crisis, together with the Limited Test Ban Treaty of 1963, undermined support for the movement. Nevertheless, its social and intellectual foundations remained in place.

THE CAMPAIGN FOR NUCLEAR DISARMAMENT: THE DOMINANCE OF RADICAL SOCIALISM

The resurgence of CND in the 1980s has been a remarkable phenomenon. Its membership grew from 3,500 in 1980 to 70,000 in 1983, with perhaps 150,000–250,000 more members in local branches. In the same period its income increased from $40,000 a year to $750,000.[4] The resurrection of CND may be attributed to several factors, but principally to fear of the alleged dangers of nuclear war. The INF issue appears to have sparked apprehension inspired by increasing awareness of an eroding theater nuclear balance in favor of the Soviet Union and a perceived Western shift to a nuclear "war-fighting" posture that includes the possibility of a nuclear war limited to the European theater. In this context, GLCMs are perceived as weapons deliberately designed to decouple, to allow the United States to fight a nuclear war in Europe while sanctuarizing itself. Worse still,

GLCMs launched from the United Kingdom are seen by antinuclear proponents as inviting a Soviet strategic response against Britain. Thus missiles in Britain pointed at the adversary are seen as more dangerous than missiles in the adversary's territory pointed at Britain. The crux of this formulation is a broadly held fundamental mistrust and resentment of the United States, as demonstrated by a poll in January 1983, which showed that 93% of the British public preferred a dual key system — one that would allow Britain to veto employment by partial physical control — should the missiles be deployed in the United Kingdom.[5] The complaint that Britain could not trust the United States to consult with the British government before launching the cruise missiles escalated to a strident, even explosive, level after the U.S. military intervention in Grenada.

CND today comprises several traditional British antimilitary elements, including Christian pacifists, secular moralists, alienated youth, and radical socialists. Christian organizations and individuals lend CND significant support (some 20,000 Quakers are members)[6] and legitimacy: secular professional associations, Scientists Against Nuclear Arms (SANA),[7] the Medical Campaign Against Nuclear Weapons (MCANW),[8] which emphasizes that there can be "no effective medical response" to a nuclear attack, and Journalists Against Nuclear Extermination (JANE), which opposes what it perceives to be a pronuclear bias in British media.[9] Discontented youth also form a significant segment of CND, as roughly 20% of the entire organization is composed of students.[10] In fact, the CND badge has been described as a part of the tribal insignia for the young. This is reflected by the fact that Youth CND (with average age of 16) is the fastest growing section of the organization.[11]

However, the radical socialist segment is predominant within the movement. Confirmation of the organization's leftist orientation comes from an internal CND survey showing that 68% of its members vote Labour.[12] Moreover, 15,000 communists (approximately 85% of the 18,000 member CPGB) are numbered among CND's supporters,[13] but the bulk of British antinuclearists are not communists. Besides communists, the radical socialist segment of CND includes feminists, trade unionists and the Labour left. Its leadership, moreover, is dominated by radical ideologues who are hostile to Western political culture in general and to the United States in particular. Thus, in the words of activist Mary Kaldor,

> the disarmament movement is a coalition of a lot of people who are in different ways dissatisfied with modern society. . . . They're doing more than opposing the arms race. They're saying we want a more humane society.[14]

The feminists are one group of activists who capitalize upon the antinuclear movement's momentum to espouse their own cause by linking it tangentially to nuclear disarmament issues. The following statement is typical:

> Most feminists see their feminism and their involvement in the peace movement as interrelated and would not accept that they were putting women's liberation on a shelf until later. For them . . . the struggle against male violence, whether on an individual level in the home or institutionalized and legitimized in the arms race, cannot be seen as separate issues.[15]

Major groups include the Women's Peace Alliance, Women for Life on Earth, and Women Oppose the Nuclear Threat. One such group attracting major media coverage is the Women's Peace Camp outside the Greenham Common Base where the cruise missiles are being deployed. A founder and major spokeswoman for the group, Mrs. Helen John, defended the continuing civil disobedience campaign and described Britain as "an American-occupied country."[16] Over Easter weekend in 1983, more than one hundred women scaled the base fences and held a short picnic while dressed somewhat anomalously as Easter bunnies and Russian bears. The camp's philosophy that men are aggressive while women are peaceful is reflected in a ban on participation by male protestors.[17] The camp was largely swept away by government forces in April 1984 as the public became increasingly critical of its goals and methods.

In September 1981 the British Trades Union Congress (TUC) voted overwhelmingly to support unilateral nuclear disarmament, a position it had been forced to adopt in 1961. It passed a motion calling for closure of all British nuclear bases; opposition to Trident and INF; opposition to "any British weapons"; a cut in arms spending; and government aid for workers displaced by defense cuts. TUC policy was explained by its Chairman:

> The policy of the Labour Party and the TUC for unilateral disarmament will mean, if implemented, a reduction in arms and allied expenditure which will release considerable resources for the manufacturing and service industries of our nation, thus benefitting the community as a whole instead of international arms profiteers. The resultant more stable situation will encourage fuller and more useful employment and a higher quality of life for our people.[18]

Strong union support for unilateral nuclear disarmament has had a galvanizing effect on the Labour party.

CND is directed by a tightly knit and highly motivated central leadership, which ranges from "soft" left to "hard" left. Monsignor Bruce Kent, the General Secretary of CND, has stated that "the Churches are handicapped by profound anticommunist feeling . . . at variance with Christian teaching."[19] Moreover, Kent underscored the importance of the CPGB to CND by appearing before the former's annual conference on November 10, 1983. Affirming that "My appearance here is something I owe you and we owe you for what has been happening over the last few years," Kent stated: "We are partners in the cause for peace in this world." The anomaly of a cleric declaring himself to be a partner with Marxists was underscored when Kent thanked the *Morning Star*—the communist newspaper which, unlike the CPGB's Executive Committee, has been moving toward Stalinism[20]—for its "steady, honest and generous coverage of the whole disarmament case."[21] This may help to explain his tolerance of substantial communist influence in the upper echelons of the antinuclear organization. At least five communists sit on the twenty-member elected National Council;[22] at least three serve as full-time officials; while the CND periodical, *Sanity*, has a communist as one of its editors as well as another on its editorial committee. The CPGB has furnished at various times the Chairman, the National Organizer, and the Press Officer of the CND.[23] Some CND members, such as CND Vice-Chairman Michael Pentz, have close ties to the British Peace Assembly and the World Peace Council, both well-known Soviet front organizations.[24] Thus, while CND can in no way be categorized as a front organization itself, disproportionate communist influence nonetheless makes itself felt at the top.

CND's main objective is simple and clear: unilateral nuclear disarmament by Britain. Monsignor Kent sums up CND's position: "The British deterrence is not independent, and above all it is not credible."[25]

CND's anti-American tilt was demonstrated by its response to President Reagan's zero-option proposal. Reagan's approach was criticized for being propagandistic and unrealistic: "The essential point is that President Reagan has not offered to remove one single nuclear weapon from Europe. He has offered to stop the siting of an entirely new generation of weapons (cruise and Pershing), neither of which are yet in existence."[26] CND deemed the Soviets unlikely to respond positively by dismantling their own weapons. In essence, then, CND regards prospects for pressuring the Soviets to disarm as unrealistic, while at the same time it refrains from expressing concern over Soviet deployments and pressures the West to disarm itself unilaterally.

Reagan's "interim agreement" proposal evoked a similar response. "We're not impressed at all with Mr. Reagan and his so-called offers," Kent remarked. Another member of CND's Executive Committee said simply, "The offer was made in the hope it would be rejected."[27] In fact, many members of the CND leadership appear reflexively to blame the United States totally for the arms race, while denying Soviet use of chemical weapons in Southeast Asia or Afghanistan.

Communist influence is manifested not only in the nature but in the specifics of the CND program. The top five priorities, according to a 1979 CND document, are the abandonment of Britain's strategic nuclear force; closure of NATO (American) bases in the United Kingdom; diversion of resources from the defense budget to social services; redeployment of workers from military production; and termination of British arms sales. These goals are identical to those of the CPGB, as enumerated in the same sequence by its Executive Committee. The sole exception was the CPGB's substitution of "withdrawal from NATO" instead of "redeployment of workers."[28] Significantly, withdrawal from NATO was added to the CND list of priorities at its November 1982 conference.[29]

The CND program was given a radically new dimension at that conference when a "nonviolent direct action" (NVDA) campaign to counter INF deployment and Trident construction was overwhelmingly approved by the delegates. Monsignor Kent has supported the move by stating that "even for conformist consciences there must be a point beyond which secular law ceases to bind."[30] A survey by CND of its national members showed that 74% approved of nonviolent civil disobedience, although 33% said they would not take part.[31]

CND mobilized demonstrations in October 1981, when 250,000 marched in London; April 1983, when over 125,000 participated in various Easter weekend activities; and October 1983, when more than 250,000 demonstrated in London against the impending arrival of cruise missiles.[32] In preparation for the Easter events, for example, CND sponsored many training sessions to enhance effectiveness and to reduce the risk of violence. Participants were instructed to dress normally, to be careful of media questions, and to communicate calmly at all times. Procedures to follow if arrested and likely penalties were also discussed. CND members planning to blockade the Royal Ordnance factory near Greenham Common were urged to approach in groups of between ten and twenty, and only after being trained in practice sessions. Walkie-talkies were used to link groups and provide organization for the protest, which was directed from a base camp nearby.

The sophisticated organization behind the demonstrations has also been evident concerning other CND-sponsored "non-violent direct action." Tarmac (the company building cruise missile silos at Greenham Common), MAN-VW (the British subsidiary of the West German firm that is manufacturing the launch vehicles), and the National Savings Bank have all been singled out by CND as targets for the NVDA campaign. Methods to be used were designed to minimize risks in order to increase the numbers of participants. CND urged Britain's 154 "nuclear-free zones" (local Labour-controlled authorities) and other local groups to boycott Tarmac and MAN-VW; to sell shares in those firms; to coordinate "phone-ins" to block the companies' switchboards; to conduct letter-writing campaigns; and to arrange local pickets and demonstrations. Local groups were notified of companies in their area thought to have links to the contractors, and were advised to persuade these companies of the CND position against the targeted firms, using stockholders meetings if necessary to get the word across. CND supporters were also encouraged to withdraw their money from the National Savings Bank to make a financial protest to the government.[33]

The CND, working through its 1,200 local groups, conducted a "peace canvas," asking whether cruise missiles should be based in Britain, whether £1 billion should be spent on Trident, and whether Britain needed nuclear weapons for defense. The operation was actually part of the election campaign against Thatcher's Conservative party. The motto was "If you can't change the government, replace the government." In pursuit of this end, the CND targeted Conservative candidates in marginal constituencies, thereby hoping to tilt the outcome toward the Labour or Social Democratic-Liberal Alliance candidate.[34] A similar strategy can probably be expected in the next election.

CND has developed into a mass movement dominated by radical socialists and led by a highly motivated, tightly knit, and sophisticated leftist leadership. Whether CND can avoid the mistakes of the past and avoid organizational fragmentation remains to be seen. Its new tactics, combined with a general disenchantment over Labour policies, have alienated some potential sympathizers. An effective government information campaign on the need for NATO missile modernization contributed to a shift in public opinion in the first half of 1983. In January 1983, when Britons were asked whether they would accept ground-launched cruise missiles (GLCMs) if the Geneva talks failed, 54% were opposed and only 35% approved. By May, however, public opinion had been reversed, with 52% approving and 34% in opposition.[35] The decisive Conservative victory in the June 1983 election represented, at least in part, a tacit acceptance of INF and a repudiation of CND's views by the general public. The antinuclear protests at Greenham Common and other sites toward the end of 1983 marked no fundamental change in the estimate that the influence of the CND had once again peaked.

EUROPEAN NUCLEAR DISARMAMENT (END): THE ANTINUCLEAR IDEOLOGUES

If the CND leadership is the heart of the radical left in the British antinuclear movement, then European Nuclear Disarmament is its brain. Composed of antinuclear intellectuals, END articulates the philosophical rationale of the majority of protestors. In this sense, END is a collective legatee of the heritage of Bertrand Russell, a fact underscored by its close relationship with the foundation named in his memory. END is practical enough to pay lip service to the desirability of promoting Eastern as well as Western nuclear disarmament; however, its relentless anti-Americanism and apologies for the Soviet Union belie this tactic.

END was launched with an "Appeal for European Nuclear Disarmament" on April 28, 1980, under the auspices of the Bertrand Russell Foundation. The appeal was circulated in Europe for the signatures of antinuclear activists. *Prima facie* balanced and reasonable in tone, the appeal stated:

> We do not wish to apportion guilt between the political and military leaders of East and West. Guilt lies squarely upon both parties. Both parties have adopted menacing postures and committed aggressive action in different parts of the world. . . .[36]

However, the specifics of the appeal betrayed a subtle bias against the Western position. Hence, the proposed nuclear-free zone in Europe would extend "from Poland to Portugal," omitting Soviet territory. The United States was called upon not to deploy or even develop cruise missiles or Pershing-2s, while the Soviet Union was merely asked to halt SS-20 deployment, a line identical to Brezhnev's freeze proposal. Moreover, END's unilateralist position was adumbrated:

> It will be the responsibility of the people of each nation to agitate for the expulsion of nuclear weapons and bases from European soil and territorial waters, and to decide upon its own means and strategy, concerning its own territory.[37]

END and the Bertrand Russell Foundation culminated this campaign in a conference held in Brussels in July 1982 to promote discussion among various Western groups concerning implementation of the appeal.

The founders of END have described themselves as non-aligned and unassociated with the East. Mary Kaldor, a founder of END and member of its Steering Committee, illustrated this by stating:

> CND had a pro-Soviet image. It was often thought of as being fellow-travelerish. . . . So we felt there was a role for a separate organization. . . . In the last few years CND has totally changed. It has largely adopted the END platform. . . . The main difference is that we [END] tend to be at the more intellectual end of the peace movement. . . . We have more of an educative role . . .[38]

The key element of END's drive to deflect criticism of pro-Eastern bias from the antinuclear movement in general and END in particular has been to pay token obeisance to panEuropeanism. Hence, Edward Palmer (E.P.) Thompson, currently the leading intellectual light of the antinuclear movement, decided to serve as END's "Coordinator" for Eastern Europe. Thompson has stated, boldly enough, that the Soviet peace offensive "is strictly for export. It has been accompanied by a stepped-up cold war at home" against peace organizations such as the Moscow-based Group to Establish Trust. "It dismays and astounds me that there should be any hesitation in the Western peace movement about coming to [the Eastern movement's] defense."[39]

However, despite such attempts to distance itself from the Soviets,

Thompson's organization made not one contact with Solidarity during the sixteen months of its legal existence.[40] More revealing sentiments were expressed in the aftermath of the crackdown on Solidarity, when Thompson described Jaruzelski as a "Polish patriot" and his action as "a Polish solution arising from Polish conditions."[41] If anyone was guilty, it was the Western governments who acted as "accomplices," as their "showy nuclear posturing was a factor beckoning on the declaration of martial law."[42] Thus, the bogey of Western INF modernization was raised as the root of all evil in Europe. In any case, according to Thompson, Solidarity "looked to the wrong friends in the West."[43] Even when END finally contacted representatives of underground Solidarity's Coordination Office in Brussels, Solidarity chose not to endorse the END Appeal.[44]

The END coordinator for Eastern Europe held comparable views concerning the Soviet invasion of Afghanistan, which he dismissed as a "client nation" of the Soviets:

> NATO played the cruise missile ball, which struck the Afghan black, which rolled neatly into the Russian pocket. It was as if Mrs. Thatcher, Mr. Pym, and Mr. Bill Rodgers were there, perched on the leading Soviet tanks, waving at the astonished people of Kabul.[45]

These convoluted apologia indicate that END's interest in panEuropeanism seems superficial at best, and most probably was adopted in order to obscure its anti-Western bias. This practical and tactical stance, as opposed to philosophical commitment, was tacitly conceded by Kaldor. She stated that Western disarmament is and should be independent of Eastern disarmament, but noted that some reciprocal moves in the East would be useful if only because they would make the job of the Western antinuclear movement easier.[46]

Nonetheless, the pretense at evenhandedness has proven a clever tactical ruse. The Soviets have perhaps recognized this, as a strangely hostile letter from Yuri Zhukov, President of the Soviet Peace Committee, sent in December 1982 to 1,500 European antinuclear activists, provided them with an opportunity to remove themselves from being associated with Moscow. Criticizing the Bertrand Russell Foundation and END in particular for attempting to "impose their conception of equal responsibility," Zhukov wrote:

> We are firmly convinced that this conception is intended on the one hand to disorient, demobilize and sap the antiwar movement, and on the other hand to conceal and justify the aggressive and militarist policy of the United States and NATO.[47]

This perhaps deliberately ridiculous allegation led to a much publicized rebuke of the Soviet *apparatchik* by END.

E. P. Thompson is certainly the most prominent of the antinuclear luminaries — indeed, its guru. His professed evenhandedness between East and West is not compatible with his pronouncements and writings, which display a deeply ingrained anti-Americanism. Thompson, a self-proclaimed "dissident Marxist," perceives the division of post-war Europe to be a deliberate partition by the United States and the Soviet Union, which has forestalled the outcome he prefers, namely a united socialist Europe. Within this frame of reference, Thompson articulates a basic perception of the United States as the aggressor state and the greatest threat to peace since World War II. Thompson finds no difficulty in attributing to free, democratic states an aggressive foreign policy. He decries those who

> assume that because the Western world is more free that *therefore* it must be more peaceful, and that its statesmen must act only with defensive intent. This is a deceptive *non sequitur*, which can be disproved by the briefest attention to history. . . .[48]

Pointing to the historical example of colonial Britain, Thompson states that "imperialism, or militarism, can perfectly well cohabit with democracy: indeed, very happily."[49]

Nevertheless, Thompson imputes to the Soviets a defensiveness born of their historical experience and a distrust of the West that is justifiable by his interpretation of past events. Thompson implies that "Chamberlain hoped . . . to divert the aggressive Nazi drive from the West, and point it in the direction of the East. Prague was to be a halfway house to Moscow."[50] This interpretation ignores the guarantees given by Britain and France to Poland and their resultant declarations of war on Germany. Thompson writes: "The basic postures of the Soviet Union seem to me . . . to be those of seige and aggressive defense."[51] He perceives the United States as the instigator of the arms race, in which the U.S. weapons program is more active and innovative, whereas that of the USSR is more reactive and imitative.[52] Thus, in sum, it is clear where Thompson's bias lies:

> The United States seems to me to be the more dangerous and provocative in its general military and diplomatic strategies, which press around the Soviet Union with menacing bases. It is in Washington, rather than in Moscow, that scenarios are dreamed up for "theatre" wars . . .[53]

Seen against the backdrop of these fundamental perceptions, Thompson's anti-American rationale for opposition to INF is clear. In essence, Thompson claims what no strategic thinker has ever suggested — that the United States is using Britain as an expendable shield:

> It makes no sense at all for decisions as to the siting of missiles — and as to the ownership and operation of American missiles on European soil — to be taken in the Pentagon, when these decisions affect the very survival of Europe.[54]

Thompson appears to dismiss American efforts at multilateral disarmament, describing Reagan's zero option as "either a tough negotiating posture or . . . a provocation."[55] He presses for unilateral disarmament by the West and violently opposes INF deployment. With consummate optimism, he urges that the first step be taken by the West precisely because the East is merely reactive, and hence will respond. The West in general and the United States in particular are to blame for the distortion of the Soviet system, according to Thompson:

> As the missiles of the West press around the borders of the Soviet Union, they serve to hold together an authoritarian regime which has long lost credibility. The utterly bankrupt ideology and methods of the Stalinist rear guard are propped in place by each new military threat. . . . The succession to the old men in the Kremlin is being determined by the actions of the Pentagon today.[56]

Thus the "Philosopher King" of the British movement professes evenhandedness while pressing for unilateral Western disarmament, blaming the West for all the world's ills, including even the nature of the Soviet state.

Where Thompson treats international relations as a category of psychology, Mary Kaldor, one of his most influential END associates, deals with more specific questions of defense. Preferring a united socialist Europe, Kaldor regards Atlanticism not only as an effort to bury nationalism but also as a conservative attempt to control socialism: "NATO provided a scapegoat, in the form of the Soviet threat, with which to eliminate, over a period of years, alternative political options."[57]

Kaldor is quick to dismiss the notion of a Soviet conventional threat as a basis for Western defensive measures:

> We *know* that the Soviet Union is heavily armed, but this is not a justification for a new arms build-up by the West. The confusion of the two issues—the Soviet military threat and the case for nuclear weapons—has provided a convenient smokescreen for evading the central arguments about disarmament.[58]

The West is seen as solely responsible for the arms race, because it is technologically more dynamic. In Kaldor's view, if the West unilaterally disarms *first*, the Soviets will follow. She sees multilateral negotiations as pointless, since they are undertaken by states in a bloc system of extremely limited flexibility. She considers the zero option to be "unrealistic" (as opposed to unilateral nuclear disarmament, which is presumably "realistic").[59]

Kaldor depicts a utopian vision for her followers. She mentions her interest in unionizing the British army and electing officers democratically, apparently along the lines of the model the Soviets tried and quickly discarded after the October Revolution. She then asks, "Do we actually want to create armed forces that are more effective militarily?"[60] As to the means for effecting British defense in such circumstances Kaldor concludes: "If any country wants to bomb us to pieces, they can. And that's something we've really got to come to terms with. Therefore, the only way to avoid attacks is political."[61]

It is clear that the ideological fount of the British antinuclear movement, END, despite its superficial pretensions at pan-Europeanism, espouses utopian unilateralism with a crypto-Marxist underpinning. Its tolerance for, and rationalizations of, Soviet actions are exceeded only by its anti-American hostility.

CHRISTIANS AND THE BOMB

While a broad strain of CND supporters are of the radical socialist/anti-American variety, many march to the beat of a different drummer. Specifically, much grass roots support comes to the antinuclear movement from those motivated by a sense of Christian moralism. Advocacy of unilateral nuclear disarmament by prominent Church organizations has lent the British antinuclear protest movement a degree of legitimacy and credibility it might otherwise lack. Groups officially advocating renunciation by Britain of an independent deterrent include the British Council of Churches, the small but active Roman Catholic organization *Pax Christi*, and several Quaker-affiliated pacifist organizations such as Quaker Peace and Service. Unilateralist sentiment has been expressed by some members of all church denominations, and has had the greatest overall effect on British society through the Anglican church itself.

The nature of the active role played by church groups in the debate on nuclear weapons has rekindled the old controversy, long dormant, that it is proper for the church to discuss the morality of nuclear war. The current debate has entered the realm of technology, military strategy and international politics to such an extent that many have charged the Church with politicizing the Gospel by intruding into secular areas.[62]

The role of Monsignor Bruce Kent as head of CND has served as a focal point for the general controversy surrounding the role of the Church in the protest movement. Much has been made of the "serious misgivings" that Cardinal Basil Hume, Kent's superior, has raised concerning Kent's role. A letter made public by the Cardinal states:

> Should the political aspects of CND develop further and become predominant in this work, it would be difficult for a priest to hold responsible office in the direction of the movement. Such a task might more fittingly be undertaken by a lay person, whose witness could more suitably be given in contentious issues of a secular character.[63]

A similar letter by the Apostolic Pro-Nuncio in Britain, Monsignor Bruno Heim, took an even more stern tone. It stated that:

Unilateralists . . . are carrying out a one-sided campaign, and it is clear which side it benefits most. Whether those doing so are consciously sharing the Soviet aggressiveness and ideology, or belong to the great number of the well-known "useful idiots," or, again, are blinkered idealists would have to be judged in individual cases, even in that of Bruce Kent.[64]

Although such concerns have been expressed in the Roman Catholic church, in the dominant Anglican church the issue has been handled quite differently. The late Canon John Collins had been a founder and chairman of CND, while Canon Paul Oestricher became a vice-chairman of the organization, raising no controversy within the church over the nature of his role. The Anglican church, in fact, commissioned a report on disarmament and deterrence by a working party from its Committee on Social Responsibility, the repercussions of which are still reverberating through the nuclear debate. The report, entitled *The Church and the Bomb*,[65] has become the bible of Christian unilateralists. It examines nuclear warfare in the context of traditional church "just war" theory, and then extrapolates to analyze the moral issues of nuclear deterrence. The working party report concluded that nuclear warfare cannot be just and is hence immoral. While conceding that circumstances could allow adherence to most requirements for a just war involving use of nuclear weapons, the report finds nuclear warfare to be morally unsupportable on several grounds. These pertain to criteria both for resort to war and the conduct of war.

Concerning resort to war, the working party first noted that the criterion for a reasonable hope for success would not be met because of the considerable likelihood that war between nuclear powers would escalate into general war; and that the evils and damage nuclear war would entail would be disproportionate to the harm it would prevent.[66] Concerning the conduct of war, the working party judged nuclear warfare to be equally unsupportable, because just war theory requires that noncombatants not be subjected to direct and intentional attack. This criterion, it was felt, would be blatantly breached in nuclear warfare and disproportionate to any legitimate end. Even limited and isolated use of nuclear weapons "would be very likely to lead to a general nuclear war."[67]

Proceeding under the assumption that nuclear warfare is in fact immoral, the working party described nuclear deterrence as a conditional pledge to act immorally. Asserting that the West has implicitly agreed to act immorally under certain circumstances, the report goes on to say that

a conditional intention implies that one has consented in one's mind to act immorally. For moral theology, sin is completed in act but begins in consent, and the consent to act immorally, even though the act is never performed, is already sinful.[68]

The working party advocated unilateral disarmament by Britain.

All Christian churches confront the same moral dilemma when they attempt to grapple with the issue of nuclear deterrence: Is it permissible, for the sake of deterring war, to threaten to do something (that is, wage nuclear war with all its potential destructiveness) although it would be immoral to carry out, because of the very large number of innocent people who would be killed by blast or fallout even in a limited counterforce nuclear exchange? Moralists opposed to deterrence argue that the fundamental intention inherent in the possession of nuclear weapons is to wage war and destroy the enemy. Moralists who appreciate the deterrent effect that the existence of nuclear weapons exerts upon the willingness of rational governmental decision-makers to go to war contend that the primary intention underlying the possession of nuclear weapons is to prevent war, and is therefore morally good. The intention to wage war if deterrence fails is a secondary and conditional one, designed to render the performance of the immoral act unnecessary. Neither group of moralists, employing exclusively moral principles, can say with certainty which course of policy action would more probably lead to nuclear war — continued participation in a system of mutual deterrence or unilateral nuclear disarmament. Estimations of probability require prudential political judgments based on empirical knowledge concerning history, psychology, strategy and the ways human beings and governments are likely to behave in varying circumstances. Those who advocate unilateral nuclear disarmament may achieve a sense of "interior moral purification," but the political realist must live with a more ambiguous conscience, while considering that balanced deterrence represents a politically surer guarantee of peace.

The report was discussed and rejected by the General Synod in February 1983, which reinforced its acceptance of the underlying principle of just war theory, that one must distinguish and pursue the lesser of two evils. In opening the debate, the Bishop of London, Dr. Graham Leonard, a prominent advocate within the Anglican church of the retention of the British nuclear deterrent and Chairman of the Church's Board of Social Responsibility, criticized the report on several grounds. Dr. Leonard, drawing analogies between pacifism and unilateral disarmament, remarked that what might be morally right as the choice of an individual ought not to be advocated as a national policy as this would demand that others not sharing the same conviction would also bear the consequences. Unilateral nuclear disarmament would allow nuclear weapons to lie solely in the hands of those without scruple about their use, either in war or blackmail. He therefore supported nuclear deterrence, stating that people "must not simply wait passively for Armageddon, nor seek a peace which was no peace, in which evil could prevail unchallenged and unchecked."[69]

The Most Reverend Robert Runcie, Archbishop of Canterbury, also spoke against the report, declaring:

Since I believe that the unilateralist approach would undermine disarmament negotiations in progress without exerting exemplary influence, I cannot accept unilateralism as the best expression of a Christian's prime moral duty to be a peacemaker.[70]

Runcie feared the international consequences concerning Britain's alliance structure should unilateralism be pursued, stating that it would have a "traumatic effect on the alliance on which the peace and stability of Europe has rested since World War II," and would strengthen American "advocates of isolationism,"[71] especially in view of the "moral inconsistency in seeking to remain within an alliance which accepts a policy of nuclear deterrence while declining to take one's share in the means by which that policy is sustained."[72] In concluding, the Archbishop of Canterbury implicitly attacked the air of moral superiority often manifested by antinuclear activists, both within and outside the church:

Principle is not the exclusive possession of those attracted to larger gestures; it also belongs to those whose moral sense expresses itself in a painstaking precision and care about detail which I have found among those actually involved in disarmament negotiations.[73]

The proposal to adopt the report was defeated by 338 to 100.

Nevertheless, the synod narrowly approved an amendment by the Bishop of Birmingham, the Right Reverend Hugh Montefiore, endorsing a "no first use" posture. Dr. Montefiore stated that a commitment by both sides to such a posture would remove at one stroke the possibility of nuclear blackmail. When pressed by Dr. Leonard to say what he would do if the West was being overrun by large conventional forces, Dr. Montefiore said to loud applause that he would not use nuclear weapons first, whatever the consequences.[74] The amendment stated that the Synod

judges that even a small-scale first use of nuclear weapons could never be morally justified in view of the high risk this would lead to full-scale warfare; . . . [and] believes that there is a moral obligation on all countries (including the members of NATO) publicly to forswear the first use of nuclear weapons in any form.[75]

In addition to this concession to the unilateralists, the synod carried another motion calling upon the dioceses to "study and pray about the issues raised in the report, *The Church and the Bomb*."[76] Thus, while defeating the spirit of unilateralism in the church, the synod failed to exorcise it completely. This has meant that the report, while not approved, still carries significant weight and legitimacy. It needs scarcely to be pointed out that the report was cited by CND to attract Christian support and to legitimize CND's goals. It was hailed as an "exciting step forward in the growing concern about nuclear weapons."[77]

Various church groups have taken initial steps in favor of civil disobedience. The International Affairs Department of the British Council of Churches, led by Paul Oestreicher, a vice-chairman of CND and a member of the working party that wrote *The Church and the Bomb*, produced a report in March 1983 favoring nonviolent direct action in support of unilateral nuclear disarmament by Britain. The document supports the principle of extending passive noninvolvement to active civil disobedience, from a mere refusal to take part all the way to positive obstruction. It suggests that the churches support the "right" of individuals to express their consciences in this manner.[78]

One member church of the council, the Quakers, has meanwhile agreed to support members of its staff who are withholding that portion of taxes presumed to be allotted to arms expenditure by the government, rather than to collect the full tax from them as its legal obligation as an employer.[79] A more direct action was taken by Christian CND when in May 1983 it demonstrated at the USAF F-111 base in Upper Heyford, Oxfordshire.[80]

While most church groups are unlikely to resort to such extreme measures, nevertheless, it is clear that support for unilateral nuclear disarmament on moral grounds has a significant base among churchgoers of all denominations. Interest by church groups and wide dissemination of *The Church and the Bomb* help stamp the imprimatur of legitimacy upon unilateralism in general and CND in particular. By providing grass roots support for CND, the church helps swell CND's ranks, mutes criticisms of the overall leftist nature of the antinuclear movement, and helps CND occupy the moral high ground in the nuclear debate.

LABOUR AND THE ANTINUCLEAR MOVEMENT

The resurgence of CND has been converted into direct political impact through the British Labour party. While Labour has not been captured part and parcel by CND, the position of mainstream Labour is more or less identical to that of the antinuclear organization.

The Labour party, from Attlee to Callaghan, formerly had a long tradition of supporting NATO, and favoring deployment of nuclear weapons by the alliance in general and by Britain in particular. It was a Labour government in January 1947 that took the decision to produce British nuclear weapons.

Labour's first flirtation with unilateral nuclear disarmament came in 1960 with the rise of CND. However, as this position was abandoned at the following year's party conference, the Labour government of Harold Wilson, which came to office in October 1964, retained the Polaris program initiated by the Conservative Macmillan government, its only sop to unilateralism being a reduction of the planned number of submarines from five to four. The Labour government also agreed to allow the basing of 70 U.S. F-111 aircraft in Britain.

The Callaghan Labour government moved further, agreeing in 1976 to an augmentation of these U.S. forces by another 90 F-111s. Moreover, it spent £1 billion on *Chevaline*, a Polaris penetration aid, that had been begun by the Conservative Heath government, and laid the groundwork for accepting U.S. cruise missiles in Britain. Even in opposition, when Labour has generally been more free with its antimilitary rhetoric, Callaghan and former Defense Minister Fred Mulley supported the INF decision.

However, CND's resurgence soon overwhelmed Labour at the grass roots level. Callaghan resigned the leadership and was replaced by Michael Foot as the Left came to dominate the party in 1980. Institutionally, the Left guaranteed a lock on the Labour electoral college, in which Labour MPs now have only 30% of the votes, while the unions have 40% and the largely radical constituency Labour parties have 30%.

The pro-CND Left has meanwhile been firmly ensconced in power throughout the party structure. Labour's annual conference voted for three successive years against a British nuclear deterrent and against U.S. nuclear bases in Britain. A narrow pro-CND majority has been established in the National Executive Committee, while 120 parliamentary Labour MPs, over half of Labour's representation in the last parliament, were members of the Commons CND Group.[81] Ironically, the institutional position of the Labour Left was strengthened after the party's crushing defeat in the June 1983 election, because the party's candidate selection process increased the proportion of Labour Left MPs in the party's parliamentary contingent. Within Labour's hierarchy, only the Shadow Cabinet has remained opposed to unilateralism.

Despite these defeats, Labour moderates have fought a rear-guard action against unilateralist sentiment within the party. After Foot's ascendance, Labour moderates took a pro-cruise but anti-Trident posture. However, their ranks were depleted owing to defections to the Social Democratic party, founded in January 1981 by senior Labour MPs Roy Jenkins, David Owen, William Rodgers, and Shirley Williams. Moreover, the remaining Labour moderates were hard hit when the unilateralist resolution passed at Labour's October 1982 annual conference with a two-thirds share of the vote, and thus became party policy.

The strength of such sentiment in the Labour party led such moderates as Roy Hattersley, Peter Shore, and Denis Healey, the shadow foreign secretary and deputy party leader, to tailor their views accordingly. Healey, who opposes unilateral disarmament, had in early 1983 renounced his earlier support for deployment of INF (even if "legitimized" by an INF agreement):

> We have a chance at this moment to start the process of multilateral disarmament by agreement on long-range theater nuclear forces.[82]

> NATO already possesses a medium-range deterrent in Europe sufficient for any rational purpose.[83]

Healey, however, did attempt to draw the line by opposing closure of existing U.S. nuclear facilities in Britain. Despite such efforts to appease the Left, the moderate Labourites still retained some strength to resist unilateralist pressures. The Labour party manifesto for the June 1983 general election was formulated with ambiguities and qualifiers in an attempt to placate the center and to diminish intraparty differences. While clear commitments were made to scrap Trident and block cruise, other unilateralist policies concerning Polaris and the closure of American bases were blurred by vague language. The fuzzy nature of the entire document may be best illustrated by the built-in contradiction of the determining paragraph on Labour disarmament policy:

> Unilateralism and multilateralism must go hand in hand if either is to succeed. It is for this reason that we are against moves that would disrupt our existing alliances, but are resolved on measures to enable Britain to pursue a non-nuclear defense policy. . . .[84]

The various qualifications in the document contradicted its basic unilateralist thrust. One Labour leader described it as "the longest suicide note in history."[85]

These modifications did not prevent the eruption of a centrist counterattack on unilateralist policy in the midst of the June 1983 election. Healey and Shore both tried to rewrite Labour policy while on the campaign trail by downplaying or even dismissing Labour's unilateralist stance, much to the consternation of party leader Michael Foot. Underscoring the importance of British participation in multilateral disarmament negotiations, Healey said: "If the Russians, contrary to what Mr. Andropov has said, fail to cut their nuclear forces, as a result of such negotiations, it would be a new situation that we would consider then."[86] Former Prime Minister James Callaghan also declared unambiguously against unilateralism:

> Our refusal to give up arms unilaterally has brought better and more realistic proposals from the Soviet Union and could form the basis of serious negotiations. Before they begin, and unless we reach satisfactory agreement, Britain and the West should not dismantle these weapons for nothing in return.[87]

Faced with majority Labour sentiment for unilateralism on one hand and with an implacable minority's opposition to it on the other, Foot's inept attempts to limit the damage were to no avail. For example, during a brief television interview, Foot underscored the dispute by saying "no" when asked if a Labour government would scrap Polaris regardless of Soviet actions, and then said "no" when asked if there were any circumstances that would cause Labour to retain it.[88]

While Labour's fractious and inept campaign undeniably cost it votes, broad British opposition to Labour's pro-CND stand was a decisive factor in its defeat. Despite a 13.3% unemployment rate at the time of the June election, the Conservatives won nearly a third of trade union votes, and even garnered the votes of one fourth of the unemployed.[89]

This time, however, defense issues seemed to dominate. Repudiation by British voters of Labour's overall pro-CND platform was demonstrated in one survey which found that 47% of British voters preferred Thatcher's defense program to 23% for Foot's unilateralist one.[90] Doubters had recourse to the SDP-Liberal Alliance, which supports multilateral disarmament measures (despite strong unilateralist sentiments among some in the Liberal Party), and which took 26% of the popular vote to Labour's 28%. This left the Conservatives with 44% and a landslide majority of 161 seats over all opposition (397 Tory seats to 209 Labour, 23 Alliance and 4 Nationalist).[91]

The election illustrates two inherent and fatal elements of CND's potential for political influence. First, while CND's efforts to capture Labour were as successful as could possibly be expected, it has proven impossible to homogenize the party. The residual centrists fought an implacable rearguard campaign against unilateralism. Thus, although CND supporters control most of the main party organs, the moderates have proven completely indigestible, as demonstrated by the pairing of the moderate Roy Hattersley, as deputy leader, with distinctly leftist Neil Kinnock as party leader. Should the strengthened Left ever select both the party leader and deputy leader from within its own ranks, and weaken the influence of the moderate Labourites even further, many senior MPs might refuse to serve under the Labour leadership. This would risk a breakdown of party discipline or a renewed wave of defections to the SDP, as one moderate Labour MP implied: "We'd just let the hard left get on with it."[92] This means that further radicalization of the Labour Party would serve to further weaken it.

Second, while CND's best hope for converting its program into national policy rests upon a radicalized Labour party, the British people have demonstrated their overwhelming opposition to such policies by repudiating a CND-aligned party even in a period of massive unemployment. Owing to the simple fact that Britons generally oppose unilateralism, democratic realities determine that the parliamentary route for CND is in actuality a dead end. CND may exert influence through sympathetic MPs, but if Labour attempts to underwrite CND's policies, it will never have a chance to govern.

Yet that is precisely what Labour seems bent on doing. The National

Executive Committee of the Labour party has published a major statement calling for a "nonnuclear defensive deterrence policy" that would include immediate cancellation of the Trident missiles; removal of all US nuclear systems, including cruise missiles, from Britain; and the decommissioning of the Polaris system. Although the policy statement rejects any increase in British conventional manpower levels or the NATO Central Front, it calls for the reorganization of NATO reserve forces and the redesigning of airforce missions to strictly defensive purposes. The Labour party statement also proposes that greater emphasis should be placed on smaller and simpler equipment that could be produced in larger quantity because of lower cost.

THE FUTURE PROSPECTS OF THE BRITISH ANTINUCLEAR MOVEMENT

The prospects are slim that the British antinuclear movement in and of itself will succeed in giving new meaning to the phrase, *Pax Britannica*. The movement, composed as it is of radical socialist and Christian pacifist elements in the tradition of British political dissent, comprises only a very small fraction of Britons. Nevertheless, the protestors have succeeded in reaching out to the population at large, focusing attention on the nuclear arms issue, and gaining support for some of their less radical ideas.

A critical element in determining the future of the antinuclear protest movement will be the degree to which the British Labour party continues to act as its surrogate in the corridors of national power. It is significant that Labour picked Neil Kinnock, a charismatic and politically adept member of the now-dominant "soft left," as the new party leader. Kinnock, himself a longtime member of CND, has affirmed his continued commitment to unilateral nuclear disarmament by Britain. He has resolved to remove all British and American nuclear weapons from British soil during the span of the next Labour government, in accordance with his belief that the British "are not masters of our own foreign policies because of our excessive state of obligation to the American Government." In marked contrast to his perception of the United States as militaristic, Kinnock opines that the Soviets suffer from a "rampant defensiveness," believing them to have no intention of ever invading Western Europe.[93] Thus, the leader of the Labour party appears to share the fundamental foreign policy perceptions of E. P. Thompson, the philosopher of the British antinuclear movement. Consequently, Kinnock has affirmed that he would never employ Britain's independent nuclear deterrent, even in response to a nuclear attack on British soil. Moreover, he chooses to repudiate the American nuclear guarantee, stating paradoxically that taking shelter under the U.S. nuclear umbrella is "the way for all of us to get killed."[94]

Despite his frequent statements in support of unilateral nuclear disarmament, Kinnock has attempted to restrain the "hard left" elements in the Labour party, largely so that some measure of party unity can be restored. He supported the Atlanticist and "multilateralist" Roy Hattersley, who has largely succeeded Healey as the banner-carrier of the residual Labour "right," for the post of deputy party leader. (Hattersley himself opposes Trident and GLCM deployment, and prefers to abandon even Polaris "if it can be negotiated away," but draws the line at removal of American "nuclear" bases from Britain.)

When Labour's annual conference of October 1983 voted overwhelmingly for the next Labour government to "unconditionally scrap all nuclear weapons systems" and to remove all American "nuclear bases," Kinnock pressed unsuccessfully to avoid the question of timing and to delete the word "unconditionally," feeling it left too little room for maneuver. (He then voted for the resolution anyway.) Kinnock also claimed rather disingenuously that a resolution for which he voted that rejected British membership in "any Pentagon-dominated military pact based on the first use of nuclear weapons," and which passed with a large majority, did not refer to NATO. In fact, on his trip to the United States in February 1984, Kinnock emphasized the importance of retaining conventional American bases in Britain. He has sought to emphasize British participation in a non-nuclear NATO, alluding to the possibility of increasing the size of the British Army of the Rhine (BAOR) with some of the savings from nuclear weapon expenditures.[95] In essence, the Labour leader has sought to carve out a position in the center of his party, though one that reflects the tremendous Labour shift to the left brought about partially by the British antinuclear surge.

Kinnock's position has been reflected in his approach to concrete matters of Labour party organizations. In formulating the Labour shadow cabinet, Kinnock divided the senior portfolios among the Labour "right" and soft-left mainstream, virtually excluding the most militant elements. This reflects the failure of the hard left to dominate the Labour Party's National Executive Committee (NEC), despite its gains in that body. The thwarting of the Labour hard left may partially be attributed to the influence of Labour's trade union power brokers, who have been taking a turn towards moderation since the devastating June 1983 election. Thus, the NEC now contains twelve "rightists," nine soft-left members, and eight hard-leftists. However, time does not appear to be on the side of the Labour party's Atlanticist segment, which is now largely confined to a small parliamentary contingent of about 30 MPs. In essence, then, Neil Kinnock has been agile in presiding over the evolution of the British Labour party from social democracy to neo-Marxism, an evolution largely catalyzed by the continuing influence of the British antinuclear movement.

An antinuclear, soft-left dominated Labour party stands significantly to the left of the broad base of British public opinion, particularly on defense issues. Nevertheless, Labour under Kinnock has managed to avoid the openly fractious behavior that so damaged its campaign efforts. Moreover, Labour appears to have been playing increasingly successfully upon British economic difficulties, ironically at a time when Prime Minister Thatcher's austere economic policies have begun to show positive results. As time passes since the rapid and disruptive rise to preeminence within the Labour Party of the soft left, so too does Labour—and through it, the British antinuclear protest movement—have an opportunity of regaining concomitantly a competitive political position within Great Britain.

Realization of the political threat Labour may begin to pose, coupled with a pragmatic perspective of British economic problems, has led the Thatcher government to moderate accordingly some of its policies and pronouncements on defense and foreign policy. While some of these changes may reflect more shadow than substance, nonetheless they indicate Conservative concern with an enhanced Labour position. At the purely economic end of the scale, the British government has announced that it will not renew its commitment to an annual 3% increase in real terms of defense spending once the NATO-wide commitment lapses in 1986. (However, the latest White Paper on defense makes clear that the emphasis will be on getting more for the defense pound.) One ramification of economizing is a British reluctance to move forward with development and eventual deployment of "emerging technology" (ET) arms, which would be designed to reduce NATO's dependence on nuclear weapons by improving conventional defenses. This results from the expense of the new technologies, and of the relatively weak ability of European industry in general, and British industry in particular, to compete in the ET area with American manufacturers. Opposition to ET complements the antinuclear movement's position that the new technologies would, somewhat anomalously, provoke an early nuclear escalation. This is alleged to be a possible consequence of the targeting of Warsaw Pact second echelons that the ET-related strategies, in accordance with the Rogers Plan, would involve.

On a purely political level, the Conservative government, recognizing the success of the antinuclear protest movement in focusing public attention on the risks of deterrence, has begun to emphasize quietly its interest in better relations with the East and in seriously pursuing nuclear arms control agreements. This was symbolized by Prime Minister Thatcher's February 1984 trip to Hungary, but is more significantly illustrated by public advocacy by senior government officials of an eventual British role in the START talks. This stems partly from a recognition that the low warhead ceiling proposed by the United States, combined with the effects of the expansion of the British deterrent force through the Trident modernization program, would tend to enhance the relative importance of the British deterrent in the overall strategic equation. (France has, however, success-fully resisted this logic.)

Moreover, a seemingly conscious effort is being made to distance the policy of the British government from that of the United States where pos-sible on non-NATO issues, such as the intervention in Grenada, and U.S. policy in Central America. Of course, Britain has remained staunchly sup-portive of most Western policies, particularly concerning Lebanon and the Persian Gulf. Criticism has been made of President Reagan's strategic defense initiative, largely on the grounds that strategic defense would diminish the utility of the British nuclear deterrent, would leave Europe vulnerable to Soviet attack in the absence of a concomitant defense against medium-range missiles, and might tempt the United States to lapse into isolationist complacency. But British industry wants a share of SDI.

The shift in the declaratory, and to a lesser extent, actual policies of the Conservative government is not exclusively a result of the impact of the British antinuclear movement. Yet it is certain that the enduring influence of the protest movement, particularly with regard to the Labour party, is having an indirect effect even upon a party with as large a parliamentary majority as Mrs. Thatcher's. The relative weakness of the Liberal-Social Democratic center Alliance has meant that the Conservatives must claim the middle ground or perhaps see it forfeited to the antinuclear Labour party. Thus, a staunch Atlanticist government is taking more moderate positions to avoid erosion of its influence within the more moderate seg-ments of British society. While the prospects for an enhanced direct role for the British antinuclear movement are dim, the repercussions of its activities within the Labour party, and even indirectly with regard to the ruling Con-servative party, may endure, even though the antinuclear issue is not likely to be the decisive factor determining the outcome of the next parliamentary election required by law to be held before the summer of 1988.

In the late summer of 1984, it seemed for a while that the defense debate in Britain might shift away from the issue of cruise missiles to the more complex question of nuclear versus conventional priorities. There was con-cern whether the United Kingdom could afford to meet all the defense demands which are likely to be placed upon it in the years ahead: to build the Trident SLBM, maintain adequate ground and air forces on the Central Front, preserve its maritime posture to carry out expanding missions in the Atlantic and out-of-area contingencies, and strengthen its capabilities for carrying out amphibious operations on NATO's Northern Flank. The cruise missile returned to the fore in September 1984, when the Liberal party at its annual Assembly at Bournemouth voted 611 to 556 in favor of a resolution calling for the removal "forthwith" of U.S. missiles from Brit-ish soil and the adoption by NATO of a pledge on no-first-use of nuclear weapons. The unilateral disarmers in the party overrode the party leader,

David Steel, who thought that such a position would make it more difficult for the Liberals to maintain their Alliance with the Social Democratic party in the next election campaign (probably before the spring of 1988). The latter stresses the need for negotiation on cruise missiles in East-West arms talks. Steel argued in vain that British voters have demonstrated over and over that they will not support a party that dodges its basic responsibility for defense.

The Annual Conference of the Labour Party at Blackpool in early October 1984 went beyond the Liberal majority and demanded unilateral nuclear disarmament across the board. It pledged that upon a return to governing power, it would cancel the Trident submarine program and remove not only cruise missiles but all U.S. nuclear bases and weapons from Britain. The party's two leading anti-unilateralists, former Prime Minister James Callaghan and former Defence Minister Denis Healey, were able to accomplish nothing more than preventing the Labour Conference from going on record in favor of excluding all American bases. Labour called for a completely nonnuclear strategy but refused to support the increased expenditures for conventional forces that such a strategy would require. The results at Blackpool, including the triumph scored by the militant Marxist leader of the Miners' Union, Arthur Scargill, were seen as a major setback to Labour leader Neil Kinnock, who wished to project the image of a more responsible party. Few observers at present think that the British electorate is anywhere near supporting unilateral nuclear disarmament or the denuclearization of Britain's strategy as a member of NATO. The fact, however, that majorities in two of Britain's four political parties now stand for extreme defense positions demonstrates to what degree the British consensus on Atlantic defense policy is disintegrating. It also shows that a large number of British politicians are convinced that the antinuclear crusade retains significance for the future.

NOTES

1. For the background of British pacifism in the early part of the century, see Peter Brock, *Twentieth-Century Pacifism* (New York: Van Nostrand Reinhold Company, 1970), pp. 25, 36, 109 and 129.
2. An article by J. B. Priestly in *New Statesman*, November 2, 1957, quoted in John Minnion, "CND: Twenty-Five Years on the March," *New Statesman*, February 18, 1983, p. 17.
3. John Minnion and Philip Polsover, eds., *The CND Story* (London: Allison and Busby Ltd., 1983), p. 17.
4. "Missiles a Major Issue in British Vote," *New York Times*, May 18, 1983.
5. "Peace Movement Takes on New Life," citing a MORI poll, *Boston Globe*, January 30, 1983.
6. "The Crowds Under the Umbrella," *The Times*, November 26, 1982.

7. See Owen Greene et al., *London After the Bomb: What a Nuclear Attack Really Means* (Oxford: Oxford University Press, 1982).

8. See *Medical Campaign Against Nuclear Weapons: A Background to the Campaign* (MCANW pamphlet, Cambridge Free Press (n.d.).

9. Peter Foot, *The Protesters: Doubt, Dissent and British Nuclear Weapons* (Aberdeen: Centre for Defense Studies, 1983), p. 33.

10. "CND Ponders Where It Goes From Here," *Financial Times*, March 2, 1983.

11. "Learning the Language of Fear," *The Times*, February 28, 1983.

12. "The Inside Threat," *Daily Telegraph*, October 26, 1981.

13. Lord Alun Chalfont, "The Great Unilateralist Illusion," *Encounter*, April 1983, p. 25.

14. "An Interview With Mary Kaldor," *Working Papers*, September-October 1982, p. 47.

15. Alison Whyte, "Thinking for Ourselves," *supra* note 8, p. 88.

16. "Oxford Resolves to Fight for Queen and Country," *Wall Street Journal*, February 17, 1983. See also "21 Peace Women Ordered to Leave,"*The Times*, March 10, 1983.

17. "Peace Movement's Human Chain Has a Few Weak Links," *Financial Times*, April 2, 1983.

18. Peter Foot, *op. cit.*, p. 28. The only major unions opposing this policy are the engineers, the electricians, and the National Union of Teachers, which have refused to affiliate with CND.

19. *Supra* note 13, p. 21.

20. "Communism Battles over the Printed Word," *Financial Times*, November 18, 1983.

21. "CND Partners of Communists Says Kent," *Daily Telegraph*, November 14, 1983.

22. Other members are appointed from CND regional organizations. Keith Best, Geoffrey Warhurst, Hans-Joachim Veen, Rodger Eling, *Playing at Peace* (London: The Bow Group in cooperation with the Konrad Adenauer Stiftung, 1983), p. 91.

23. *Supra* note 13, p. 24.

24. *Supra* note 13, p. 20. Stanslav Levchenko, a KGB officer who defected to the United States in 1979, in referring to possible Soviet use of "agents of influence" in the European protest movements, stated: "I think that 99.9 percent of the people active in the peace organizations are honest," adding: "But they want a leader or two. They want somebody who stays late to write out the platform when they go home to bed. Those people stay busy. Sometimes it's just a slogan. But the degree of Soviet success so far has been great. The buildup of criticism on nuclear weapons by these groups has gone basically in only one direction—against NATO." "KGB Officers Try to Infiltrate Antiwar Groups," *New York Times*, July 26, 1983.

25. "Disarmers Hit a Sensitive Nerve," *Financial Times*, October 26, 1981.

26. "CND Exposes Reagan's Nuclear Fraud," *Morning Star*, November 19, 1981.

27. "Outflanked by Thatcher, Missile Foes Look Past the Law," *Wall Street Journal*, April 6, 1983.

28. Lord Alun Chalfont, *op. cit.*, p. 24.

29. "CND Votes to Use Civil Disobedience Tactics in Anti-Missile Protest," *The Times*, November 29, 1982.

30. "Outflanked by Thatcher. . ."

31. Sarah Benton, "CND Mass Politics," *New Statesman*, December 3, 1982.

32. "600,000 March in Europe Over Arms Buildup," *International Herald Tribune*, October 26, 1981; "U.S. Nuclear Missiles Protested in Europe," *ibid.*, April 4, 1983; and "Missiles are Fine, if They are British," *The Economist*, October 29, 1983, p. 58.

33. "Campaign Against Missile Site Firms Launched by CND," *Daily Telegraph*, May 4, 1983; "CND Prepares Action Against Cruise Companies," *The Times*, May 3, 1983; and "Tarmac Protests at CND Blacking Campaign," *The Guardian*, May 4, 1983.

34. "CND Takes Nuclear Weapon Debate to the Doorstep," *The Times*, March 26, 1983;

"Missiles a Major Issue in British Vote," *New York Times*, May 18, 1983; "CND Will Concentrate its Attack on Tories in Marginal Seats," *The Times*, April 18, 1983.

35. "British Peace Movement is Down But Not Out," *Christian Science Monitor*, June 22, 1983.
36. E. P. Thompson and Dan Smith, eds., *Protest and Survive* (Harmondsworth: Penguin Books Ltd., 1982), p. 224.
37. *Ibid.*, p. 225.
38. "An Interview With Mary Kaldor," *op. cit.*, p. 47.
39. "One Clear-Eyed Unilateralist," *Washington Post*, February 25, 1983.
40. Scott McConnell, "The 'Neutralism' of E. P. Thompson," *Commentary*, April 1983, p. 31.
41. Timothy Garton-Ash, "The Myth of 'Self-Liberation'," *Spectator*, August 21, 1982, p. 12.
42. *Supra* note 40, p. 31.
43. *Supra* note 40, p. 31.
44. *Supra* note 41, p. 13.
45. *Supra* note 40, p. 30.
46. Presentation by Mary Kaldor for the Study Group on Nuclear Politics and Society, Harvard Center for European Studies, March 4, 1983.
47. "Meddling in Anti-Nuclear Movement?" *Boston Globe*, April 4, 1983.
48. E. P. Thompson, "Human Rights and Disarmament," in E. P. Thompson, ed., *Beyond the Cold War: A New Approach to the Arms Race and Nuclear Annihilation* (New York: Berlin Press, 1982), p. 93.
49. E. P. Thompson, "Freedom and the Bomb," *New Statesman*, April 24, 1981, p. 9.
50. *Ibid.*, p. 10.
51. E. P. Thompson, "A Letter to America," *The Nation*, January 24, 1981, p. 17.
52. E. P. Thompson, "Notes on Exterminism, the Last Stage of Civilization," *supra* note 48, p. 47.
53. *Supra* note 51, p. 17.
54. *Supra* note 48, p. 167.
55. E. P. Thompson, "Zero Option: A Nuclear-Free Europe," in *Beyond the Cold War*, p. 128.
56. *Supra* note 52, p. 12.
57. Mary Kaldor, "The Role of Nuclear Weapons in Western Relations," in Mary Kaldor and Dan Smith, eds., *Disarming Europe* (London: Merlin Press, 1982), p. 110.
58. Mary Kaldor, "Is There a Soviet Military Threat?" in Michael Clarke and Marjorie Mowlam, eds., *Debate on Disarmament* (London: Routledge & Kegan Paul Ltd., 1982), p. 29.
59. *Supra* note 14, p. 48.
60. Louis Mackay and David Fernback, eds., *Nuclear-Free Defense* (London: Heretic Books, 1983), p. 145.
61. *Ibid.*, p. 94.
62. See, for example, "God or the Big Battalions," *The Times*, February 27, 1983, and "Turbulent Priests," *New Statesman*, February 4, 1983, p. 12.
63. "Hume's Concern Over CND's Catholic Leader," *The Times*, April 27, 1983.
64. "CND Chief Comes Under Attack From Papal Envoy," *The Times*, May 14, 1983. The letter included an extract from the Pope's address to the U.N. General Assembly of June 1982: "In current conditions, 'deterrence' based on balance, certainly not as an end in itself, but as a step on the way towards progressive disarmament, may still be judged morally acceptable."

65. *The Church and the Bomb: Nuclear Weapons and Christian Conscience* (London: Hodder and Stoughton, 1982).
66. *Ibid.*, p. 95-96.
67. *Ibid.*, p. 97.
68. *Ibid.*, p. 98.
69. "The Dilemma Facing Christian Pacifists," *The Times*, February 11, 1983.
70. "Archbishop of Canterbury Fears for Negotiations in Progress," *The Times*, February 11, 1983.
71. "Church of England Rejects Call for Nation to Scrap Nuclear Arms," *International Herald Tribune*, February 11, 1983.
72. *Supra* note 70.
73. *Supra* note 70.
74. "General Synod Rejects Unilateral Nuclear Disarmament," *The Times*, February 11, 1983.
75. "Church Appeals Against First Nuclear Strike But Rejects Unilateralism," *The Times*, February 11, 1983.
76. "Mass Destruction Condemned," *The Times*, February 11, 1983.
77. "Bishop Denies Report is Challenging the State," *The Times*, October 19, 1982.
78. "How Civil Disobedience Could Become a Weapon of the Church," *The Times*, May 3, 1983.
79. *Ibid.*
80. *Supra* note 33.
81. "CND Ponders Where it Goes From Here," *Financial Times*, March 2, 1983.
82. "Healey Shoots Down Unilateralists," *The Guardian*, November 6, 1981.
83. Denis Healey, letter to the editor, *The Economist*, March 12, 1983, p. 4.
84. *The New Hope for Britain: Labour's Manifesto 1983*, p. 35.
85. "Labor Stumbles in British Race," *Boston Globe*, May 23, 1983.
86. "British Laborites Split on Missiles," *New York Times*, May 26, 1983.
87. "British Labor Split on Arms," *International Herald Tribune*, May 27, 1983.
88. *Supra* note 85.
89. "Conservatives Win 100-Seat Majority in British Election," *New York Times*, June 10, 1983.
90. "Thatcher: Cool and Confident," *Newsweek*, May 30, 1983, p. 76.
91. "How Britain Voted," *The Economist*, June 18, 1983. The Alliance received only a minute share of seats owing to Britain's 700-year old winner-take-all system on which the American system is based. Proportional representation on a national basis would have given the Alliance a far more significant share of seats.
92. "MPs Say Morale Will Collapse if Meacher Wins Deputy Leadership," *The Times*, July 1, 1983.
93. "Turnouts are Thin at German Arms Protests," *New York Times*, October 18, 1983.
94. Michael Getler, "Labor Party Leader Tangles With Shultz Over U.S. Policies," *Washington Post*, February 15, 1984.
95. William Buckley, Jr., "Neil Kinnock and the Bomb Over Cardiff," *International Herald Tribune*, March 6, 1984.

Chapter 4

The Antinuclear Movement in West Germany: *Angst* and Isms, Old and New

Clay Clemens

ANGST AND THE ROMANTIC STATE OF MIND

Spokesmen for the West German antinuclear campaign insist theirs is an entirely spontaneous phenomenon born of public outrage over NATO arms policy, while the movement's critics instead often see it largely as the product of outside manipulation. Although the movement indeed coalesced around resistance to INF deployment and has been skillfully exploited by the Soviet bloc, the attempt to understand it should not begin with a discussion of missiles or an attempt to demonstrate subversive influence. The origins, extent, character, and impact of today's antinuclear sentiment owe much to certain enduring thought traditions which have shaped German attitudes throughout history—*Angst*, romantic anti-modernism, illiberal anti-parliamentarism and Christian pacifism. These ideas are again at work in several segments of contemporary society. The impact of these thought traditions is clearly evident in the deep distrust many young people and intellectuals feel toward their country's establishment, a mood which leads them to engage in public protest over a number of issues, including nuclear arms policy.

The role these thought traditions play in today's antinuclear protest is frequently overlooked or underrated because they rarely take a very tangible form. No consistent ideological threads can be drawn from the past to the current mood of protest. Instead, the continuity lies in certain ways of thinking, often rather vague tendencies or impulses which, today, engender hostility toward nuclear weapons among young people, intellectuals and students. (Polls show 80% of today's antinuclear activists are under 35 and one fourth are university students.)[1]

One thought tradition of particular significance is the peculiarly German sense of anxiety or *Angst*. This is not ordinary, momentary, personal fear, but a deep-rooted cosmic despair. Historian Karl Dietrich Bracher describes "fear of the future" as "an old pattern of human thought, related to forms of archaic superstition," and it is particularly strong in the German experience.[2] As Fritz Stern asks, "Can one understand German history of the last century without paying particular attention to the element of fear, of *Angst*?"[3]

The state of mind defined earlier as romanticism has, in countless guises, long affected every aspect of German life and thought. Romanticism, strictly speaking, denotes the genre of cultural expression prevalent in Germany and throughout Europe during the first half of the 19th century. Yet romanticism also describes a broader way of thinking, which is traceable to the Middle Ages and visible today. Its essential elements have been characterized by historian Gordon Craig as "that peculiarly German sense of inwardness, or remoteness from reality, of intimate community between self and the mysterious forces of nature and God."[4] Drawing its strength from sources beyond reason—emotion, sentiment, spirit, nature—the romantic state of mind reduces the world to what sociologist Ralf Dahrendorf calls "'dismal dichotomies' between pure good and pure evil,"[5] and gives rise to powerful passions in modern German history. *Angst* and romanticism have influenced German life and thought at all levels of society, intellectual and popular.[6]

The manifestation of romantic impulses and *Angst* in German abstract philosophy has been a pronounced tendency toward anti-rationalism. As early as the late 18th century, Johann Gottfried Herder and J.G. Fichte were stressing spirit and sentiment over reason, and positing an organic as opposed to mechanistic philosophy. By the turn of the 20th century, Friedrich Nietzsche was leading a full and very pessimistic revolt against rationalism, a path followed by Martin Heidegger. Max Weber himself argued the limits of reason, and emphasized the role of intuition and empathy. Sigmund Freud's psychoanalytical thought—the role of the subconscious in human action—fits well into the antirational tradition.

Romantic impulses, and, to a lesser extent, *Angst* have inspired artistic expression more deeply than abstract philosophy. This can be seen not only in the original romantic era in the early 19th century with its spirited rejection of classical art forms, but in the struggle to escape from the constraints of reality, reason and order which has characterized German literature, music and painting ever since. From Goethe, Schiller and Beethoven, to Heinrich Heine, Stefan George and Thomas Mann, German poets, writers and composers have worked endless variations on romantic themes. The apogee was reached with Wagner; like many others, he drew his material from ancient German folktales, which were already redolent with idealized notions of the pastoral life, Germany's magical forest, and noble yet simple and often doomed heroes—Siegfried or Parsifal. Although such 20th century artists as the Expressionist painters or Bertolt Brecht satirized standard romantic themes, they themselves also displayed a most markedly romantic tendency toward escapism. Manifestations of *Angst* and romantic impulses can be traced clearly in the streams of thought that have largely shaped today's antinuclear sentiment—social anti-modernism, political illiberalism and Christian pacifism.

ANTI-MODERNIST TENDENCIES AND THE PROTEST MOVEMENT'S SOCIAL DIMENSION

It is significant that many observers have used the label "ecopeace" to describe Germany's current protest movement. Organizationally, politically and—most important here—thematically, the campaign against nuclear weapons has evolved as an outgrowth of opposition to nuclear power, industrial pollution, housing shortages and even the very pursuit of economic growth. Reflected in this "ecopeace" connection is an intense dissatisfaction with modern technological society, which clearly stems from a type of pessimist, romantic impulse quite common in German social criticism.

Despite its virulently anti-capitalist tone, today's mood of protest owes relatively little to the strong streams of strictly socialist thought in Germany. Indeed, the reformist tradition that attempts to secure material benefits for workers and has been so influential in German social democracy is seen by the movement as bureaucratic and even as an unwitting tool of capitalism. Marxism has had an ambivalent impact on the thought climate among those in today's peace movement. Its comprehensive critique of capitalist society appeals to many young Germans and intellectuals who are drawn above all to the theologies of class struggle and alienation. Yet the orthodox Marxian view of social transformation, which stresses economic progress and industrial expansion, does not resonate with the ideas of the "ecopeace" movement. Moreover, the Marxist notion of historical inevitability demands obedience to one rigid system of thought, while the protest movement emphasizes heterogeneity and the ideal of a broad church. Finally, Marxism is still discredited in some eyes by its association with communism in Eastern Europe and above all East Germany.

The term anti-modernist may be used to describe the entire socio-cultural dimension of the romantic impulse, whether in the early 19th century or the early 1980s. Its essence is partly captured in the classic sociological dichotomy between *Gesellschaft* and *Gemeinschaft* (roughly translated as urban, impersonal commercial society versus traditional, rural, religious community): while the former suggests a heterogeneous, atomized milieu, the latter has the connotation of an organic, tightly knit and secure setting. Unlike Marxism, romantic anti-modernism lacks systematic theories of social change and instead reflects a certain sense of negativism which is almost reactionary.

Among the striking historical manifestations of this anxious, romantic anti-modernism was anarchism: the violent reaction to the transition from traditional to modern society. Anarchism in theory was radically egalitarian and involved a complete rejection of authority, features that distinguish it from other brands of anxious, romantic anti-modernism. By the same token, anarchism was a European wide, leftwing movement, while there have been more specifically German cases of the anti-modern mindset on the right. The *Völkisch* movement, a 19th century forerunner of National Socialism which celebrated "German values" and had racialist, anti-Semitic overtones, struck out against modern society and upheld the virtues of agrarian German culture. Most important of all, however, is "cultural pessimism," a label attached to the ideas of many pre-World War I and Weimar-era German intellectuals like Paul Lagarde and Moeller van der Bruck who deplored industrial society as soulless, uncreative, preoccupied with the mediocre, tainted by foreign influences and lacking in real values. They implied the need for radical violent change in order to revitalize Germany. Sociologist Ralf Dahrendorf called cultural pessimism the most general expression of the romantic attitude in intellectuals, for, as historian Fritz Stern points out, they "emulated the German romantics' esthetic and spiritual interpretation of politics and history, and their disdain for the empirical and material fact."[7]

Writers have traced anti-modernism, particularly the cultural pessimist stream through the course of 20th century Germanic life, finding strong samples of it in the writings of Frank Wedekind, Heinrich Mann, Oswald Spengler, Thomas Mann, Gerhart Hauptmann and Martin Heidegger; in the activities of pre-Nazi, "back to nature" German youth groups, including the famed *Wandervogel* movement, in the imperialist goals of some Wilhelmine leaders as well as those of countless foes of the Weimar Republic. Hitler's Reich marked in many ways the zenith of right-wing cultural pessimism and its critique of modern society, intermixed with ideas drawn from corporatism, Italian-style fascism, and anti-Semitism.

Anti-modernist impulses have also strongly influenced left-wing, even

Marxist, thought in the 20th century. Herbert Marcuse, Max Horkheimer and Theodore Adorno, theoreticians of the "Frankfurt School," combined a neo-Marxist critique of capitalist society with Freudian analysis (anathema as a sickly bourgeois science in the Soviet Union), resulting in a theory that stresses that repressive aspects of modern society, consumerism, and the manipulated media destroy class consciousness; workers living in such a manipulated society cannot recognize how alienated they are from their own interests. This backing off from historical inevitability, bleak outlook, and anti-consumerism (and its concomitant anti-Americanism, resulting at least in part from their years as emigrés in the United States) clearly demonstrate the influence of cultural pessimism.

These various anti-modernist impulses were not entirely dormant during the Federal Republic's halcyon days of unparalleled economic growth, the *Wirtschaftswunder* (economic miracle). Many critics deplored the alleged German willingness to sacrifice traditional values and culture on the altar of prosperity; the *Leistungsgesellschaft* (accomplishment-oriented society) did produce relatively little in the way of art, theater, music and literature, especially when compared to Germany's brilliant cultural heritage (though this may have been a consequence of the necessary concentration on recovery). Yet much of the criticism, even that from conservatives and those who politically supported the Republic, appeared insignificant when seen in light of such rapid technological and economic advances and the *Wirtschaftswunder's* residual benefits — funding for a comprehensive social welfare program, and a growing worldwide status for the Federal Republic as an economic powerhouse.

The anti-modernist impulse had a substantial impact among young radicals in the second and third decades of the FRG. Students of the New Left during the Vietnam War absorbed, often in vulgarized form, the Frankfurt School's amalgam of Marxism, Freudianism and cultural pessimism, not to mention anarchism, in their battle against bourgeois society. *Angst* and romanticism influenced even the disenchanted and the discontented members of the middle class. After the 1960s student movement dissolved, these ideas influenced the violent terrorist groups who, significantly, chose a large department store as their first major target of attack.

Anti-modernism also inspired another major protest mood which, unlike the New Left, generally shuns elaborate and systematic social theories — the "Alternative" cultural movement that gained popularity in many urban areas, especially such larger predominantly Protestant cities as Berlin, Hamburg and Frankfurt. This movement is an amalgam of university students, of whom roughly 25% support it and 12% belong to it,[8] dropouts from the academic and professional worlds, and unorthodox political leftists. This secular ascetical movement professes a contempt for market economics and planning by governments which show no compassion for people, human rights, feminists, homosexuals, drug addicts and those in desperate need of housing. Alternatives see official policies as inherently corrupt, designed to line the pockets of businessmen, bureaucrats, politicians and trade union officials with money. The Alternatives claim to be seeking a new set of post-materialist values and constructing a counterculture. In some cities there is a full counterestablishment, with Alternative stores, newspapers, drug clinics and anti-system politicians.

In the mid-1970s, yet another anti-modern impulse emerged in a backlash against the reputed ecological dangers of policies which, despite "warning signs," continued to foster high growth rates. Pollution of Germany's air and water, a perception that the country's forests were shrinking and, above all, the widely publicized risks of civilian nuclear power gave new life to traditions which stressed the virtues of nature and the pure, pastoral life. The term *ecologist* "is really shorthand for a variety of specific outlooks and relates to a collection of social issues . . . [which] has broadened out into a full-scale attack on the values of modern society" and appears "as a latter-day version of the traditional phenomenon of cultural pessimism with an anti-'1984' orientation".[9] Ecologists declaim against massive factories, roadways, airports, shopping malls, and power plants, things that not only fail to serve human-oriented needs, but that also destroy forests and fields, poison the air and water, and—in the case of nuclear energy— threaten a horrible catastrophe. Their professed philosophy is *Klein aber rein*, ("small but pure"), a "back-to-nature," "small is beautiful" mindset which partly reflects anarchistic tendencies as well as the peculiarly German tradition of cultural pessimism.

By the late 1970s, other issues had emerged which shook the confidence of many Germans in their system and gave the anti-industrialist, anti-capitalist, and anti-bureaucratic impulses of romantic anti-modernism their greatest resonance in years. A second "oil shock" and a worldwide recession aroused doubts about the prospects for continued economic growth, and Bonn's leadership was depicted by critics as so ill-equipped to adapt its policies to these new circumstances that confidence in it was shaken. Books echoing the theme of limits to growth and the social consequences of a failure to grasp those limits, were popular; the movies of Rainer Werner Fassbinder, with their charges that West Germany had prostituted itself to materialism, were a sign of the times. When, by 1982, unemployment had reached unprecedented heights and housing shortages were headline news, a question on the cover of *Der Spiegel* characterized the new pessimism: "Are the Good Times Past?" Nowhere did the anti-growth bias exert a stronger influence than among students and intellectuals who claimed that new values were needed in Germany's post-industrial society.

MANIFESTATIONS OF ANTI-MODERN THOUGHT IN THE ANTINUCLEAR CAMPAIGN

Dissatisfaction with Germany's modernist ethos stemming from a modern-day romanticism and *Angst* has helped shape the current antinuclear protest. Ecologists and "alternatives" are the peace movement's foot soldiers; originally mobilized to oppose nuclear plant construction or urban housing shortages, they quickly shifted their emphasis to antinuclear protest. Social scientist Hans Ruhle notes that ecological demonstrations tapered off as the peace cause gained momentum, and believes the latter cause has permanently absorbed the former.[10] Polls do indeed show an almost perfect correlation between those who oppose nuclear plants and those active in the anti-weapon movement or supportive of it.[11] The Green party, originally ecologically oriented, shifted its emphasis to the antinuclear cause with little difficulty, as did the Alternative lists in cities like Hamburg and Berlin. Clearly, many prominent figures in the peace movement—Erhard Eppler, Heinrich Albertz, many left-wing Social Democrats and Liberals, as well as the Green leaders—were initially active in other causes stemming from the antimaterialist, anti-modernist impulse of contemporary sociocultural romanticism.

This "ecopeace" connection in terms of organization and personnel is understandable. Erhard Eppler, a recognized leader of the ecological and nuclear pacifist cause, has articulated the case against Germany's current social trends. His book on *Paths Out of Danger*, required reading for activists, is a diatribe against "growth." Eppler scoffs at faith in technical innovation and material progress, showing how time and again, economic targets are not reached, yet entail unseen costs and hazards. Politicians are absorbed in managing details rather than considering consequences. The "expertocracy" actually determines policy by determining available options. All of this activity conceals the economic interests that propel us along the same path. Far from calling themselves doomsayers, Eppler observes, ecologists and alternatives claim only to point out the misdirection of current policy; growth as a good in itself produces neither wealth, jobs nor equity, and must be supplanted. No others, least of all those motivated by self-interest or blinded by the exigencies of political self-perpetuation, can lead Germany out of danger. The process of positive change needs the ecologists and Alternatives, who alone offer the right blend of realism and idealism, objectivity and selflessness.

For Eppler, nuclear weapons are manifestations of the same sickness. Just as economic compulsions lead to the concept of "growth," so military compulsions produce that of "power balance"—never defined and in practice undefinable. Eppler claims the faith in technology and bureaucracy engenders the evils associated with growth and nuclear weapons: "There is probably no other area where the 'expertocracy' still governs so completely as in the realm of arms, arms control and arms limitation." For him the prime example of nuclear weapons being thrust upon Western society by experts is the INF decision.[12]

Eppler has plenty of anti-modernist company. Peter Bender, a leading advocate of a European policy "between the Superpowers," defends neutralism and antinuclear tendencies by lamenting the "values that have long since disappeared as articles of consumption in the West's modernity."[13] Like Eppler, his words recall those of earlier cultural pessimists. The same could be said of Berlin pastor Heinrich Albertz, a leading Protestant activist and strong supporter of his city's Alternative subculture: "It is no longer generally understood that one speaks of progress while we are running to our destruction, practically like lemmings. . ."[14]

Certain Marxist theorists demonstrate the pervasiveness of the antimodern impulse stemming from *Angst* and a romantic state of mind, so much so that they no longer espouse an orthodox Marxian faith in progress. The most significant example is Rudolf Bahro, an exiled East German intellectual who has become a major Green party figure and espouses a "red (non-Soviet)-Green" alliance.

> The contemporary peace movement is built on the new formation which originated as a response to the ecological crisis, i.e., the crisis of human evolution itself. Confronted with a capitalist system whose destructive consequences now penetrate to the very core of human identity and which threatens to drag us all down in its collapse, the general action programme of the peace movement aims at a radical transformation in the great urban centres, a life revolution with a spiritual perspective which will bring about a sustained reconstruction of the material foundations on which we no longer stand secure. The spirit of the state and the various parties, with their logic of power and their computerized rationality will be no match for it.[15]

The same blend of radical left rhetoric and theory with a fundamentally romantic impulse is seen in the writing of Johano Strasser, a former "Young Socialist" leader and in the 1960s one of the Marxist student spokesmen:

> If there is a new social question, it is this: How can we protect people from the consequences of a process of progress which has gotten out of their control? How can we prevent them, in their belief that they are promoting their own happiness, from plunging into the most abysmal alienation by unconditionally subjugating themselves to the dictatorship of the technological and bureaucratic apparatus?[16]

Gone from the proclamations of these left-wing writers, fervent supporters of the entire ecopeace movement, is any reliance on many traditional Marxist concepts — above all the inevitability of historical progress. Not coincidentally, they explain the limited involvement of workers in the ecopeace cause by stressing modern consumerism's distorting effect on class consciousness. Their anti-technological, anti-bureaucratic, anti-consumerist, anti-materialist, and anti-rationalist view of society owes much more to cultural pessimism and romanticism than to Marx.

Other writers and artists who propound fervently anti-bourgeois themes have helped form the existing climate of opinion, particularly among younger people. Nobel Prize winning author Heinrich Boll's books — *The Clown, Billiards at Half-Past Nine* — were, remarked American historian, Gordon Craig, "unflattering portraits of the booming economic growth of the Federal Republic . . . [demonstrating his belief that] the simple virtues of courage, responsibility, honor and love [were] unavailing in a callow and bureaucratized society that believed–only in power, influence and money."[17] Another activist celebrity, actress Hanna Schygulla, gained notoriety for her roles in the movies of Rainer Werner Fassbinder, such as *The Marriage of Maria Braun*, where she played a woman who prostitutes herself for success — clearly meant as a symbol for the Federal Republic's postwar materialism.

Though anti-American sentiment is common in Europe, many observers believe it is strongest in Germany and particularly among young, educated Germans who are attracted to the "ecopeace" cause.[18] Students in the 1960s often espoused a dogmatic leftist anti-Americanism, but many of today's protesters find it easy to despise U.S. policy largely because they reject the cultural model the U.S. provides — a model they believe alien to their heritage.[19] *Amerikanisierung* (Americanization) has come to mean the crass materialism, hollow values, and the despoilation reputedly inflicted upon postwar Germany by U.S.-style capitalism. America is the very epitome of what 19th century cultural pessimists, such Weimar figures as Bertolt Brecht, and today's protesters fear Germany has become. Typical of the sentiment are these letters, written to a major newsweekly following its publication of an article on German-U.S. relations:

- It is not only the weapons of the warmongers. We want out of the Americanization of life, which is after all nothing more than the molding of men for the purpose of money.
- As long as I still have a brain that is capable of functioning to some extent, I will not allow myself to be degraded to the role of marionette, neither for bubble gum nor Bonanza nor atomic weapons.
- Sex and crime, American crime series on German television. Drugs (every third American soldier is hooked), Cola and sandwich culture, comics as

spiritual nourishment for children and youth, supermarkets with their consumer terror and much more that shows how poor the U.S. is in real human values.[20]

This anti-Americanism has been heightened by often inaccurate perceptions of "neo-conservatism," "the New Right," and "Reagonomics." United States President Reagan is depicted as a cowboy and an unsophisticated amateur, an archetype of his society. Thus while German youth continue to wear blue jeans and enjoy American rock and roll, demonstrators frequently burn U.S. flags, hang Reagan and Uncle Sam in effigy, and denounce not merely American policy, but also American society in sweeping terms. Even a pro-movement newspaper, the *Frankfurter Rundschau*, felt compelled by such sentiments to warn against an "arrogant and ignorant" anti-Americanism that believes the United States only represents hamburgers and fails to acknowledge that New York — not a German city — is the world's leading cultural center.[21]

This same combination of anti-Americanism and antinuclear sentiments is expressed by journalist Peter Bender, who defends neutralism and antinuclear tendencies by declaring that Europe "must be careful that it itself does not become further Americanized" and indeed should help Russia "avoid Americanization." Indeed, while Europe struggles to free itself from America's "spiritual distractions" and "civilizational demagogery," it can learn from the East which, because of its backwardness and despite its ideology, has preserved old-fashioned values.[22]

Youth revolt is a recurrent feature of the German anti-modern mindset according to historian Peter Merkl:

Is the present generation really very different from earlier German generations of this century? We know that it shares its predecessors' revulsion toward materialist values and bureaucratized life, as well as toward such old German tendencies as quasi-religious longings of varying content, idealism, and inclinations toward romantic utopias.[23]

Historian Karl Dietrich Bracher stresses that this anxious, romantic anti-modernism gives today's protest an especially passionate appeal among young Germans: "Today's fears of the fall of civilization and catastrophe are so great because they coincide with a conflict between the generations," namely disenchantment among educated youth in particular with the Germany they have inherited from their elders.[24]

Antinuclear activists are not comfortable with the anti-modernist label. Eppler maintains that any similarities between the current movement and past romanticism are superficial: Today's antinuclear ecological and Alternative protesters, he insists, are not anti-urban and "do not dream of the restoration of the splendid agrarian society"; they are in the main "progressive" and any reactionary romantic rhetoric comes from right-wing fringe elements of the ecological campaign; and, he asserts, they display no tendencies toward elitism, nationalism, and hero-worship comparable to those of 19th century pessimists.[25]

Scholars remain unconvinced by these attempts to sever the current protest movement's very evident historical ties to older traditions. Hans-Joachim Veen, director of the Social Science Research Institute of the Konrad Adenauer Foundation, who himself criticizes the Federal Republic's overemphasis on materialism and prosperity as its source of legitimacy, nonetheless notes that today's mood of dissatisfaction with German society is "neo-romantic." [26] William Griffith characterizes this view even more clearly when he states that

> . . . this movement is part of the current revival of German romantic cultural pessimism (*Kulturpessimismus*). Over the past decade, a minority of educated Western German youth have been gripped by a romantic disdain for materialism, consumerism, economic growth, bureaucracy, liberalism, bourgeois lifestyle, and conventional morality.[27]

ILLIBERAL ANTI-PARLIAMENTARIANISM AND THE ANTINUCLEAR MOVEMENT'S POLITICS

Today's wave of protest reflects a distinctly negative perception of pragmatic, bureaucratic politics and a rejection of liberal parliamentarianism. This same "illiberal" tendency has been visible throughout modern German history.

Just as it would be a mistake to examine the protest movement's social thought solely in light of socialist ideas — a mistake frequently made — so it is misleading to trace the campaign's political antecedents to any particular party traditions. To be sure the movement clearly does draw substantial support from the Social Democratic party (SPD) left wing, whose spokesmen phrase their antinuclear proclamations in the terms of party programs and party goals. "The parties of peace and detente" should by definition oppose an arms race. Today's mood of protest is also reminiscent of the original Social Democratic party's opposition to arms during the Weimar Republic and to rearmament during the 1950s. In the latter case, a majority of the SPD rank and file, as well as such leaders as Kurt Schumacher, vigorously resisted West German entry into NATO and later the deployment of U.S. nuclear weapons on German soil. Both moves of the Adenauer government were said by Social Democrats to expose Germany to terrible risks while reducing the likelihood of reunification and perpetuating the country's division by contending superpower blocs. Current antinuclear writers often argue that contemporary events prove how right many West Germans were to oppose rearmament.

Yet the current mood of peace protest owes relatively little to party political programs or traditions. While the overall movement's critique of NATO nuclear policy is often indistinguishable from past and present SPD left-wing views, the campaign's impetus in terms of political ideas does not derive from any particular party or parties. No identifiably Social Democratic political ideas have shaped the current climate of opinion. Indeed the movement claims to be—and clearly is—bipartisan, or non-partisan, in its political origins as well as its political character. Many activists make a point of voicing their contempt for the SPD by echoing chants from the 1960s, such as *"Wer hat uns verraten, Sozialdemokraten!"* ("Who has betrayed us—Social Democrats!")

To understand the movement's political dimensions, it is necessary to examine not German party traditions, but tendencies which cut unevenly across party and to some extent ideological lines. Liberal parliamentarianism, espoused originally by parties bearing the "Liberal" tag, became the political mode of all those in the Bismarckian and Wilhelmine era who opposed unrestricted and unaccountable crown or ministerial power. With the support of center-left and center-right, parliament became the locus of governmental responsibility in the Weimar Republic but was eventually undermined by its enemies. Only in the Federal Republic did parliamentarianism truly gain the ascendancy, as all major established political groupings fully supported it. Parliamentarianism essentially entails a readiness to become engaged in representative government with the confidence that this system is best-suited to developing effective policies while safeguarding the rights of the majority and the minorities alike. Implicit in parliamentarianism is the tolerance of opposing views and, inevitably, the tolerance of partisan politics.

The peace movement's antecedents in terms of political thought lie in a reaction against liberal parliamentarianism Today's mood of protest bears the imprint of an illiberal, anti-parliamentarian tendency often seen in German history. The romantic backlash against reason and reality in much of German thought spawned a contempt for liberal institutions and values, a feeling compounded by the exaltation of culture and anti-modernist hatred for bourgeois society. Thus the most passionate illiberal anti-parliamentarians were the turn-of-the-century cultural pessimists. According to Fritz Stern, "Above all, these men loathed liberalism. . . . They attacked liberalism because it seemed to them the principal premise of modern society."[28] Even thinkers like Thomas Mann, Friedrich Naumann, and Ernst Troeltsch often expressed their contempt for liberal parliamentary politics.

As observed by historians, illiberalism has traditionally generated or compounded a great many other impulses—the tendency always to think in terms of friend and foe, to become self-righteously "anti-political" or "unpolitical" and "rise above" mere partisan squabbling. An illiberal bias has often made Germans overly susceptible to "evil fantasy" and "paranoid simplifications," such as Bolshevik or Jewish conspiracies. The illiberal anti-parliamentarian bias in German political thought has continually manifested itself—in Bismarck's effort to circumscribe the power of his class enemies, by Wilhelmine leaders' attempt to perpetuate their brand of Caesarism, by Nazis and Communists alike who undermined the Weimar Republic, and by Hitler in establishing his totalitarian regime. All could count on touching a responsive chord by denigrating parliamentary liberalism, dissent, debate, and tolerance.

Animosity against parliamentary government was submerged in the Federal Republic's early days. Until the mid-1960s, vocal dissatisfaction with West German's liberal political system was heard primarily from the far left and from maverick critics who exerted little influence. Younger Germans and students traditionally classified themselves as apolitical in the 1950s. In the following decade, however, several developments combined to heighten the political activism and discontent of left-wing groups as well as students. The Marxist-oriented Students for a Democratic Society (SDS) became disenchanted with the centrist orientation of its parent party, the SPD. In the 1960s, the SDS increasingly agitated within the universities against traditional educational policies, as well as broader social and foreign policy trends in the Federal Republic.

Developments in the universities coincided with a change at the highest level of German politics: in 1966, the SPD and Christian Democratic Union/Christian Social Union (CDU/CSU) formed a Grand Coalition government. For some critics, this signaled that power would be monopolized. Right-wing resistance to Bonn's Grand Coalition generated support for the neo-Nazi National Democratic party. On the other extreme, left-wing critics moved into "extra-parliamentary opposition" (Apo)—a collection of generally Marxist sects. The Apo's and the SDS formed a New Left milieu, dogmatically Marxist and characterized by radical contempt for bourgeois capitalism, conservative university tradition, and Bonn politicians, as well as American policy in Vietnam, South African apartheid, and right-wing military dictatorships. As early as 1961, historian Stern wrote, "The present crisis of German universities shows that illiberalism is still strongly entrenched in some sectors of German society."[29] Violence marked demonstrations in Berlin and at universities around the country during 1967 and 1968.

Lacking any coherent notion of an alternative, the New Left disintegrated as political conditions changed. After 1969, Willy Brandt's SPD-FDP government held out the attractive prospect of social reform along with a dynamic *Ostpolitik*, and radical opposition to the Bonn establishment mellowed. Many former student activists became engaged essentially in a long-range effort to infiltrate the establishment by participating in government, the mainstream parties (above all the SPD), citizen action groups, or the more orthodox left. Structurally the Apo's dissolved into still radical, but increasingly small and insignificant Marxist, often Maoist, sects such as the new Communist party of Germany or KPD (not to be mistaken for the traditionally pro-Moscow KPD banned by decree in 1957 and legally reestablished in 1969 as the DKP). At the edge of the extreme, radical leftists like Ulrika Meinhof and Andreas Baader organized terrorist cells. This brand of radical violence reached its highpoint in the mid-1970s, winning some sympathy from German youth and leftists by prompting government "crackdowns" on dissent which many viewed as threatening to civil liberties in general.

Two remnants of 1960s radicalism among German youth and leftists survived the 1970s and constitute an important part of today's protest milieu. One, generally described as the Alternative Subculture, includes "dropouts," ex-leftists, and the eighth to a quarter of the current university student population that rejects both the establishment and dogmatic leftism. During the 1970s, these alienated elements turned inward, forming their own "alternative" communities in major cities like Berlin, Hamburg, and Bremen — "self-sufficient" counterculture life styles with an instinctive rejection of traditional values. Politically, the Alternatives have often appeared genuinely anarchistic, propagating such slogans as "All Power in Nobody's Hands," "Make Cucumber Salad of the State," "Legality, Illegality, It Makes No Difference." The term most frequently applied is "spontaneous" — an anti-establishmentarianism manifested in proposals for the radical reorientation of urban housing and environmental policies and an intrinsically unorganized, *dis*organized activism, cynically disdainful of doctrinaire leftism. By the late 1970s, "*Sponti*" (for "Spontaneous") lists of candidates were attracting substantial support in city elections.

A residue of the 1960s brand of left-wing antiestablishment sentiment has lived on inside the SPD itself. Those leftists integrated into the party by Willy Brandt rapidly lost their faith in their ability to effect social and political change. Ever since it dropped its revolutionary Marxist orientation with the 1959 Godesberg Program, the SPD has been viewed as *the* establishment party — a target more than an agent of radical protest. Particularly after free marketeer Helmut Schmidt replaced Brandt in 1974, the party left took a vocal stand against their own government's nuclear energy policy and its pro-NATO, pro-U.S. orientation.

If the vehicles of protest against Bonn politics — the Apos, the SDS, the Alternatives, the SPD-Left — often got bogged down, there was no shortage of the grass-roots dissatisfaction with West Germany's political system, which to some extent had propelled them all. In the late 1970s, two issues emerged which gave new life to this lingering discontent with Bonn's liberal political establishment: nuclear power and nuclear weapons.

Throughout the 1970s, increasing numbers of citizens—by no means all left-oriented—became concerned about pollution and the potential danger of a nuclear accident. Grass-roots groups, petition drives, "initiatives," and local "Green" candidate lists proliferated. By 1982, there was a federal Green party which had become a major political factor—an obstacle to unhindered SPD governance in several regions. With a 6 to 8% share in public opinion polls, the party for a time topped Bonn's traditional third political force, the FDP. In 1983, the Greens won enough votes to exceed the 5% threshold needed to earn seats in the Bundestag, the first party aside from the three main ones to do so for decades. They gained twenty-three seats, enough to form a *Fraktion* and thereby receive committee assignments and speaking privileges.

The Green party has challenged Bonn's establishment even more vigorously than other outsiders or splinter parties (aside from the radical-dogmatic left). It is a function of the party's character and program to treat the system with hostility. Cooperation with mainstream parties would risk purity of principle and thus has been restricted; cooperation with smaller, generally left-wing allies—namely urban "Alternative" lists—poses no such danger and is thus encouraged. In general, the party pictures its political role as an omnibus for minorities, picking up all the outsiders and discontented political groups—including Communists who are not excluded from party ranks despite the wishes of some "pure" Greens. A difficult decision has been whether to become a "party" with a staff and firm program, or whether to remain a dynamic movement.[30] According to Gertrud Schilling, a Green official, the party hopes to abolish Parliament, replacing it with referenda and "basis" or "grass-roots democratic" processes.[31]

THE PEACE CAMPAIGN'S ILLIBERAL TENDENCIES

Among educated German youth and intellectuals, satisfaction with German liberal parliamentarianism has reached its nadir in the campaign against nuclear weapons. Remnants of the 1960s protest, the SPD left and many Alternative circles (if not most Marxist sects), have led the dissent against nuclear weapons, and their complaints against the establishment's unresponsiveness have been picked up by other groups in the antinuclear campaign with little political experience, such as the various Christian pacifist organizations. Thus anti-parliamentarian sentiment in the Federal Republic has proliferated with the peace movement. There is reason to fear that the movement, while proclaiming respect for democratic values and institutions, harbors a profoundly illiberal perspective which could in many ways endanger the first truly healthy democracy in German history.

Such apprehensions arise first from the very nature of the movement's desire to see itself as "unpolitical" — a tendency familiar in the evolution of anti-parliamentarian attitudes throughout German history. The movement, leaders as well as rank and file, have no patience with political debate and compromise. Peace activists see "nuclear death" as a question of human existence which permits none of the "give and take" designed to accommodate dissenting views. Green party leader and Marxist Rudolf Bahro observes that

> . . . political is the last thing we should aspire to become. We shall not get anywhere by accepting a notion of commitment to peace that is *conditioned* by politics, if that means that everything has to be filtered through the power relations in the party, the coalition, the state governments and in NATO, so that the original impulse vanishes and the original intentions are distorted and turned upside down. There have always been other modes of political action.[32]

One observer speaks of a "fanaticism that abhors crossing swords with dissenters;" frequently this leads to a "dropout mentality that prohibits even listening to arguments put forward on specific issues."[33] After witnessing an unruly "peace forum" in Berlin, where SPD representatives were hooted down, a *Die Zeit* correspondent wondered what to make of "a movement that writes 'non violence' on its banner and then with force prevents discussion."[34] At the 1981 Church Day in Hamburg, Defense Minister Hans Apel was also virulently harassed and required bodyguards and shields for fear of eggs and tomatoes being hurled from the assembled Protestant peace activists. Even Eppler mildly rebuked this display of intolerance.

For their role in creating the nuclear problem, the Social Democrats, Christian Democrats, and Free Democrats are often treated as enemies. As Gerhard Wettig put it, "This can even go to the point where anybody who seeks a dialogue with 'them' in Bonn is *a priori* regarded as an enemy."[35] Political foes are villified as "treacherous."

Dissatisfaction with the parties (and the Social Democratic party in particular) manifests itself in the unconventional types of political action the movement has undertaken. SPD party discipline has broken down. Backbench protest and grass-roots activism is generally directed against that party's hierarchy. Green campaigns and participation in Länder parliaments have been avowedly antiparliamentary in character. The Greens adamantly refuse to form parliamentary coalitions which they fear will cause them to compromise on goals.

The very fact that the peace movement is a movement — something working largely *outside* the realm of party politics — further demonstrates how little faith its members have in the parliamentary system. Mass demonstrations, disruption of meetings, citizen initiatives, and other unconventional forms of political action are central to the peace movement's method of operating. Movement leaders, moreover, frequently appeal for "direct action" — a willingness not only to circumvent normal political channels, but also, as one commentator put it, to work outside "the existing structures and laws of the social system."[36] A prominent ecopeace activist, Jo Leinen, noted the movement's strategy has called first for an "appeal phase," then a "demonstration phase" — both unconventional forms of protest clearly underway during 1981–1982 — and finally an intensive "direct action" phase which began to be implemented in the "hot autumn" of 1983, as Pershing-2s started to arrive at Mutlangen. The Three Year Plan was worked out at a 1981 meeting of leading ecopeace organizers (including major Green party figures) and envisioned the defacing of military facilities with blood, mass hunger strikes, and widespread civil disobedience.[37]

The militant peace movement's political orientation may be called "plebiscitary," for it relies on the image of sheer numbers and presents a starkly simple, yes-or-no choice between its own proposed course and the frightful alternative of nuclear death. Eppler's thesis of reform in *Paths Out of Danger* stems from his rejection of "elitist" political expertise: "If salvation grows out of anything today, it is not from the tops of the institutions, but there, where men try humanely to live with one another."[38]

The weakness of the antinuclear movement's commitment to a liberal democratic system is evident in its willingness to tolerate law-breaking and on occasion even violence. Aside from the merely disruptive and unruly political conduct described above, most peace activists define "direct action" as "civil disobedience," or law breaking. According to ecopeace activist Jo Leinen, "unrest must rule the country" during the third phase — intensive direct action — of the Three Year Plan for peace protest.[39] The tactics included blockades of barracks and military installations, as well as "die-ins" (demonstrators feigning death by radioactivity) — all designed to obstruct implementation of the INF plan. There was fear that peace activists would target the missile sites or missile convoys, leading to violent confrontations with U.S. soldiers. Other civil disobedience tactics in the plan included occupation of churches, work stoppages, the refusal to pay government and church taxes as well as electricity bills. More dangerous proposals include taking pictures of "provocative" military installations and publishing them, jamming military radio broadcasts during maneuvers, disrupting NATO air facilities with balloons, and causing breakdowns on the Autobahn to stop military convoys.[40]

The willingness to break certain laws is not restricted to marginal elements in the movement: peace activists in the armed forces have regularly broken rules against their participation in protests, and polls indicate an overwhelming majority of peace activists already support the illegal occupancy of unused houses, for example, while a similarly large proportion are unwilling to serve in the army.[41] Indeed, Green-Alternative party representatives have put the government on notice that they themselves will disobey "unjust" housing laws.

There is greater ambiguity when it comes to *violent* illegality. The movement does not glorify violence in the same way as did turn-of-the-century cultural pessimists. Leaders disassociated themselves from such incidents as the bombing of U.S. military facilities and attacks on American personnel, and only fringe groups in the movement have openly advocated violent tactics. Surveys show German youth in general and peace rally participants largely reject forcible means of protest. Nonetheless, about 15% consider it permissible, and there remains a not inconsiderable reservoir of sympathy among younger Germans, Alternatives, and left-wing intellectuals for the Red Army Faction (RAF), remnants of the Baader-Meinhof gang.[42] Demonstrations against distinguished American visitors to Berlin and Bonn (including Reagan, Haig, and Bush) became full-scale battles with police. The willingness of demonstrators to confront NATO soldiers and occupy NATO installations indicates that the militants do not fear a violent encounter with German or U.S. authorities. A minority undoubtedly hoped to provoke incidents leading to a forceful response from American soldiers. Realizing how adverse the consequences would be, the authorities took precautions to make sure that German police units would handle disturbances.

The movement has turned away no antiparliamentarian allies. Numerous communist-front organizations, as well as the pro-Soviet German Communist party, are openly active in opposing INF. Their affiliation with and financial dependency on the East bloc are well known. A substantial number of Communist and other left-wing political organizations, certified by the Office for Protection of the Constitution as extremist, are actively involved in the peace campaign.[43] One study showed that 17% of German university students, a segment of society from which the movement draws much of its support, identify themselves as Communist or radical left and show a strong "principled anti-parliamentarian" orientation.[44]

Mainstream peace movement leaders treat the Communist K-groups and other extremists warily for fear of arousing criticism from conservatives. At a planning session for the June 1982 Bonn rally, Communists stacked the hall with party members and rammed through blatantly pro-Soviet resolutions. Although this incident and the general nature of Communist activity in the anti-INF cause have aroused bitterness, most Green activists and Christian pacifists in particular stress that the movement must remain ecumenical. The words of a Green leader characterize this view that all peace activists share a common overriding goal, whatever their tactical difference: "One must take up every sincere person who is ready to demonstrate for peace and to be active."[45]

The far-left Alternatives and their press have been more suspicious of Communist influences than the Christians or ecologists, signifying a distrust born of infighting among radical groups. The Alternative newspapers *spontan* and *radikal info* have published exposés of such Communist fronts as the Committee for Peace and Cooperation, the German Peace Union, and others. Left-wing writer Klaus Rainer Rohl, himself a one-time intimate of the Communist left, warned that "useful idiots are almost always cheap"—a reference to pro-Moscow elements in the peace campaign.[46] But the awareness that a close association with Communists taints the peace cause has not been enough to prevent "K-Groups" from entering the movement or to prompt the movement as a whole to repudiate them and refuse to cooperate with them.

It is when movement members speak about the type of political change they favor that the illiberal, anti-parliamentary streak in today's antinuclear campaign emerges most clearly. Activists express their contempt for *Parteienherrschaft*—the rule of parties they consider particularistic and closed—and, in the words of Green party leader Petra Kelly, they "want another republic."[47] Erhard Eppler's own ideas of political change include plebiscites (not used in Germany since they were misused in the Naza era) that could "loosen up" the system, and permitting extremists into representative bodies.[48] The Greens have endorsed measures designed more explicitly to do away with Parliament; the depth of their animosity toward the current system was most clearly evidenced when a group of Greens visited Libya in 1982, where several told strongman Muammar el Qaddafi that they shared some of his views on political theory and hoped themselves eventually to abolish Bonn's Parliament.[49] Nevertheless, leading spokesmen for the movement vigorously deny that its political orientation is illiberal. To the contrary, they assert that fellow peace activists simply desire to "purify" German democracy. Eppler argues that the Federal Republic's political system was well-designed to ensure against the type of instability which undermined the Weimar Republic, but he insists it now works against openness and reform: "Could it not be that our danger today lies more in rigidity than in the lack of stability?"[50]

Yet while even many conservatives may acknowledge that there is scope for reform in the Federal Republic's political system, deep-rooted doubts about the peace movement's commitment to liberal democracy are unavoidable. Too much evidence—the movement's intolerance and anti-pragmatism, its advocacy of direct action and plebiscitory measures, and its passive acceptance of some violence and deep Communist involvement—

points toward a strong stream of illiberal anti-parliamentarianism. For many observers, the antinuclear campaign represents one of the most serious dangers yet to the Federal Republic's attempt to secure its own political Westernization.

THE RELIGIOUS DIMENSION OF THE PEACE MOVEMENT

Angst and the romantic state of mind have helped form those religious thought traditions in German history that have most influenced current antinuclear sentiment. Although the spiritual and secular power of both major churches made Christianity an overwhelmingly significant force in Germany through the centuries, the religious currents which have so powerfully shaped today's protest do not really flow from the orthodox churches. Instead, the impulses of greatest importance emanate from Christian ways of thinking that historically were reactions against established church authority, conventional practice, and often even orthodox tenets of Catholicism and Protestantism. Pacifism, which has always cut across confessional lines, was clearly one such tradition.

There are several reasons why mainstream Catholicism and Protestantism have not generally fed the currents of today's antinuclear opinion. Ever since the Reformation, German Catholicism as a social institution has developed an internal cohesion to help preserve itself from external pressures, such as Bismarck's anticlerical *Kuturkampf*; it became a self-contained community, firmly established in Bavaria and the Rheinland. Consequently, respect among Catholics for the German church hierarchy's authority has been strong. Though not always strictly conservative in doctrinal or political matters, the German bishops have nonetheless generally used their own powerful position and their church's cohesion to preserve traditional tenets of the faith and to discourage internal dissent. Although its status since World War II has suffered somewhat from a belief that church leaders acquiesced in Hitler's takeover, and from an increasing secularization of German society, mainstream Roman Catholicism as defined by the hierarchy still commands adherence. Twice as many Catholics as Protestants attend church regularly.[51] There they hear warnings against the temptation to make decisions on moral grounds without taking into account the ramifications such decisions may have beyond the personal sphere. In political affairs, the church has always adhered to the doctrine of just war, while resisting pacifist tendencies; it has also used its authority to support the Federal Republic's security policies, including deterrence, while condemning the threat posed to Christianity by Soviet communism.[52]

Lacking Catholicism's overarching institutional and doctrinal cohesiveness, Protestantism by definition has spawned a wider variety of thought traditions, some of which have helped to generate antinuclear sentiment. The confession's common denominators are the Lutheran doctrine of justification by faith and the priesthood of all believers, which reduce the role for religious authority beyond the dictates of scripture and one's own conscience. Mainstream Protestantism has historically emphasized that this freedom of the spirit makes faith an inward experience, engendering both doctrinal conservatism and political conservatism. Luther was firmly convinced that secular authorities are ordained of God to preserve order among sinful men. This conservatism dominated Protestantism for centuries; not unjustified charges that it failed actively to resist Hitlerian rule (except for the "Confessing Church," those Protestants who opposed Hitler's attempt to take over the churches)[53] combined with modern Germany's secularization, have compelled postwar Protestantism to secure itself against any charge that it is collaborating with evil by making room for dissenting streams of thought.[54] Nonetheless the German Protestant church (EKD) contains strongly conservative elements. The EKD's official policy on nuclear weapons (though under challenge) still offers a justification for deterrence policy. [55]

Given Catholic traditionalism and Protestant conservatism on such questions as the Christian's political obligations and the specific issues of nuclear deterrence, neither mainstream confession could be described as the major religious contributor to today's antinuclear mood. What has fed the currents of peace sentiment are those Christian traditions always regarded as dissenting. In today's peace movement, as in the past, many Christians have believed they could only overcome a pessimistic, even despairing uncertainty about the state of their souls by demonstrating their faith actively and externally, unconstrained by established dogma and, when necessary, even in violation of both spiritual and secular authority. Whatever else separated these various nonconformists or anti-establishment streams of religious thought from one another, they have shared a common disdain for dogma. In many respects, these same features of past Christian dissent demonstrate the strength of the romantic reaction against reason and reality. They asserted the primacy of emotion, spirit, and sentiment and disdain for the scholastic, bureaucratic dogmatism represented by established religious authority.

Even in pre-Reformation times there were small Christian breakaway groups labeled "Millenarian" — radically egalitarian, anti-urban, and alienated from society. In preparing for the millenium, most saw the need for radical change and even violent change in earthly society, including quite often the elimination of secular as well as religious authority; many such groups saw the Church of Rome as the anti-Christ, and they desired to restore pure, primitive Christianity.[56]

Dissent was particularly pronounced in later centuries among Protestants who rejected the conservative interpretation of Luther's emphasis on the individual and independent conscience, that is, those who denied that Christianity was an entirely inward faith. To some extent, this dissent against Lutheran conservatism began with Thomas Munzer, one of Luther's contemporaries. Munzer, a forerunner of the modern liberation theologians, believed the individual Christian must manifest faith externally: Only by helping create the Kingdom of God on earth was a Christian truly obeying the dictates of conscience as well as New Testament scripture, and thus overcoming anxiety about personal salvation and the salvation of mankind as well. Munzer's doctrine stands in clear conflict with Lutheran teachings.[57]

The peace protest has also been influenced by Pietism, which carries to an extreme the Lutheran concern with individual conscience by stressing the need to manifest one's faith through a pure life, pure deeds, and acts of social amelioration. *Angst* has been a particularly important element in pietism, which sees moral renewal as achievable only "by passing through the anguish of contrition into the overwhelming realization of the assurance of God's grace." Although not an explicitly political tradition, pietism's absolutist, introspective, reformist impulse has tended to put its adherents at odds with religious and often political authority; laws were passed against it in the 18th century. But activist, zealous protest against the bureaucratization of religion survived and prospered in such regions as Prussia, Saxony, or Wurttemburg,[58] where peace activist Erhard Eppler is a leading political figure.

Pacifism in German religious thought was partly interwoven with these various anti-dogmatic, anti-establishment tendencies. Some of the medieval sects opposed soldiering. While Munzer himself was not an anti-militarist, many of his contemporaries and spiritual descendants saw him as such, and radical pietists in the 17th century began to preach nonviolence.[59] Pacifism has long been a particularly compelling response to personal anxiety about salvation as well as survival. Taking New Testament teachings as a basis for the complete renunciation of force is the primary pacifist principle. The admonition of "turn the other cheek" and Christ's Sermon on the Mount have over the centuries been political prescriptions for many believers. In Germany, this tendency received its greatest impetus from smaller Reformation era groups known as the free churches, including, above all, the Mennonites. Early 16th century Anabaptism, which espoused adult baptism but collapsed from internal dissension and external pressure, had produced several off-shoots, including the groups who followed Menno Simons. Proclaiming, among other things, complete nonresistance, the Mennonites foreswore proselytizing, became closed sects, and often emigrated, all to avoid persecution. And although their pacifism flagged somewhat under pressure from authorities in the era of mass conscription, Mennonites established a tradition of Christian nonresistance which, in North Germany, for example, won respect.[60] Within German Protestantism itself, there was also a pacifist strain, typified by those pre-World War I and interwar ecumenical movements which hoped to establish nonviolence as the universal Christian peace ethic.[61] The traditionally widespread Roman Catholic acceptance of a just war doctrine did not prevent the emergence after World War I of a small counter-movement in the German Catholic church which tried to establish a "natural law" basis for pacifism, and which failed partly because of its overly moralistic tone.[62]

After 1945, with the established churches discredited for a failure fully to propagate Christian faith in the Nazi era, all these dissenting and pacifist streams of thought gained greater resonance. Although some, like the Mennonites, were harshly repressed by the Nazis, their ideas gained greater credence. Groups within the EKD and the Catholic church undertook extensive works of social and political amelioration, including the establishment of aid programs to developing countries, works of atonement in Eastern Europe and Israel, and the promotion of arms control. Pacifist tendencies were particularly strong, as seen in the fact that certain EKD groups led opposition to German rearmament in the 1950s, resistance to NATO's initial deployment of nuclear weapons on German soil (the Anti-Atomtod Movement), and the subsequent Easter peace marches of the 1960s. Accordingly, the EKD's major official statement on nuclear weapons—the 1959 Heidelberg Theses—was an effort to reconcile conservative and pacifist ideas by calling them complementary paths to peace.[63] Still, the presumption against established authority led some Protestant pastors to support the 1960s student movement, insist upon guarantees that the rights of terrorists and terrorist suspects would be defended and actually defend the ecological movements. At the demonstrations against construction of the Brockdorf nuclear plant, pastors offered "field masses" for the protesters, lending an air of sanctity to their cause. Despite their newly won influence within established churches, these various dissenting schools of thought during the Federal Republic's life have been especially important among those Germans who classify themselves as non-denominational, as "Christians without Churches."

CHRISTIAN ANTI-DOGMATIC DISSENT AND ANTINUCLEAR SENTIMENT

These various traditions of Christian dissent, all bearing the imprint of *Angst* and the romantic reaction against reality, have strongly influenced contemporary antinuclear sentiment in West Germany. In content, form, and moralistic tone the peace movement often gives the appearance of a religious crusade. One indication of the continuity between past religious dissent in Germany and today's peace movement is seen in the character of those religious groups involved in antinuclear protest. They themselves scorn traditional dogma and the spiritual authority of the church hierarchies in the same manner as their spiritual predecessors. At the EKD's 1981 Church Day, one panel was entitled "Impatience with the confessions," that is, the churches and speakers boasted that they were "on the fringes."[64] Catholic theologian Norbert Greinacher, for example, a strong backer of antinuclear activism, observed that "Popes and bishops are only one element of the Church," and rejected as "false" the "old theological instruction" that there is no salvation outside the Church.[65] Polls reflect a similar disdain for traditional dogma. Only 2% of all young Germans regularly visit church. Among those who consider themselves antinuclear activists only 4% go to services often (at least once per month), while nearly half never attend. Even those activists who classify themselves as "pacifists" are unwilling to expose themselves to mainstream religious influences: only 21% go to church regularly, one third stay away completely. An analysis of such poll data suggests that compared to the overall population, a disproportionate share of those involved in antinuclear protest have minimal contact with "the clerical milieu" and are as a rule "removed from the influence of religious organizations."[66]

Today's antinuclear Christians echo the pietist charge that an overly bureaucratized, authoritarian religious hierarchy ignores *real* matters of faith — above all a way out of nuclear death; to become caught up in the religious establishment's dogmatism when the arms race threatens mankind would endanger salvation. Maverick Social Democrat and Protestant activist Erhard Eppler, director of the EKD's 1983 Church Day, thundered against the hierarchy that "a church that would remain silent when the existence not only of the entire people, but ultimately of all living things, is at risk, would surely also be no church of Jesus Christ."[67] Heinrich Albertz suggests that the established churches have been coerced into silence on delicate issues by the wealthy taxpayers who finance them.[68] Catholic activists have increasingly taken up similar themes: theologian Greinacher charged that his church is ruled from above by a bureaucracy "which no longer serves the people, but revolves around itself," an establishment that "strangles" Catholics "through repression" and an "unpreparedness for dialogue." Christ, he fears, given the choice, would not be a Catholic today.[69]

Rather than explicitly breaking with their respective church leaderships, today's dissenters prefer to designate themselves as "basis-church" movements that will purify Christianity by restoring its "real values" through a type of activism which makes faith relevant. A "Church from Below" movement within German Catholicism stresses the antinuclear theme, along with such causes as permitting married, female and homosexual priests to administer the sacraments. Greinacher hopes such openness would include greater acceptance of atheists "from whom we can learn," and believes these reformist trends mark "a return to the original Church."[70]

Today's dissenters see themselves—and only themselves—as expressing pure, true, relevant Christian concerns because of their antinuclear stand and social activism; such a sense of exclusive purity characterizes the pietist streak in German Protestantism, while the notion of faith through engagement recalls the Munzer tradition. Resolutions and working groups at the 1981 EKD Church Day reflect this emphasis on social and political engagement: most dealt with such issues as apartheid, development, human rights (in Chile, Taiwan, and other such countries) and—above all—disarmament.[71] Berlin pastor Helmut Gollwitzer characterizes this attitude that dissenters are, by virtue of their purity and engagement, true Christians; more radical interpretations come closest to the real meaning of Christian ideas because they have not been compromised. Phrases or questions such as "Would Francis of Assisi be with the Greens Today?" and "Today the Lord Jesus would live in Kreuzberg" (the Alternative-culture section of Berlin) characterizes this sense of purity.[72] Antinuclear activism is the mission of the Christian. Heinrich Albertz argues that "resignation is the real Christian original sin."[73] Although peace activists in number are overwhelmingly Protestant—polls suggest 70%—this sense of *Angst*, so long considered a product of Protestantism, is now shared by many Catholics.

Many observers have somewhat misleadingly labeled the entire antinuclear movement "pacifist" because the element of Christian-based non-resistance is so marked within it. Polls show that 60% of all activists in fact consider themselves pacifist.[74] The New Testament admonition to "turn the other cheek," traditionally interpreted as a rule for the individual who would give heroic witness to Gospel values is converted into a program of public policy for the state and is reflected in a whole range of the antinuclear campaign's slogans, proposals, and statements. "Living Without Weapons" is the title of one initiative which has attracted several thousand signatures for a pledge to get along entirely without military defense; "Create Peace Without Weapons" was the theme of a major 1981 demonstration. Generally these initiatives are sponsored by groups within both confessions which are also largely pacifist in complexion: the "Action Reconciliation and Peace Service" and "Service for Peace," both headed by Protestant pastors and largely responsible for major peace demonstrations, as well as the "Union of Young Catholics" and Germany's branch of *"Pax Christi."* A whole cottage industry has grown up around publications on nonviolence; Gandhi and Martin Luther King are taken as models, while the Sermon on the Mount is held out as the scriptural basis. Catholic groups such as the Bensberger Circle stress the "New Testament as instruction for political behavior."[75]

Leading Protestant peace spokesmen and politicians, Erhard Eppler and pastor Albertz, deny that they themselves are pacifist: both express doubts that Christ's Sermon on the Mount could effectively govern political conduct and national policy, and they do not think the Protestant community could be brought to renounce weapons altogether. Nonetheless both Eppler and Albertz welcome pacifism and the religious rationale for it as a means of restraining governments and they have cultivated it within the rank and file of the movement. Albertz, for example, believes complete nonresistance is a perfectly understandable interpretation of Christ's teaching and that the world could only gain by moving closer to the point where the Sermon on the Mount becomes a guide for policy.

In content, Catholic Christian opposition to INF is only a slight variation on the Protestant critique, with the obvious difference that the former draws heavily upon papal and conciliar appeals for peace. The touchstone is Vatican II's concluding statement, *Gaudium et Spes*, which denounced wars of mass destruction and termed the arms race "mankind's most terrible wound." Without explicitly condoning or condemning deterrence, the Council urged that genuine arms control be adopted quickly. Many Catholic youth and church peace activists in general (especially those associated with *Pax Christi*) contend that this later goal of *Gaudium et Spes* has gone too long unachieved. Although not all are pacifists, most question the continued ethical justifiability of deterrence. This contention is occasionally phased in terms of church doctrine on peace (an interpretation of the just war concept for example), but more often activists stress the self-evident moral urgency of arms reduction, especially in light of world tensions. They also refer to the "concrete utopia of a world without weapons" urged in *Pax Christi's* 1981 Program, without mentioning the fact that Pope John Paul II has specifically warned against utopian thinking.

This sense that moral purity is found largely among dissenting Christians has bred an intolerance which often conflicts with the movement's own stated desire to open the churches up and democratize religion. At the 1981 EKD Church Day, attended by thousands of young Christian peace activists, a leading Social Democrat who tried to defend government policy said, "They consider us non-humans;" government spokesmen were heckled or ignored, and despite bodyguards and shields, Defense Minister Apel was eventually stopped from speaking. Although movement spokesmen like Eppler denounced such intolerance, he himself conveys the self-righteousness of many Christians involved in antinuclear protest: In denouncing the Heidelberg Theses, for example, he argues that this compromise "cannot be permitted to continue." Catholic activists, according to *Der Spiegel* "are also no longer prepared to tolerate silence" on the arms issue.[76] In viewing this tolerant tendency, Helmut Schmidt stated:

> The people in the Church must make sure that they do not lapse, under the pressure of the peace movement into a God-is-with-us theology, i.e., into an inverted imperialism a la William II. During the days of Emperor William II, the belt with which the soldiers were issued bore the inscription: God is with us. And people imagined 70 years ago that the policy pursued by the then German Reich under William II was indeed blessed by God and that it accorded with God's wishes. Today, we must pay attention lest many people with critical views on the policy which is necessary for Germany start to believe that their opinions are the only ones of substance in God's eyes. We have no use for a God-is-with-us theology or a God-is-with-us policy in the sense that somebody holding a different view has the sole right to invoke God and Christ.[77]

CONCLUSION: THE PEACE MOVEMENT AND GERMANY'S FUTURE

Pierre Hassner has observed that "West German generations have a remarkable power of subterranean transmission to their successors."[78] Today's peace movement is heir not only to traditional tendencies toward *Angst* and romanticism, but also to the perspectives which those basic impulses have shaped: social anti-modernism, political illiberalism and anti-dogmatic Christianity. The same despairing, pessimistic uncertainty and radical rejection of reality which generated dissent in Germany's past are at work in the current peace movement. Antinuclear sentiment has emerged as a function of traditional and fundamentally anti-Western tendencies. The peace movement's rejection of modernism, liberalism, and traditional Christianity has engendered a mood which sees missiles and their own government's willingness to deploy them as a reflection of all that is wrong with the Western model of social, political, and religious development.

The antinuclear protest is a tangible expression of an identity crisis among those Germans — youth and intellectuals above all — least inclined toward the West. The antinuclear movement's national-neutral orientation in foreign affairs and its often unconscious emphasis on national ideas and symbols are logical extensions of its fundamental antipathy toward the Western model which has its origins in those basic tendencies toward *Angst* and romanticism.[79] The movement is overwhelmingly neutralist in tone and in its policy preferences (one poll shows 87% of peace activists advocate neutralism) again reflecting not only its opposition to German involvement in the Western nuclear security framework, but also a fundamental estrangement from the Western experience as a whole.[80] Many observers, including some of the peace movement's sympathizers, soberly wonder where these sentiments might take Germany in the future. Even if the national-neutralist extension of this anti-Western orientation does not immediately prevail in the Federal Republic, it may nonetheless be counted upon to strain the country's cohesion and create further dissension over Germany's future direction, internal and external. Political scientist Günther Schmid has noted that the younger generation is for the most part pessimistic about the future and that "the more pessimistic their view of the future, the more frequently and more engaged will be their support or participation" in protest.[81] According to sociologist Helmut Schoeck, this pessimism is being perpetuated by the media and "a new industry" which provides "an almost professional training to young spirits with an aptitude for dissent or a penchant for protest":

> never before in our history have we seen the spectacle of politicians, and pastors, pedagogues and best-selling writers, teachers and hit-songsters, all vying with each other to impress our children with the ugliness of the prospects facing them, with the horror (partly real, partly freely made-up) of all life's problems that will soon overwhelm them disastrously.[82]

It is difficult to say where the alienation, pessimism, and anxiety described in the foregoing pages will lead Germany during the next few years. Much depends, of course, upon how much resonance they have in the population as a whole, and on how their strength will compare to that of the ideas, attitudes, and social forces which have sustained the Federal Republic's ties to the West since the beginning of the Adenauer period. If it were merely a question of one or two million militant protesters carrying banners and placards in the streets, this would not necessarily constitute an unmanageable challenge to the policies of West Germany, the United States, and NATO. Indeed, the fact that a few Pershing-2 missiles were deployed on schedule in the Federal Republic in December 1983 demonstrated that Moscow could not count on the developments of the "hot autumn" to reverse the implicit consequences of Chancellor Helmut Kohl's electoral victory of the previous March. NATO had proved its determination to show that it could at least begin to implement the December 1979 INF decision and thereby negate Moscow's effort to veto the West's right to see to its security, while monopolizing the Soviet right to modernize weapons systems that would increase Western Europe's hypothetical vulnerability to military attack and real vulnerability to even greater political intimidation in the future.

So far as the antinuclear campaign in West Germany is concerned, it has lost a preliminary skirmish but not the war. The Greens' MP Marieluise Beck-Oberdorff spoke defiantly to Chancellor Kohl: "You will get your cruise and Pershings but it will be a Pyrrhic victory because the real debate is only beginning" — and the real debate will be about German membership in NATO.[83] Until quite recently, campaign leaders preferred to direct most of their venom against U.S. nuclear weapons policy because they recognized that most of the German people who were opposed to new INF missile deployment were also favorably disposed to NATO as the only available guarantor of the Federal Republic's security. But over the course of four years NATO governments, in spite of stresses and strains, had maintained complete unanimity in their semiannual reaffirmations of the December 1979 decision. Henceforth, therefore, it will be necessary to attack NATO head-on.

The West German peace movement can be expected to stress the following propaganda themes during the next few years: (1) the NATO "dual track" strategy failed because of U.S. intransigence in the Geneva arms negotiations; (2) the United States was mistaken in thinking that by pursuing a "tough" course it could motivate the Soviet Union to make concessions. (3) The deployment of the new NATO missiles, by provoking the USSR to accelerate its deployment of nuclear weapons in Eastern Europe, puts West Germany in a more dangerous position than ever. (4) The Federal Republic perhaps could once entrust its security to NATO and the United States with confidence, particularly when the United States held strategic superiority, but the global system has changed to such an extent that membership in NATO is now more of a liability than an asset. (5) During the last two administrations, U.S. leadership has become more erratic (a proposition on which both major parties might agree). (6) Earlier assumptions concerning the indefinite effectiveness of nuclear deterrence are eroding as a result of talk on both sides — first in the East and now in the West — about waging and winning nuclear war, combined with the development of new technologies and air-land battle scenarios which make war more thinkable and more probable. (7) Membership in NATO entails an increasingly humiliating national subservience to the United States, the leading imperialist power which has set out to recolonize the Third World. (8) The bright future of West Germany lies in moving toward a safety shelter in withdrawal from NATO and neutralism as roads toward eventual national reunification, or at least toward enabling the German people, west and east, to begin reversing their victimization as pawns in the rivalry of the superpowers.

How successful the peace movement is in keeping these goals high upon the agenda of West Germany's public debate over security policy will continue to depend in part on the credibility of the Green party. The Greens' success in gaining entry into the federal parliament in the March 1983 election was followed by a period of slight confusion and consolidation. Internal disputes over their approach to parliamentary politics and actual formal cooperation with the SPD at the state level strained party unity; conflicts over socio-economic policy and overly-virulent anti-Americanism tested the Greens' cohesion even further, the latter culminating in the resignation of former NATO general Bastian, whose membership had enhanced the party's credibility. Nonetheless, the Greens performed well in local and state elections in 1983 and 1984, and obtained over 8% of the German vote in the 1984 European Parliament elections. Invigorated by an ever-present whiff of scandal in Bonn politics and continuing public dissatisfaction with both socio-economic and environmental policy, the Greens—according to almost all opinion analysts—have won at least a semi-permanent share of the Federal Republic "protest vote." This in turn assures that the party will remain a major vehicle of antinuclear and anti-NATO protest.

As in the past, the Greens and the overall peace movement will be able to magnify their impact upon West Germany's nuclear arms debate by their leverage over the SPD. Fearful of being outflanked on the left, Willy Brandt in late 1982 began to steer the SPD in the direction of both cooperation with and co-optation of the eco-peace movement, a strategy reinforced by the desire to placate his party's own left wing. Freed from the burdens of government, which West German Social Democrats have historically found distasteful, substantial elements of the party were more than willing to cut their ties with the Helmut Schmidt era. This meant a change in the party leadership's composition, including the rehabilitation of left-wing spokesmen like Erhard Eppler, plus the complete abandonment of INF. Both processes began after the 1983 federal election, and accelerated as the November date for an INF decision approached, with first each local party group, then the national party executive—against the reservations of Schmidt's by then miniscule minority—and ultimately the SPD parliamentary delegation voting against deployment. At that point, most party centrists, however, relieved to have disassociated themselves from the missile plan, were ready to exercise greater caution. Never entirely at ease with the peace movement and worried about the SPD's image among voters as well as in Allied capitals, party leaders like Hans-Jochen Vogel worked toward a period of consolidation. There was relatively greater sympathy for the warnings of moderates like former Defense Minister Apel; the party pledged to update and reinforce the Godesberg program, the 1959 party declaration which opened the way for formal endorsement of West German membership in NATO: Vogel himself journeyed to Washington in an effort to demonstrate that the SPD still wanted to play an active role in Alliance affairs. But the party's leftward lurch into the peace movement camp had already substantially altered the character of its security policy, for it was not only in regard to INF that the SPD had backed away from Schmidt's policies. Party spokesmen were challenging official estimates of Soviet conventional military strength, figures largely in line with those published by the Schmidt government, and echoed peace movement charges that new defense concepts such as AirLand were "offensive" oriented. The SPD's 1984 Party-Day in Essen called for Western concessions at the MBFR talks on the grounds that aiming for a military balance was unrealistic. At the same gathering, delegates endorsed an INF moratorium, a policy of no-first-use, nuclear-free zones in Europe, and further unilateral cuts in NATO's tactical nuclear stocks. Observers found unmistakable tones of "national-neutralism" and essentially "left-wing-Gaullism" in the party's efforts to stress a security policy increasingly separate from that of the United States and France. Most observers agreed that, given the constant pressure of peace activists both within and outside of the party, the SPD's security policy was likely to move further in this direction before the federal elections scheduled for 1987.

There can be little doubt that the antinuclear movement has created a most delicate political situation in West Germany. A twenty-five-year-old bipartisan consensus on the requirements of FRG security has begun to unravel. The task of policy makers responsible for the deterrence of war is bound to become increasingly difficult. There will be strong pressures upon the Bonn government to enhance the prospects for East-West arms negotiations by urging upon the NATO allies a cessation of all INF deployments after the emplacement of a minimal number of missiles — once NATO has made a necessary point about its ability to carry out a decision. This, of course, would still leave NATO's capabilities at a lower level than needed for the restabilization of the European balance.

Because the traditional tendencies toward *Angst* and romanticism will remain deeply-rooted in German society, particularly among the country's youth, the "bureaucratic middle" which has long guarded the uncertain foundations of German Westernization will be under fire for years to come. Until the early 1980s, liberals and conservatives — Christian Democrats, Free Democrats, and Social Democrats — maintained Bonn's Western orientation in internal and external policy, but the domestic pressure against them has never before been so deep and broad. Co-opting a movement so firmly entrenched may not prove successful, and the situation has gone beyond the stage where "tactical party political maneuvers" or minor concessions will suffice. Any solution must encompass new ideas and experimentation without sacrificing basic principles, and it will require the involvement of all parts of the Federal Republic's establishment — political, socio-economic, and religious.

The peace movement was further discredited in the fall of 1984 when antinuclearist groups organized "human chains" to disrupt the autumn maneuvers of the Bundeswehr and U.S. forces. The West German press, reflecting a rising tide of resentment against violent attacks on troops and military installations, began to demand that such criminal behavior be punished appropriately. Some editors, noting that the size of the demonstrations were only one-third or one-quarter as large as the year before, suggested that the leaders of the movement, recognizing their growing isolation and helplessness, were beginning to thrash about frantically looking for ways to restore momentum. The loss of *elan* was probably due to several factors. There was no longer a single clear-cut goal—preventing the installation of the missiles—to be achieved as a specific deadline approached. Moreover, the public perception of the Soviet threat underwent a subtle change in the light of reports that the USSR had deployed a hundred mobile SS-20s of 900-kilometer range in the GDR and Czechoslovakia, and that a staff exercise of the Soviet 3rd Spearhead Army, monitored by radio, indicated that Moscow was war-gaming on the basis of an offensive doctrine which presupposed that Soviet forces would seize West German cities and move toward the Rhine. Perhaps the most important change was in the political climate of Russo-German relations. The Kohl government continued its patient policy of trying to improve relations between the two German states even after the cancellation of East German leader Erich Honecker's planned visit to Bonn. As Moscow stepped up its strident propaganda campaign against West German "revanchism," there seemed to emerge a vague notion that perhaps Germans—all Germans—had better draw closer together in the face of an uncertain future. Another factor affecting the situation, by no means insignificant, was the realization that NATO's determination to proceed with carrying out its December 1979 decision probably had helped to persuade Moscow that it was time to think seriously about entering into business-like negotiations with the West for equitable agreements on nuclear arms. The Soviet leadership, however, can be expected to keep watching the antinuclear movement in the Federal Republic as a potential lever to be exploited for the purpose of intervening in both German and NATO affairs.

NOTES

1. Peter Nissen, "Prospects for a Realignment of the West German Party System: The Impact of Oppositional Movements and the 'Green' Party," paper delivered at the University of California, May 19–20, 1982 (analysis of data from the September, 1981 survey by EMNID for *Der Spiegel*), pp. 10–11.
2. Karl Dietrich Bracher, "Afraid of the Future," *Scala* (April 1982), p. 45.
3. Fritz Stern, *The Failure of Illiberalism: Essays on the Political Culture of Modern Germany* (New York: Knopf, 1972), p. xxxviii.
4. Gordon Craig, *The Germans* (New York: G. P. Putnam's Sons, 1982), p. 190.
5. Ralf Dahrendorf, *Society and Democracy in Germany* (Garden City, New York: Anchor Books, 1969), p. 271.
6. Stern, *The Failure of Illiberalism*, op. cit., p. 7.
7. Dahrendorf, *Society and Democracy*, op. cit., p. 271.
8. Fritz Stern, *The Politics of Cultural Despair*, p. xi. See also Christian Krause, Detlef Lehnert, Klaus-Jürgen Scherer, *Zwischen Revolution und Resignation? Alternativkultur, politische Grundströmungen und Hoch-Schulaktivitaten in der Studentenschaft* (Bonn: Verlag Neue Gesellschaft, 1980).

9. Geoffrey Pridham, "Ecologists in Politics: The West German Case," *Parliamentary Affairs*, 31 (Autumn 1978), p. 438.

10. Hans Ruehle, "Zur politischen Bewertung der Kernenergie Kontroverse," in Hans Ruehle, Hans-Joachim Veen and Heinz Riesenhuber, editors, *Die Zukunft der Kernenergie, Forschungsbericht, Fachtagung der Konrad Adenauer Stiftung vom 13. – 16. Dezember, 1981 in Bonn* (Melle: Verlag Ernst Knoth, for the Konrad Adenauer Stiftung, 1982), pp. 65–67.

11. Nissen, *Prospects for a Realignment*, op. cit., p. 6.

12. Erhard Eppler, *Wege aus der Gefahr* (Hamburg: Rowohlt, 1981), pp. 79, 82.

13. Peter Bender, *Das Ende des ideologischen Zeitalters: Die Europaisierung Europas* (Berlin: Severin and Siedler, 1981), pp. 267–68.

14. "Der Herr Jesus wurde in Kreuzberg wohnen," Interview with Heinrich Albertz, *Der Spiegel*, August 31, 1981, p. 38.

15. Rudolf Bahro, "The SPD and the Peace Movement," *The New Left Review* (January–February 1982), p. 27.

16. Johano Strasser, cited in Reinhard Meier, "West Germany's Disoriented Left," *Swiss Review of World Affairs*, 30 (July 1980), p. 21.

17. Craig, *The Germans*, op. cit., p. 222

18. Jim Cooney, "Germany, Europe and the United States: Is Anti-Americanism Significant?," Report on the Aspen Institute Conference, Berlin, 1981.

19. John Vinocur, "Anti-Americanism in West Germany," *New York Times*, July 5, 1981.

20. *Der Spiegel*, August 24, 1981, pp. 7–10.

21. Hans-Herbert Gaebel, "Antiamerikanisches Gift," *Frankfurter Rundschau*, July 11, 1981.

22. Bender, *Das Ende des ideologischen Zeitalters*, op. cit., pp. 267–68.

23. Peter Merkl, "Pacifism in West Germany," *SAIS Review* (Spring 1982), pp. 84–85.

24. Bracher, "Afraid of the Future," op. cit., p. 42.

25. Eppler, *Wege aus der Gefahr*, op. cit., pp. 134–44.

26. Hans-Joachim Veen, "Jugend heute: Als Burger eher unterfordert: Daten Zur politischen Psychologie ihrer Zufriedenheit und ihrer Proteste," *Das Parlament*, August 14–21, 1982.

27. William Griffith, "Bonn and Washington: From Deterioration to Crisis," *Orbis*, 26 (Spring 1982), p. 118.

28. Stern, *The Politics of Cultural Despair*, op. cit., p. xii.

29. Stern, *The Failure of Illiberalism*, op. cit., p. xxii–xxiii.

30. Gunter Hofmann, "Die Grünen – Gegner oder Partner? Warum der Umgang mit der neuen politischen Bewegung so schwierig ist," *Die Ziet*, July 23, 1982, p. 4.

31. *New York Times*, July 27, 1982.

32. Bahro, "The SPD and the Peace Movement," op. cit., p. 26.

33. Gerhard Wettig, "The New Peace Movement in Germany," *Aussenpolitik*, 23 (Fall 1982), pp. 226–27.

34. Karl-Heinz Janssen, "'Es Muss Unruhe herrschen im Lande': Das Alternativprogramm der Pazifisten: gewaltfrei, gesamteuropäisch, gesamtdeutsch," *Die Zeit*, November 6, 1981, p. 2.

35. Wettig, "The New Peace Movement," op. cit., p. 227.

36. Gert Schmidinger, "The peace movement and what it stands for," *Saarbrucker Zeitung*, in *The German Tribune Political Affairs Review*, June 27, 1982.

37. Peter Meier-Bergfeld, "Strategiepläne der 'Friedenskämpfer': Sturmlauf auf die Kasernen: Teile der Sogenannten Friedensbewegung gehen vom gewaltfreien Anti-Atom Protest zur subversiven Aktion über," *Rheinischer Merkur Christ und Welt*, July 3, 1981, p. 3.

38. Eppler, *Wege aus der Gafahr, op. cit., p. 111; "Frieden in Bewegung: Gesprach mit Dr. Erhard Eppler,"* Evangelische Kommentare (November 1981), p. 645.

39. Janssen, "'Es muss Unruhe herrschen im Lande'," op. cit.
40. Meier-Bergdorf, "Strategiepläne der 'Friedenskämpfer'," op. cit.
41. Nissen, "Prospects for a Realignment," op. cit., p. 6.
42. Veen, "Jugend heute"; *Der Spiegel*, July 13, 1981, pp. 47, 50; *Der Spiegel* August 3, 1981, pp. 68–69.
43. *Deutsche Presse Agentur*, October 11, 1981, cited in *Foreign Broadcast Information Service—Western Europe*, October 13, 1981, p. J10.
44. Krause, et al., *Zwischen Revolution und Resignation*? p. 166.
45. "Die DKP schadet der Bewegung," Interview with Ernst Hoplitscheck, *Die Zeit*, April 16, 1982, p. 6.
46. Klaus Rainer Rohl, "Die Geschäfte des Herrn Oberst," *Spontan*, May 1981, p. 2.
47. Petra Kelly, cited in Josef Joffe, "The Greening of Germany: Not 'Deutschland über alles,' but 'Leave us alone!'," *The New Republic*, February 14, 1983, p. 19.
48. Eppler, *Wege aus der Gefahr*, op. cit., p. 18.
49. *New York Times*, July 27, 1982
50. Eppler, *Wege aus der Gefahr*, op. cit., p. 17.
51. Craig, *The Germans*, op. cit., pp. 83–103; Georg Denzler, "SS-Spitzel mit Soutane: Wie die Katholischen Bischofe im Dritten Reich mitschuldig wurden," *Die Zeit*, September 10, 1982, p. 9.
52. "On the Current Peace Discussion," Statement adopted by the plenary assembly of the Central Committee of German Catholics, November 14, 1981.
53. Craig, *The Germans*, op. cit., pp. 83–103.
54. Dietrich Strothmann, "Mit der Kirche Über Kreuz: Vom Altar zum Aktionismus: Die Schwierigkeit, ein Protestant zu sein," *Die Zeit*, December 31, 1981, p. 7.
55. Erwin Wilkens, Editor, *Christliche Ethik* und *Sicherheitheitspolitik* (Frankfurt am Main: Evangelisches Verlagswerk, 1982).
56. Griffith, "Bonn and Washington," op. cit., p. 119.
57. Craig, *The Germans*, op. cit., pp. 85–86.
58. Ibid., pp. 87–88.
59. Peter Brock, *Pacifism in Europe to 1914* (Princeton, New Jersey: Princeton University Press, 1972), pp. 60, 101, 248–49.
60. Ibid., pp. 407–441.
61. Armin Boyens, "Ökumenische Friedensethik," in Wilkens, *Christliche Ethik*, pp. 138–152.
62. Harald Oberhem, "Zur Kontroverse um die bellum-iustum-Theorie in der Gegenwart," in Norbert Glatzel and Ernst Josef Nagel, eds., *Frieden in Sicherheit: Zur Weiterentwicklung der Katholischen Friedensethik* (Freiburg: Herder, 1981), pp. 49–55.
63. "Die Heidelberger Thesen zur Frage von Krieg und Frieden im Atomzeitalter," in Wilkens, ed., *Christliche Ethik*, pp. 237–47.
64. *Deutscher Evangelischer Kirchentag Hamburg 1981: Dokumente* (Stuttgart: Kreuz Verlag, 1981), pp. 350, 396, *passim*.
65. "Wäre Jesus heute römisch-Katholisch? Der Katholische Theologieprofessor Norbert Greinacher über Amtskirche und 'Kirche von unten'," Interview with Norbert Greinacher, *Der Spiegel*, August 29, 1982, pp. 83–84.
66. Nissen, "Prospects for a Realignment," op. cit., pp. 7, 12.
67. *Frieden in Bewegung*, op. cit., p. 648.
68. "Der Herr Jesus würde in Kreuzberg wohnen," op. cit., p. 45.
69. "Wäre Jesus heute römisch-Katholische?," op. cit., p. 83.
70. Ibid., p. 84.
71. Luhmann and Neveling, eds., *Deutscher Evangelischer Kirchentag*, pp. 544–45.
72. "Wäre Franz von Assisi heute bei den 'Grünen'? Ein Gespräch über die Aktualität eines

frühen Reformators, mit Adolf Holl," in Peter Hertel und Alfred Paffenholz, eds., *Für eine politische Kirche: Schwerter zu Pflugscharen: Politische Tehologie und basiskirchliche Initiativen* (Hannover: Verlag Schmidt-Kuster, 1982), pp. 150–59.

73. "Die Grösste Gefahr ist die Resignation. Ein Gespräch über die aktuelle Politik und den Realismus der Bibel, mit Heinrich Albertz," in Hertel and Paffenholz, eds., *Für eine politische Kirche*, pp. 119–30.

74. Nissen, "Prospects for a Realignment," op. cit., p. 6.

75. Bensberger Kreis, Editors, *Frieden — für Katholiken eine Provokation*? Ein Memorandum (Hamburg: Rowohlt, 1982).

76. *Der Spiegel*, August 29, 1982, p. 81.

77. "Should Politics Be Left Exclusively to the Politicians?" Replies by Federal Chancellor Helmut Schmidt to questions put to him during the Protestant Church Congress, St. Trinitatis Church, Hamburg, June 19, 1981, *Relay from Bonn: Statements and Speeches, German Information Center*, Vol. 4, July 7, 1982, p. 15.

78. Pierre Hassner, "The Shifting Foundation," *Foreign Policy* (Fall 1982), p. 6.

79. Michael Naumann, "German Identity and the Emergence of German Neonationalism," *Partisan Review*, Vol. L (Spring 1983).

80. Nissen, "Prospects for a Realignment," op. cit., p. 6.

81. Günther Schmid, *Sicherheitspolitik und Friedensbewegung: Der Konflikt um die 'Nachrüstung'* (Munich: Gunter Olzog Verlag, 1982), p. 251.

82. Helmut Schoeck, "A Letter from Germany: Protesting for a Brave, Green World," Vol. LIX (December 1982), p. 50.

83. Walter Schwarz, "The German debate in no man's land," *Manchester Guardian Weekly*, December 4, 1983.

Chapter 5

The Antinuclear Movement in the Netherlands: A Diagnosis of Hollanditis

Clay Clemens

Today's continent-wide peace movement received much of its initial impetus from the activities of Dutch organizations. Many observers refer to the impact of "Hollanditis," a term first used by political scientist Walter Laqueur in describing Dutch resistance to missile deployment and the epidemic of antinuclear attitudes which has struck Western Europe.[1] A more whimsical commentator has called this infectious mood "the Dutch qualm disease." To an extent few thought possible, events in the Netherlands have jeopardized plans for deploying enhanced radiation weapons (ERW) and modernized theater nuclear forces not only in that country alone but also throughout Western Europe. There is fear that this antinuclear, and often explicitly neutralist, campaign could even undermine the Netherlands' future credibility as an Alliance partner and cast serious doubts upon NATO's future.

What accounts for the depth of antinuclear and even neutralist feeling in a country that was the first European ally to accept nuclear weapons and one which has traditionally espoused NATO solidarity, and what gives these changing public attitudes such resonance elsewhere in Western Europe? Certainly much of the explanation lies in ideas that predate the first stirrings of a peace movement in the Netherlands and attitudes that involve a good deal more than nuclear weapons. This chapter will analyze the broad, powerful tendencies in Dutch thought that have helped to shape today's antinuclear malaise.

CHRISTIAN-BASED MORALISM, SOCIAL LIBERATIONISM, AND THE EFFECTS OF GEOPOLITICAL INSIGNIFICANCE

Close observers of Dutch society agree that religion has been the most significant formative influence on popular as well as intellectual attitudes. Every social and political institution in the Netherlands has evolved in a way that reflects the impact of various religious thought traditions. Even the avowedly secular elements of Dutch society bear the imprint of the Christian legacy.

Somewhat paradoxically, these important religious traditions have historically taken the form of both intense intraconfessional differences and a strong tendency toward toleration. Dutch Calvinism gained a firm grip in northwestern Europe during the Reformation and was a major factor in the long civil war which finally saw the Netherlands break away from the Catholic Hapsburg Empire. In the 19th century, a split occurred in the Calvinist community: strictly orthodox members broke with the larger Dutch Reformed church and established their own separate Reformed church. Dutch Catholicism also remained a vital force in the Netherlands and sank deep roots in the country's south, but was long considered a minority church until it emerged with a "plurality" in recent decades. Largely in reaction against these entrenched religious groups there emerged an avowedly *secular* community in the Netherlands which spawned in the 19th century both liberal and labor-socialist political movements. As a result of religion's impact, Dutch society became highly pluralistic, since each religious group, and even to some extent the secular bloc which resisted Christianity's pervasive influence, developed its own social, educational, and political institutions, producing a condition the Dutch call *verzuilung* or "vertical pillarization."[2]

In the postwar Netherlands, these different communities are still clearly delineated: roughly 40% of Dutch Christians now classify themselves as Catholic, while about 20% are Dutch Reformed and 10% Reformed. The remaining 30% profess no religious affiliation, but since only about one half of Dutch Christians attend church regularly, some writers place the modern "secular bloc" at over 50% of the population. Even though the lines of division today are less stark, each community still has its own political representatives: the Labor and Liberal parties are drawn from the secular bloc, while the Dutch Christian Democratic party (CDA) which was for several years a loose coalition of Catholic, Reformed, and Dutch Reformed political factions,[3] became more united in 1980 with the merger of the Catholic People's party (KVP), the Anti-Revolutionary party (ARP), and the Christian Historical Union (CHU).

Religious division produced a strong tradition of toleration. The need for toleration was stressed by such great Dutch religious and secular thinkers as

Erasmus, Arminius, Grotius, and Spinoza. Although some Calvinist elements wanted to establish a state church, the major religious groups — especially the Dutch Reformed church — came to see the value of toleration in a pluralistic society, for in its absence any consensus on vital questions would be impossible. Thus the Dutch learned the art of accommodation among themselves and the Netherlands' doors were also opened to religious minorities — Mennonites, Jews, and others.

Yet this tolerant spirit is limited. One writer has observed that the Dutch "people have to live together in peace, but not necessarily in a spirit of compromise," which today accounts for the "peculiarly Dutch characteristic combining tolerance with a refusal to yield principle."[4] This inflexibility is often traced to the modern-day legacy of Calvinism. Although Calvinism never held a monopoly over Dutch Christian beliefs, it has shaped the attitudes even of Catholics and avowed secularists in the Netherlands. The postwar secularization of Dutch society diminished the power of all religious orthodoxy, particularly among the young. There remains, nevertheless, a strong Calvinist residue in social and political thought, which takes the form of underlying feelings of personal guilt and generalizes them into fears of societal failings. There is a remarkably widespread belief that conduct must be a perfect reflection of pure and consistent intentions, and there is a belief in the transcendent obligation to obey one's own conscience before all other authorities. As one critical church official observed, "any statement made with an appeal to conscience is immediately construed by many as *ipso facto* absolutely true."[5]

Whether they attend church regularly, or not at all, the Dutch often demonstrate an intense moralism in many aspects of political life. Since personal and collective guilt, a desire to manifest good intentions, and complete submission to conscience dictate personal conduct, these factors also frequently govern political conduct. It has been observed that "the unwillingness to compromise one's personal principles does not make for very effective political solutions to real problems."[6] Pragmatism is acceptable only in solving those problems on which the country's various socioreligious groups are divided by interest and principle; thus for purposes of reconciliation in a pluralistic system, the "politics of accommodation" is applied. Nevertheless a moralistic tone is always prevalent. Moreover the emphasis on personal conviction makes power "a dirty word,"[7] politically unpalatable. It also leads to what one Dutch scholar describes as "a disbelief in authority" — the Dutch love to be against the government.[8]

The religious intensity with which the Dutch often pursue secular matters is due not only to its historical strength but also to the *decline* of traditional religion in Dutch life, for it was, above all, postwar Holland's secularization that "redirected missionary zeal from the other world to this one."[9] The same changing, socio-economic circumstances which helped rechannel much Dutch religious energy also gave rise to a whole new current of thought: affluence, consumerism, the democratization of society, and the expansion of education all spawned what one writer described as "liberationism," a mind-set among young people and intellectuals in particular which rejected established social structures and, in often vastly different ways, sought to create alternative life styles. As early as the 1960s, Dutch cities were plagued by gangs of discontented youth who in their boredom sought any kind of disruption in the prevailing social order, violent or not. They quickly blended into a growing antiestablishment movement among students and intellectuals who declared their intention to liberate Dutch society from traditional constraints. In the name of new, "authentic" values, they encouraged experimentation with alternative life styles of all sorts. Initially this liberationism took the form of a prosperous hippy culture, but it expanded to include new religious cults, student radicalism in the universities, feminism, homosexual activism, ecologism, displays of pornography, the widespread use of drugs, and later a squatters' campaign to gain free housing. Occasions ranging from the 1961 murder of Congo's Prime Minister Patrice Lumumba to the 1980 installation of Queen Beatrix were seen as provocations for civil disobedience and violence against the established order and established standards.[10]

Although such illegal activities were restricted to a few groups, the liberationist mind-set offered substitutes for older Christian standards and was adopted with equivalent "Calvinist" zeal by people throughout society.

> Many Dutchmen left their churches and embraced new values—authenticity, liberty, dialogue with the ardour of the converted . . . a lumpen-intelligentsia arose: people who had lost their points of reference and who sought compensation in a naive and redemptory commitment consisting of pidgin-Marxism and the bric-a-brac of the media.[11]

So entrenched has liberationism become that "few people any longer raise an eyebrow at any kind of nonviolent transgression of former ethical codes."[12] Universities became the centers from which the new worldview emanated.

Naturally this stream of thought had an impact on Dutch political attitudes. Liberationist parties arose and, although the establishment's initial response was hostile, it gradually tried to co-opt the various countercultural movements by substantially relaxing laws and restrictions detrimental to alternative life styles. The adoption of minimal penalties for drug use made Amsterdam a haven for hippies. Discipline was relaxed in the army. Troops were allowed to organize unions. Dutch foreign policy took on a new dimension, as "action groups" claiming that new values were important in external matters exercised considerable leverage; to take one example, Frits Bolkestein observes that "at times it seemed as if, for the Dutch, southern Africa was the world's most important issue."[13]

The Netherland's geopolitical status in modern history has also greatly influenced Dutch life and thought. A small, relatively powerless country situated in an arena of great power conflicts, Holland has long been aware of how little weight it carries in foreign affairs. Dutch national interests came to be defined in terms of those conditions necessary to further maritime commerce, namely peace and stability. This national outlook has reinforced the moralistic tendency in Dutch socio-political life. Powerlessness has bred a disdain for strength, especially in its military forms, as an appropriate expression of Dutch nationalism. Patriotism exists, but it does not follow the traditional pattern. A corollary of the disdain for power is the Dutch preference to remain aloof from international politics and traditional diplomacy. Instead there has been in the Netherlands an often quite strong strain of what historian J. C. Voorhoeve calls international idealism—a high priority on goodwill and a faith in good intentions as the necessary underpinnings of international relations.[14] Skeptical Dutch politicans have observed that their fellow citizens believe they can make up for a lack of international experience by "moralizing meditations," forgetting that "it was not Dutch virtues but the balance of power which made this policy of abstentionism possible."[15]

MANIFESTATIONS OF DUTCH THOUGHT TRADITIONS IN THE PRESENT-DAY PEACE MOVEMENT

As early as 1962 the Dutch Reformed church condemned nuclear weapons, forbidding any Christian involvement in nuclear war. The Catholic church more cautiously moved toward a more moderate antinuclear position in the 1960s and 1970s. But what really lies at the center of today's Dutch movement is a lay organization called the Interchurch Peace Council (IKV), founded in 1966 ostensibly to propagate world harmony by pressing for increased development aid to the Third World and arms limitation. The IKV is affiliated with and receives support from all major Dutch confessions—and thus is legitimated by these ties—but it does not speak for the churches as a group or individually. Equally active in the Netherlands opposing nuclear weapons program, is the country's national chapter of *Pax Christi*, a worldwide voluntary Catholic peace organization, not officially part of the church. Mennonite pacifists, too, have spoken out strongly against NATO nuclear modernization.[16]

Christian antinuclear activists frequently state their case in explicitly doctrinal terms. Christ's Sermon on the Mount is cited in nearly every IKV proclamation, with the strong implication that it should directly inspire day-to-day public policy. Moreover, IKV argues that nuclear weapons are among the false gods proscribed in the First Commandment. Christians should not worship them by supporting their deployment. Since nuclear weapons would massively destroy "image bearers" of God, they are condemned on doctrinal grounds. At the same time, few IKV leaders admit to being absolute doctrinaire pacifists like the Mennonites.[17]

Today's peace activists reflect the Dutch religious legacy by adopting a moralistic tone even when they condemn nuclear weapons on purely political or strategic grounds. For young people and intellectuals, Holland's Christian (especially Calvinist) legacy seems to lead to a missionary zeal regardless of whether dogmatic considerations are involved. They do not deny that the antinuclear campaign is a political one waged on political terms. IKV executive director Mient-Jan Faber prefers to make use of political arguments.

Individual conscience, good intentions, and the need to expunge guilt are set forth as the only reliable guides for one's approach to secular, political questions. IKV literature resounds with the theme of one's duty to obey conscience: "A judgment arrived at in good conscience transcends the rules and commands of the government."[18] Dutch *Pax Christi* emphasizes that Christians "are responsible for this world—we hold it in trust—and this realization and nothing else will bring about our survival."[19] A Dutch NATO official observes that for many activists moral concern is translated immediately into a policy imperative: "They are opposed by emotion to nuclear weapons, and their churches have taught them not only to follow their consciences, but what their consciences tell them is objectively true."[20]

IKV leaders alike are so convinced of their own sincerity and their correctness that they spend little time in give and take with opponents. Activists state frankly that they "do not accept the starting points" from which others might argue, and their attitude makes discussion fruitless.[21] Opposing views are summarily dismissed or condemned on the basis of ethics. Those who disagree often find not their opinions but their integrity challenged: A NATO official notes that since 1979, public discussion over INF has become "a purely Dutch-style debate about whether the politicians are hypocrites."[22]

The antinuclear movement is generous in its treatment of the Soviet Union. A leading churchman addressed an open letter to President Carter suggesting that human rights violations by the Communist state stemmed from its fear of the West, while many members of IKV assert that it is morally wrong to attribute evil intentions to Moscow, since all people are of equally good will. They imply that the West should feel obligated to make a gesture of its own good will, and that Holland can set the example for the whole world by renouncing nuclear weapons. Such moves would help atone for any Western guilt in creating the horrible arms race and represent an ethical way out of it.

Beyond this almost exaggerated sense of moral propriety there are strong indications that the antinuclear movement's ideas have also been formed by the recent trend toward social "liberationism" in the Netherlands. The Dutch ecological movement, with its large-scale protests against the construction of nuclear power plants, has at times worked in close conjunction with the "peace" campaign. Both streams of protest reflect the widespread appeal of the "liberationist" countercultural attack against the prevailing social order, based on the charge that bourgeois Holland is shallow and dangerous, and must be replaced by a more open community of alternative life styles with "authentic human-oriented values." The liberationist outlook is inherently skeptical of those forces which sustain the prevailing social order, especially technological expertise and political authority. Among youth and intellectuals in particular, it has paved the way for a complete rejection of nuclear weapons, instruments of the *ancien regime* which would have no place in their utopian conception of a socially liberated Holland. Faber has said that "the problem of nuclear weapons is only the start. We are really interested in much more: the construction of a completely different culture."[23] There is some significance in the fact that it is an IKV leader who here sets Holland's antinuclear cause in the broader context of countercultural dissatisfaction with established Dutch society. For many Dutch youth and intellectuals the main task of the churches should be "to point an accusing finger at the injustice of the existing economic order" and now nuclear weapons as well.[24] Thus the "liberationist" stream of thought and the strong current of traditional moralism which has its origins in Calvinism are mutually reinforcing in their antinuclear critique. Consequently, Dutch peace groups, especially IKV, have been willing to cooperate actively with radical left and Communist organizations in the Netherlands and in the Soviet bloc. Some observers have charged that the international "Christians for Socialism," a branch of Moscow's World Peace Council has gained a dominant influence over IKV, though that claim has been vigorously refuted.[25]

Like so much of Dutch thought throughout history, today's antinuclear sentiments emerge from a consciousness of the Netherland's special position in world affairs. All the traditional tendencies which are part and parcel of the small maritime country's self-image — a sense of powerlessness, a disdain for power, an inclination toward abstentionism, internationalist idealism — have been at work in today's Dutch peace movement. They take many different forms and create not only an antinuclear mood but also, IKV denials notwithstanding, a neutralist disposition.

An awareness of the Netherlands' inherent military weakness shows up quite explicitly in reference to its minimal importance for the NATO alliance: Not only peace activists but many Dutchmen stress that their country can add very little to the Western side of the scales in balancing Soviet power. They see the country as merely a battlefield for superpowers' conflicts, a place whose fate is decided by others. This leads to a fear that U.S. missile deployment could mark the prelude to Holland's devastation, and the sense of victimization has strongly anti-American overtones. Because Holland is small and powerless, the line goes, Washington policy makers take advantage of her. It is a refrain that organized peace activists can play with great effect because it touches a chord among many Dutch citizens, evoking such reactions as: "You [Americans] should feel the fear!"[26]

Equally influential in shaping antinuclear attitudes is traditional Dutch abstentionism, a feeling that its unimportant status permits, even obligates, the Netherlands to remain aloof from power politics. Because NATO still holds a symbolic appeal among even those Dutchmen close to the peace movement, many activists are careful not to call for withdrawal from the Alliance. Nonetheless, the IKV program reflects a marked tendency toward abstentionism, which has helped to breed antinuclear and of course neutralist sentiments. An IKV memorandum outlines how the Netherlands could "break away from the nuclear protection of the Superpowers." Other proposals espouse the value of a "bloc-free" Europe which must of course begin with Dutch renunciation of nuclear weapons. Such abstentionist impulses are equally evident in calls for "liberation from the American protectorate." In short, the movement's desire is for the Netherlands to "opt out" of the existing power political framework of Europe and the struggle for hegemony between the superpowers, and a key element in that process is the elimination of nuclear weapons.

If the Netherlands' limited role in world affairs has generated feelings of powerlessness and tendencies toward abstentionism, it has also given rise to a corresponding spirit of internationalist idealism which has similarly helped form Dutch antinuclear sentiments. Many peace activists in the Netherlands claim to have taken upon themselves a mission which begins with opposing INF modernization, but concludes only when the world is also free of such weapons and at peace. IKV's slogan is "Help rid the world of nuclear weapons and begin with the Netherlands" and to that end it proposes several complementary lines of action. The Netherlands as a small power can, of course, lay the groundwork for this European peace structure by helping to convene a European disarmament conference, establishing closer relations with non-aligned countries, encouraging talk about political problems and the future of Europe, and above all, renouncing nuclear weapons. William Bartels, head of IKV, calls Dutch nuclearization "co-operative unilateralism":

> This should not be seen as an element of an approach towards complete unilateral disarmament, but as a first step, which is unilateral and independent yet designed to promote a bilateral and multilateral process towards disarmament and also to function as a confidence-building measure, a step that should

be drastic enough to reflect an alternative approach, but at the same time small enough to enable allies and others to respond to it on the military and political level.[27]

This step, it is expected, would be greeted by other European publics in Scandinavia, Germany, and wherever "independent" antinuclear movements are at work. Such a step-by-step denuclearization (and an end to European economic integration) would lead to a general loosening of the blocs by depriving the superpowers of the instruments they use in their struggle for hegemony and by reducing traditional Soviet fears of the West. Thus, through unilateral measures, it would encourage the Soviets to begin disarming. As an IKV pamphlet declares, Moscow could be persuaded that Western policy is no longer dictated by the U.S. desire to bring about "the fall of the Soviet empire and reinforcement of their own [American] influence in Europe." When all hint of such Western hostility vanishes under the peace movement's guidance, "sensible" groups in Moscow would prevail, with the result that the blocs could be replaced by "a far more complex system of relations between European states" entailing total disarmament, close cooperation, and even unification. In this anti-bloc sense, IKV sees itself as a Western counterpart to Solidarity."[28]

The hope for liberalization in Eastern Europe offers the West another reason to disarm. Faber argues that ideology is dead in Soviet controlled Europe, where "it exists solely to legitimize the power of governments. . . . " Thus since there is no real domestic imperative for repression in Communist Europe, it follows that East-West confrontation largely explains the strict limitation of human rights. Faber has outlined this view:

> The Solidarity people in Poland have said many times that in a way they are the victims of Western freedom. The modernization program of NATO is seen by the Russians as a threat, and so they feel that they have to be strong in their own camp, which means not only weapons but political identity and uniformity in Eastern Europe. If you can build up a situation — and it will take a very long time, at least 20 years – where Eastern Europe sees no threat from Western Europe and vice-versa, then perhaps the Soviet Union will allow more political freedom in Eastern Europe, and movements like Solidarity will continue.[29]

In short, Western military strength threatens human rights, as well as peace. Reduce that strength and there will be both liberalization and accommodation. The peace movement often portrayed itself as a "protector" of Solidarity. Moscow had a "stake" in continuing Western antinuclear protest and would not want to risk it by reacting brutally, as in Hungary (1956) or Czechoslovakia (1968). Although some IKV leaders admitted that the Soviet-inspired crackdown in Poland was a setback, they publicly insist that "bloc pressure" was responsible for such action and add that because we cannot accept "another Poland," Western denuclearization is all the more urgent. Thus IKV pamphlets declared that "Russian prudence on Poland would be encouraged by growing success of the Western peace movement."[30] Two years after Jaruzelski's crackdown, however, Solidarity appeared to have been effectively suppressed, in spite of the Western "peace movement's protection."

For the IKV, antinuclear activism is part of a broader, global peace strategy which epitomizes the exaggerated internationalist idealism of the Dutch. The current campaign will lead the Netherlands not only to the renunciation of nuclear weapons but also to a complementary coalition of similarly "peace-oriented" states.

> The IKV government propagates the idea of a "small-power policy" *(kleine landen politick)*. This concept is related to the notion that the Netherlands should be the "guiding nation" *(gidsland)*, i.e., a progressive guide to the rest of the world by setting an example of international behaviour. Thus, Holland is to take the lead in forming an alliance with other small powers, such as Belgium, Denmark, Romania, Mexico, Nicaragua, Angola, Mozambique, Tanzania, Sri Lanka, etc. Together with other small nations, it should also join the group of 21 non-aligned countries which operate in the United Nations Disarmament Commission.[31]

Such notions of Holland as a *gidsland* serve to illustrate how the various forces in Dutch thought which have generated antinuclear sentiment, especially moralism drawn from a Christian heritage, a distinctive national brand of internationalist idealism, and an awareness of the country's limited geopolitical significance, are mutually reinforcing and together create a powerful inclination to set an example by instigating a new "peaceful world order." Dutch historian M. C. Brando remarks that people can be heard to say, "Let's make [Holland] a city on a hill, the conscience of the West . . . Good intentions can do so much."[32]

The desire to view Soviet behavior in the best possible light reflects that same idealistic impulse and moralistic tendency to speak no ill of an enemy while attributing good intentions to him. The same high-minded restraint does not always apply to the United States. The anti-American overtones to Dutch antinuclear attitudes do not arise solely from traditional Dutch feelings of victimization which reflect the Netherlands' powerlessness. Social "liberationism," arch-critical of modern society, decries America as the worst example of what Holland could become, and helps create a powerful presumption against U.S. policy. In other words, antinuclear attitudes in the Netherlands are the product of a common milieu which was formed by often exaggerated and distorted versions of several traditional Dutch thought traditions or thought trends. How extensive these were and how enduring were their impact upon Dutch public opinion and official policy is examined in the following section.

The Dutch people, of course, are not naive. Many believe there is also substantial Soviet involvement in the Dutch peace movement. A well-known story in the newspaper *Reformatorisch Dagblad* reported that a Soviet embassy official made the following claim:

> Do you know that all those well-meaning people in the Netherlands are being taken for a ride? They believe that the antineutron bomb movement and the reaction against the cruise missiles and other NATO activities have grown out of a pure idealism based on compassion for and concern with the fate of one's fellow man and his children. Oh, if those people just knew that everything is taking place according to a blueprint in Moscow, how they are being manipulated by a small group of communist ideologues who receive their instructions through me. If Moscow decides that 50,000 demonstrators must take to the streets in the Netherlands, they take to the streets. Do you know how you can get 50,000 demonstrators at a certain place within a week? A message through my channels is sufficient. Everything is organized with military precision under the leadership of essentially conscientious objectors. I should know because not only am I daily involved with these clandestine activities, I am also one of those who transmit the orders coming in from Moscow.[33]

Observers acknowledge the effectiveness of Soviet lobbying, propaganda, disinformation, and public diplomacy in the Netherlands. Another embassy officer was awarded a prize in Moscow for his work in cultivating Dutch anti-ERW sentiment. Most commentators believe that Moscow's real significance has been manifested more in exploiting than in creating public pressure against nuclear weapons. Few antinuclearists would deny that role. Virtually all are willing to condone the active cooperation of the Dutch Communist party in what they regard as a cause of overriding importance. Many justify the cooperation with the assurance that it is quite ethical from a political standpoint so long as it is undertaken with no illusions concerning the party's ulterior motives.

THE PEACE MOVEMENT AND DUTCH PUBLIC OPINION, POLITICS, AND POLICY

The impact of Dutch antinuclear sentiment on official policy can best be gauged by first examining public opinion in the Netherlands as a whole. IKV ideas have been shown to have deep roots in Dutch thought traditions, but do they have a broad appeal today? Certainly IKV has been well placed to propagate its major themes. With 10,000 active members in 400 local chapters, it is considered the envy of political parties. It claimed to have obtained 1.2 million signatures (a figure that was challenged) for an anti-ERW petition. The IKV can claim a large measure of responsibility for the parliamentary impasse which was created in December 1979, forcing the government to postpone the decision to deploy INF in the Netherlands after it had voted with all the allies for NATO deployment of the missiles.

Its massive anti-INF rally in Amsterdam in November 1981 had nearly 400,000 participants.[34]

The effectiveness of the organization and its appeal is born out in a rapidly growing antinuclear mood, even among those people who are not personally active in protest. Surveys as late as 1979 revealed only about 10% support for any sort of unilateral action towards disarmament; two years later, although a large percentage still favored Dutch membership in NATO, over 60% opposed having nuclear weapons of any sort, especially INF, in Holland; nearly 50% endorsed IKV's slogan ("To help rid the world of nuclear weapons, begin with the Netherlands"); and over one-third said that there should be no nuclear deterrent in Europe.[35]

As for how enduring the antinuclear appeal will be, one indication is found in the extent to which young people will support the peace campaign. IKV and *Pax Christi*, as well as the demonstrations they sponsor, are composed primarily of people in their twenties and thirties. Polls confirm that the antinuclear movement is largely, though by no means exclusively, a youth phenomenon; moreover, 40% of men between ages 18 and 24 years say they would not fight in the event of war, with just under half considering themselves strict pacifists. There are also signs that the peace campaign has reached down to younger children.[36]

Because IKV and the peace movement as a whole are so well organized and clearly strike a positive chord in public opinion, antinuclear themes have dominated Dutch politics for several years. Perhaps more than anywhere else in Europe, political parties in the Netherlands feel compelled to place disarmament atop their agenda; almost every major political organization must present itself as "a peace party," although the VVD or Liberal party, which largely eschews antinuclear appeals, has managed to strengthen its position in recent years by providing a refuge for the still sizable minority (25%) who have wearied of the peace campaign (several very small traditionalist Calvinist political factions have also proven immune to the antinuclear fever).

Most vulnerable to antinuclear pressures has been the Dutch Labor Party (PvdA); indeed partly because of the peace campaign, the PvdA nearly split between 1979 and 1982. Throughout the initial years of public debate over nuclear weapons, first with ERW and then with INF, moderate, one-time Premier Joop den Uyl led the PvdA. He advocated a relatively cautious, compromise approach to disarmament that would lead the Netherlands gradually away from involvement with nuclear arms. But more passionate antinuclear sentiments deeply penetrated the Labor party. Among PvdA activists "liberationist" ideas had found political support in the 1960s, and even before the nuclear debate was underway these same tendencies were pushing the party away from its traditional support of nuclear deterrence toward unilateralism. Radical disarmament measures earned widespread support over the protests of den Uyl and other party moderates, including one-time Foreign Minister Max van der Stoel. Although van der Stoel and others in the party leadership continued to state that PvdA's official stand on INF was to await the outcome of negotiations in Geneva, there was a consensus in the party as a whole on several points: The SS-20s posed no substantially new threat to Western Europe; there was, therefore, no need for NATO INF; steps to create a theater balance would decouple Europe from the U.S. nuclear deterrent; and thus the dual decision must be "reconsidered" and INF should not be deployed. In the PvdA view, arms control should be the response to any Soviet weapons build-up, but the zero-option proposal of Ronald Reagan, which van der Stoel endorsed, was unacceptable to Moscow and thus "absolutely not negotiable" in the view of the PvdA majority. In 1982 de facto PvdA opposition to the missiles stiffened, and it was the Labor party's persistent effort to have the Dutch government officially urge that NATO's decision be "reconsidered" which made it unable to join a CDA-led government. The PvdA refuted charges that Dutch pleas for "reconsideration" and Dutch refusal to undertake sitings for the missiles would damage the Netherlands' ability to remain involved in NATO procedures right up to the deployment decision, arguing that the belated start of U.S.–Soviet arms talks made it likely that Dutch deployment would not take place until perhaps as late as 1986. Thus the Labor party continued to speak about doing away with the missiles without expressly advocating unilateral Dutch renunciation of them.

> . . . the PvdA probably would like to make it clear that what is most important is the best possible Netherlands contribution to a security policy with the major objective of reducing nuclear arms levels. For this, a "clear No" from the PvdA to the deployment of 48 cruise missiles would not be out of place, although many observers in The Hague are saying that the PvdA will have to make do with a "No in effect."[37]

The Labor party also generally rejects Holland's other "nuclear tasks" — deployment on its soil of six different types of tactical nuclear systems — and called in 1980 to eliminate all but one or at most two. The latter exception was made only because den Uyl refused to lead the party in the 1981 election campaign if its platform contained a totally antinuclear plank. The PvdA mirrored the IKV view that antinuclearism represented the Netherlands' best effort to bring about peace. Neither the IKV nor the PvdA advocated withdrawal from NATO, membership in which remained popular with the Dutch public. Both organizations ignored the contradiction between their avowed loyalty to NATO and their repudiation of a unanimous NATO decision deemed necessary to maintain effective deterrence in Europe.

The Netherlands' other major left-of-center party, Democrats'66, claiming to be the "true liberals" took a more ambiguous position on the specifics of nuclear policy, continuing to hold that the dual-track decision was "regrettable," without unconditionally rejecting it. Like the PvdA, D'66 felt pressure from antinuclear groups and was a major IKV target. Party leader Jan Terlouw in 1981 proclaimed the need for "responsible unilateral steps in the direction of disarmament" and, although D'66 has recognized Soviet SS-20s as a threat to Europe, it proclaims no arms imbalance exists and insists that at any rate, NATO could live with a "limited inferiority" in weapons. Wishing to maintain sufficient flexibility to enter a coalition government either with the Christian Democrats or Labor or both, D'66 said in its platform that "deployment is unacceptable *under the present circumstances,*" leaving the door open to a compromise, perhaps a result of work by moderates such as Hans van Mierlo, who did become Defense Minister in the new government formed in September 1981. In a similarly ambiguous manner, the party criticized Ronald Reagan's zero-option proposals for excluding Anglo-French nuclear forces, yet greeted it as an "opening offer." Nonetheless, D'66 echoed IKV positions on ERW, the need to reduce the Netherlands' tactical nuclear tasks and the desirability of convening a European disarmament group that did not involve the superpowers.

Naturally the Netherlands' smaller left-wing parties — the Pacifists, Radicals, and Communists — unambiguously reflect the peace movement's rejection of nuclear weapons.

The most volatile relationship between the antinuclear campaign and a political grouping involves the Christian Democratic Appeal, the loose centrist coalition of traditional religious parties that has been at the center of most Dutch governments since the 1970s. The anti-ERW movement struck a deep chord in the CDA and many elements in the Appeal echoed IKV's moralistic condemnation of the weapon; a CDA Defense Minister resigned because the cabinet would not follow the CDA parliamentary delegation in opposing the U.S. decision to produce components of the neutron warhead. Since then the CDA has continued to resist ERW, and seeks — along with the PvdA and Communist party — to reduce the Netherlands' tactical nuclear tasks. The Dutch peace campaign's ideas have had a particularly strong resonance within one wing of the CDA, the Anti-Revolutionary party (ARP), which has in turn applied pressure on its colleagues; this has been especially evident in the CDA's dilemma over the NATO double-track decision. Although originally affiliated with the arch-traditionalist Reformed church, the ARP — like all of Dutch society — underwent secularization; it opened up to the new liberationist philosophy yet retained a certain Calvinist intensity. As a result, ARP members have been the locus of moralistic antinuclear sentiment within the CDA. When the CDA-VVD government in late 1979 was attempting to solidify support within its own ranks for NATO's December INF plan, the best it could achieve was a compromise agreement to defer a decision on missile deployment for two years pending the outcome of U.S.-Soviet arms reduction talks. But ten ARP members created difficulties for Prime Minister Dries van Agt by bolting to the opposition, endorsing a motion to reject the double-track plan altogether. Van Agt only barely held his party (and his government) together by insisting that the Netherlands had made no firm commitment to deploy if the talks failed. Since then the party center-right and antinuclear sympathizers have vied for dominance. Prior to the November 1981 IKV demonstration in Amsterdam, the CDA again compromised with itself—declining to help organize the event yet agreeing to participate in it. Peace activists and Laborites argued that the CDA in 1981 moved slightly from its noncommittal position when it asserted that the NATO deployment plan was a necessary "point of departure" in arms reduction talks; the CDA also endorsed Ronald Reagan's zero-option and interim proposals, which were greeted with far more skepticism by IKV. At the same time, the party has remained ambiguous about actual deployment. While voicing formal support for preparation of the missile sites throughout 1983, it nonetheless assured antinuclear critics that only "administrative" or "passive"—as opposed to "active"—measures would be taken.

IKV and the "peace movement" as a whole have had a substantial impact not only on Dutch public opinion and Dutch political parties, but as a result, on the process of forming governments and shaping public policy. No individual "antinuclear" party has had a dominant hand in government policy, but three of the four largest parties—PvdA, D'66, and the CDA—house strong antinuclear forces. As *Der Spiegel* observed about Holland, "No government can be formed there without the opponents of nuclear weapons."[38] Over two thirds of Dutch voters in elections since nuclear weapons became a major issue have chosen parties which contain significant virulently antinuclear blocs. It should be noted, however, that the Liberal party's waxing political fortunes in 1982–1983 suggest that the Netherlands' pro-INF minority eventually consolidated and grew during this period.

Almost every major decision on nuclear issues taken by Dutch governments between 1977 and 1983 has borne the imprint of antinuclear pressure. IKV and left-wing resistance to ERW in 1977–1978 quickly swept up all major parties but the VVD, and neutron weapons have remained completely off the agenda of policy issues in The Hague ever since. Governments even made their consideration of other NATO nuclear policies contingent upon stopping any further Alliance reference to ERW. Many leading political figures base their objections on the arguments that ERW would spark an arms race and obstruct arms control because it would eliminate the necessary firebreak between conventional and nuclear weapons by being so "usable," but unquestionably the peace campaign's propagandistic condemnation of the "neutron bomb" as "the perfect capitalist weapon—designed to kill people without damaging property" is what sparked public, and governmental, resistance to the system's deployment.

Pressure has been directed with equal force against all the Netherlands' involvement with other NATO tactical nuclear weapons such that it is official Dutch policy to reduce the country's battlefield nuclear tasks. Here the strength of IKV's moralistic campaign has been matched by a sophisticated argument in government circles that such low-level systems do little to enhance deterrence. All governments, whether center-left or center-right, have held to the viewpoint of then Prime Minister Dries van Agt's cabinet in 1981 when it promised to be "energetic in promoting examination within the alliance of how defense can be responsibly maintained with fewer nuclear weapons. In this connection the reductions in the Netherlands' nuclear forces will be discussed."[39] Clearly, the protest movement's effort to denuclearize the Netherlands has borne fruit.

After the inconclusive elections of May 1981, despite continuing differences in emphasis and slightly different evaluations of the zero-option proposal of Ronald Reagan, the CDA, PvdA, and D'66, all members of the new governing coalition, continued to preserve the only feasible basis for consensus: a decision not to decide. In December 1981, two years had elapsed since the Netherlands chose to defer for two years a deployment decision pending the outcome of arms talks, but since the Americans and Soviets had only begun to discuss reductions, that deadline was extended. PvdA members' talk of "reconsidering" the NATO plan altogether was disregarded by the tripartite coalition. Nonetheless, formal government policy continued to reflect an unwillingness to disturb the fragile consensus based on deferring a decision. Prime Minister van Agt said:

> (The) results of the negotiations on medium-range nuclear arms will play a major role when the cabinet comes to consider the timing and contents of a decision. As far as the NATO dual decision is concerned the cabinet is aware that there are divergent views on this point in the various political parties. The differences of opinion primarily surround the question of whether this is the correct military and political response to the modernization and buildup of the number of medium-range nuclear weapons in the Soviet Union.
>
> The decision has been made, it exists and forms NATO's point of departure for the negotiations between the United States and the Soviet Union. We are of the opinion that given the present situation, pressure within NATO for a reassessment of the decision would harm the chances of a successful conclusion to the negotiations.[40]

Differences in emphasis over the missiles partly determined the form of a new government in late 1982, but the policy of postponing a decision remained. The PvdA had continued to press for an official "reconsideration" of the deployment plan and vowed it would have nothing to do with stationing missiles. In response, the CDA claimed that "nothing should be done or omitted that could damage the talks in Geneva." This precluded further unilateral Dutch steps toward a renunciation of the cruise missiles.[41] As a result, the CDA turned to the Liberals who had been strengthened by the 1982 elections. Although this meant cohesive support for a unified backing of the American position at Geneva, the CDA could still not afford to buck IKV-inspired resistance to deployment. The Hague continued to defer a decision. Though many Dutch politicians favored deployment so as not to weaken Holland's "role and voice within NATO,"[42] and though one report suggested that CDA Prime Minister Lubbers would follow Bonn's lead,[43] it became clear by late 1983 that the CDA as a whole would ultimately support stationing only if the Geneva talks failed due to "an outright *nyet* from Moscow."[44] Indefinite deferral of a firm decision remained the only formula that could hold the Dutch government together. A clear choice unsatisfactory to either the pro-INF Liberals or anti-INF elements in the CDA could bring the coalition down, force new elections, and perhaps lead to a victory by the unconditionally antinuclear Labor party. Lubbers' government had kept postponing the decision until June 1984, hoping that the example of Britain, West Germany, Italy, and Belgium (all of which had agreed to accept the missiles and the first three of which had already begun to deploy them) might build support for the weapons in the Netherlands. Dutch popular resistance to cruise missiles, however, was reported to be increasing, while NATO was pressing The Hague for an answer. A public opinion poll showed 63% of the population willing to support a parliamentary vote against deployment, including 45% of the Christian Democrats and 34% of the Liberals interviewed. Even the Christian Democrats in the Cabinet were split, Foreign Minister van den Broek favoring deployment and Defense Minister Jacob de Ruiter adopting a much more equivocal position. Lubbers first proposed compromise called for the deployment of fewer missiles than the forty-eight allocated by NATO (probably sixteen to start with), the phasing out of two more of the country's nuclear tasks*—atomic demolition mines and the Navy's Neptune anti-submarine weapons—and an increase in the Netherlands' financial contribution to NATO's conventional forces.[45] The NATO allies were not happy with this idea, fearing that any breaking of alliance ranks on the December 1979 decision would constitute a payoff to Moscow for its political warfare campaign and might rekindle the flagging controversy in Britain and West Germany. U.S. Defense Secretary Weinberger, during a visit to The Hague, and also at a NATO Defense Ministers meeting in Turkey,

---

*The Netherlands had already scheduled the replacement of Nike surface-to-air nuclear missiles by Patriot missiles carrying non-nuclear warheads.

while denying any intention of intruding into Holland's internal political affairs, warned that any decision short of full deployment could lead to the unravelling of NATO's carefully worked out plan and reduce pressure on Moscow to resume arms control negotiations.[46] Next, the Christian Democratic leadership, in an effort to hold the badly split party together, floated the idea of a "crisis deployment" option under which the Dutch portion of the NATO missiles would be stored in other member countries of the alliance (such as West Germany and the United States) and flown into pre-prepared sites in the Netherlands at a time of crisis. This plan also encountered heavy criticism from the United States and NATO on the grounds that rushing the cruise missiles into the Netherlands under such circumstances would probably exacerbate the crisis.[47]

Many Dutch leaders were worried lest their country appear to be an unreliable ally. Conversely, other NATO governments did not wish to be seen as imposing from the outside a decision that would bring down the government and force an election which the strongly anti-deployment PvdA (Labor party) would be almost certain to win. The allies were sympathetic with the domestic political plight, but they refused to back away from their insistence upon full deployment. On June 1, 1984, the Dutch government announced its compromise. It offered to cancel deployment of its share of nuclear missiles if the Soviet Union would freeze its SS-20 arsenal at the level of that date. If the Soviet Union continues its build-up for the next seventeen months, the Netherlands will accept its full quota of forty-eight missiles. If a U.S.-Soviet arms limitation accord is reached before November 1, 1985, the Netherlands will accept and deploy its full share of NATO's permitted number of missiles. Meanwhile, physical preparations for siting the missiles will continue. In other words, the Dutch promised to make their final decision on November 1, 1985 (when the Lubbers Cabinet would complete its third year of ruling), but this postponement pushed the final siting date, originally scheduled for 1986, to 1988. Lubbers had to produce a compromise which provided for the possibility of fewer than forty-eight missiles, theoretically down to zero, to placate the antinuclearists in his own party and also for the full quota of forty-eight in order to keep the Liberal party from abandoning the coalition. Under the compromise, the Netherlands became the first member of the alliance to break ranks on the NATO deployment timetable. This was the only victory over the official policy of a NATO government to which the West European antinuclear movement could point.[48]

Dutch antinuclear sentiments have not had an impact on the Netherlands alone. IKV's ties with West German (and to a lesser extent East German) church groups have helped intensify the religious opposition to nuclear weapons in that country. Dutch activists have actually participated in great numbers in German antinuclear rallies, including the two large Bonn demonstrations in November 1981 and June 1982. In early 1983, IKV began a campaign in France, but there was serious doubt whether its antinuclear critique could take hold there. But the "Dutch disease" has spread in even greater measure to Belgium. Flemish sections of the country read and watch the Dutch media and the Flemish Socialist Party has taken up many IKV themes. Other Belgian antinuclear organizations with Dutch ties include the national chapter of *Pax Christi* and the Flemish Students Union. Aside from Brussels, Antwerp on the Dutch border has been the site of Belgium's largest peace rallies.

All of the important cases—ERW, debate over battlefield tasks, and especially INF—indicate that IKV and its allies have had so great an impact on Dutch public opinion as to define the limits of what the parties and the government see as acceptable nuclear policy. The movement's appeal has in the process drawn upon and revived historic Dutch tendencies toward broader feelings of pacifism, unilateralism, and neutralism, but there is less certainty about whether these tendencies have gained sufficient strength to determine political priorities to the same extent and thus severely constrain the Netherlands' conduct of foreign policy.

Faber denies altogether that his movement is a pacifist one, claiming it includes soldiers and seeks "less aggressive," "alternative defence structures."[49] Others are unconvinced by such distinctions and openly label the antinuclear campaign a pacifist one. Critics claim that much of IKV's rhetoric leads young people to believe that "dialogue is a substitute for defence" and that problems are never solved by force. The aforementioned poll showing how many young Dutch men would not fight an invader is also taken as a disturbing sign of the peace campaign's impact.

Unilateralism and neutralism are other parts of the peace movement's appeal which stem directly from Dutch thought traditions and may threaten to become as irresistible as the strictly antinuclear sentiments to which they have contributed. Again, IKV defends itself from such criticism by pointing out that the organization and its allies in the peace movement, like the "Stop the Neutron Bomb" campaign of 1977–1978, have not renounced NATO; Faber insists that his campaign is not for unilateral disarmament and is not aimed against alliances, but merely seeks greater say over what the superpowers do in Europe.[50] Yet peace activists have tried to compel the Netherlands' government to withdraw from various nuclear programs regardless of what other Alliance members do; IKV's slogan—"Rid the world of nuclear weapons and begin with the Netherlands"—further manifests a unilateralist impulse. Critics fear the movement would like the Dutch government to go the unilateralist, neutralist way and "turn their backs on the world."

But even the movement's critics point out that the most important impact of these pacifist, unilateralist, and neutralist streams in the peace campaign has been to reinforce strictly antinuclear tendencies; phrasing protests against the missiles as protests against war or against the blocs has given antinuclear rhetoric a greater appeal. But when the nuclear issue is set aside, the peace campaign has nonetheless not had so substantial a pacifist, neutralist, or unilateralist effect on Dutch politics and policy as a whole. After all, polls show that *most* youth would still defend their country, and the Dutch army is regarded as effective. Public opinion is also less unilateralist than the peace campaign might assume: even in the Dutch Reformed church there is suspicion of the IKV's slogan's unilateralist tone.[51] Public support for NATO membership remains above 70%. International events also helped to slow any move toward pacifism or unilateralism: Ronald Reagan's zero-option and interim proposals mitigated America's image as a "war-monger," while the Soviet arms build-up and repression of Solidarity reawakened recognition that force *does* play a role in world affairs and that there are differences between the blocs. Aside from some stirrings in the PvdA, the major parties have stopped far short of complementing their position on nuclear arms with explicit calls for a renunciation of military defense or withdrawal from the blocs. Counter groups advocating strong defense and loyalty to NATO began to emerge in 1982, and in that year the conservative VVD made enormous electoral gains. Beginning in mid-1982, many Dutch observers began to discern a slowing down of the entire peace movement's momentum; not only were explicitly pacifist, neutralist, and unilateralist pressures being blunted, but the more powerful antinuclear drive itself had tapered off. Joris J. C. Voorhoeve felt encouraged to declare that the movement as of mid-1982 presented "less of a threat to a responsible foreign and defense policy than it did during the last three years."[52] Although IKV remained strong and the government's ability to implement NATO's INF policy remained uncertain, the situation stabilized somewhat. VVD politician Frits Bolkestein observed that there is no compelling reason why the Netherlands should not remain committed to NATO.[53] Commentators like Voorhoeve and Bolkestein believed the best insurance against a renewed, even stronger peace campaign lay in Washington's maintaining a visible arms control plan and providing for consultation within the Alliance, combined with a forthright government policy within the Netherlands itself. Despite the broad thought traditions and trends which have given rise to the movement, historian Voorhoeve points to factors from the country's past which may help mitigate against a further erosion of the Dutch position within the Western Alliance:

> There is no reason to assume that the Dutch, who have fought totalitarianism and advocated liberty and democracy for generations, have suddenly lost their senses. All Dutch know of the sea, that it respects only the well-maintained dikes. Many still know that this also applies to potential aggressors. In Dutch history, the dike-builders are always the ones who prevail.[54]

The Dutch people on the whole are not pacifist. They certainly cannot be regarded as naive after centuries of fending for themselves in an arena dominated by larger powers. Defense efforts and defense spending can hardly be called popular with them. As budget priorities they are ranked lower than such socio-economic issues as housing, social security, pollution control, employment programs, and so on. But in this regard the Dutch do not differ significantly from other West European publics, none of which can become enthusiastic about increasing military appropriations. Indeed, virtually all of them are inclined to think that if public sector spending must be cut for the sake of fiscal solvency, the funding for guns should go down before the funding for butter.[55] This view is characteristic of public opinion everywhere throughout NATO because of two common beliefs: (1) the danger of war in Europe is infinitesimally low; and (2) much military equipment is now being purchased at artificially and exorbitantly inflated prices. Unlike governments, publics can seldom appreciate the political and psychological subtleties involved in the deterrence equation, or the long-range consequences of gradual intimidation which may increase precisely because war in Europe has become "unthinkable" for all normal people.

Actually, the Netherlands' record was better than average for Alliance members when it came to fulfilling the NATO goal of increased defense spending in real terms (after inflation) set in the late 1970s. Three quarters of the Dutch people grudgingly concede the need for military defense and NATO, which they recognize as providing security at relatively low cost — a factor not to be ignored by an economy-minded people. But their evaluation of nuclear weapons has become gradually more negative over the years, as their presence on Dutch territory has become more dangerous with the growth of Soviet nuclear power. Rather than admit that they are afraid for themselves, the Dutch would prefer, not insincerely, to universalize their moral and humanitarian concern by projecting it to the whole world. They would like to be rid of nuclear weapons if at all possible. Without calculating the costs that would be involved, they prefer a shift from nuclear to conventional deterrence and have worked for such a shift within NATO in recent years. They are particularly anxious to eliminate what they regard as the most dangerous and least useful nuclear weapons now on their soil, especially the short-range howitzers. In the end, they might be willing to retain a very small number of nuclear "tasks" such as Lance rockets or air-launched missiles. But they will probably remain unalterably opposed to the introduction of enhanced-radiation warheads, the prospect of which initially triggered their protest. The ground-launched cruise missiles scheduled to be put in Holland have been, of all nuclear weapons, the most unpopular because they were seen as new, unnecessary, symbolic of a wasteful escalation of the arms race and provocative enough to heighten international tensions and increase the probability of nuclear war. Whether the government will be sufficiently determined and able to overcome the powerful opposition to INF generated by the IKV is a question that cannot yet be settled. As 1984 drew to a close, the government at The Hague continued to adhere to that position, although some Dutch politicians were expressing doubt that Moscow was seriously interested in the Netherlands' offer, especially in the light of reports that the USSR was preparing new basing sites for SS-20s. NATO observers expected the Soviet Union to keep manipulating the issue of the SS-20s for the purpose of influencing the Dutch decision on deployment.

NOTES

1. Walter L. Laqueur, "Hollanditis: A New State of European Nationalism," *Commentary* (August 1981) pp. 19–26. For the view that Laqueur's characterization may have been somewhat overdrawn and that the current Dutch consensus is more pragmatist than pacifist, see Richard C. Eichenberg, "The Myth of Hollanditis," *International Security*, 8 (Fall 1983), pp. 143–159.
2. Bartholomew Landheer, ed., *The Netherlands* (Berkeley: University of California Press, 1944). The term *verzuiling* is explained in Frank E. Huggett, *The Modern Netherlands* (New York: Praeger, 1971), pp. 62, 64.
3. Arend Lijphart, *The Politics of Accommodation: Pluralism and Democracy in the Netherlands* (Berkeley: University of California Press, 1968), pp. 17–32.
4. Hal Piper, "'Dutch Disease' Causing Complications for NATO," *Baltimore Sun*, June 5, 1981, p. 1.
5. Monsignor Dr. R. P. Bar, "Views of Church Groups in the Netherlands on War and Peace," *NATO Review*, 30 (February 1982).
6. Piper, op. cit.
7. Frits Bolkestein, "Neutralism in Europe: The Dutch qualm disease," *The Economist*, June 5, 1982, p. 44.
8. Barry Newman, "European Voice: Dutch Peace Council Feels Misunderstood Despite Some Success," *Wall Street Journal*, January 28, 1982, p. 1.
9. Bolkestein, op. cit.
10. Gerald Newton, *The Netherlands: An Historical and Cultural Survey*, 1795–1977 (Boulder, Colorado: Westview Press, 1978), p. 198–99.
11. Bolkestein, op. cit., p. 43.
12. Newton, op. cit., p. 203.
13. Bolkestein, op. cit., p. 44.
14. Joris J. C. Voorhoeve, *Peace, Profits and Principles: A Study of Dutch Foreign Policy* (The Hague: Martinus Nijhof, 1979).
15. Frits Bolkestein, "The Netherlands and the Lure of Neutralism," *NATO Review*, 29 (October 1981), p. 2.
16. Newman, op. cit.
17. Bar, op. cit., and *IKV-berichten 1982/83-nr.1*, August 1982.
18. Bolkestein, "Neutralism," op. cit., p. 45.
19. Mark J. Kurlansky, "The Concern of People Living on the Battlefield . . . ," *International Herald Tribune*, Supplement November, 1981, p. 115.
20. Richard Eder, "Dutch in the Vanguard of Missile Skeptics," *New York Times*, September 18, 1981.
21. Colonel Mozes W. A. Weers, "The Nuclear Debate in the Netherlands," *NATO Review*, 9 (Spring 1981), p. 68.

22. Eder, op. cit.
23. Bolkestein, "Neutralism," op. cit., p. 44.
24. Bolkestein, "The Netherlands," op. cit.
25. "Soviet Subversion, Involvement with Peace Movement," *De Telegraaf*, July 22, 23, 25, 29, and August 1, 1981, *Foreign Broadcast Information Service—Western Europe.* (herein after FBIS.)
26. Newman, op. cit.
27. William Bartels, speech before the United Nations' Second Special Session on Disarmament, June 24–25, 1982.
28. *IKV-berichten 1981/1982—nr. 2.*
29. *New York Times*, February 21, 1982, p. E3.
30. *IKV-berichten 1981/1982—nr. 2.*
31. J. A. Emerson Vermaat, "Neutralist Tendencies in the Netherlands," *The World Today*, December 1981.
32. Piper, op. cit.
33. J. G. Heitink, "Soviet Subversion, Involvement with the Peace Movement," *De Telegraaf*, July 22, 1981, in *Current News, Foreign Media*, October 28, 1981, pp. 3–4.
34. *The Economist Foreign Report*, December 19, 1979, p. 3. Kurlansky, "The Concern."
35. "Poll Reveals Majority Opposes Cruise Missiles," *Handelsblad*, August 15, 1981, *FBIS.*
36. *Die Zeit*, January 21, 1983, p. 22.
37. "Labour Party Maneuverings on Cruise Issue," *De Volkskrant*, September 22, 1982, *FBIS*, September 27, 1982, F1.
38. *Der Spiegel*, June 15, 1981, p. 30.
39. "Van Agt Against Review of NATO Dual Decision," *De Volkskrant*, November 17, 1981, *FBIS*, November 20, 1981, F1.
40. *FBIS*, November 20, 1981, p. F1.
41. "Missile Issue Delays Cabinet Formation," *De Volkskrant*, September 28, 1982, *FBIS*, October 1, 1982, p. F1.
42. *International Herald Tribune*, November 8, 1982.
43. "Country Will Follow German Example on Missiles," *NRC Handelsblad*, June 16, 1983, *FBIS*, June 21, 1983, p. F1.
44. "Missiles could be explosive here too," *The Economist*, April 23, 1983, p. 46.
45. Priscilla Painton, "Dutch Leaders Seek Solution to Dispute Over Cruise Missiles," *Washington Post*, March 7, 1984; R. W. Apple, Jr., "Dutch Government in Quandary Over Stationing of NATO Missiles," *New York Times*, March 24, 1984.
46. Fred Hiatt, "Dutch Warmed to Accept U.S. Missiles," *The Washington Post*, March 27, 1984; Brad Knickerbocker, "Weinberger in Europe will urge on missiles, assuage allies' fears," *Christian Science Monitor*, March 28, 1984; Fred Hiatt, "Weinberger Says NATO Ministers Underline Need of Dutch Solidarity," *Washington Post*, April 5, 1984.
47. Fred Hiatt and Michael Getter, "Dutch Inclined to Take Missiles Only in a Crisis," *Washington Post*, April 25, 1984; William Drozdiak, "Dutch Seeking Formula to End Missile Dilemma," ibid., May 15, 1984.
48. William Drozdiak, "Dutch Link Missiles to Soviet Halt," ibid., June 2, 1984; "Text of Dutch Statement on Delay in Deploying of Missiles," *New York Times*, June 2, 1984.
49. Eichenberg, "The Myth of Hollanditis," op. cit., pp. 148–149.
50. Interview with Mient-Jan Faber, *New York Times*, February 21, 1982, p. E3.
51. Bolkestein, "Neutralism in Europe: The Dutch qualm disease," p. 45.
52. J. C. Voorhoeve, "Pacifism in the Netherlands," *Freedom at Issue*, July-August 1982, p. 4.
53. Bolkestein, "The Netherlands and the Lure of Neutralism," p. 5.
54. Voorhoeve, "Pacifism in the Netherlands," p. 5.
55. See Richard C. Eichenberg, "The Myth of Hollanditis."

Chapter 6
The Antinuclear Protest in Italy: A Nonstarter?
Diane K. Pfaltzgraff

INTRODUCTION: THEMES IN THE ITALIAN PEACE MOVEMENT

The antinuclear protest movement in Italy is somewhat unique. It does not lend itself easily to comparison with that of any other country in Western Europe. The situation in Italy is quite unlike that in France, where all the major parties favor nuclear deterrence and the *force de frappe*. It is also different from that of the other NATO allies—Britain, West Germany, Netherlands, and Belgium—where there has been politically significant opposition to the scheduled emplacement of intermediate-range missiles. The protest in Italy has produced no major impact—at least not yet. This may be due to the fact that there is no Protestant tradition to speak of in the distinctly Catholic culture which still pervades the historic center of Christendom. Although Northern Italy, which is oriented toward continental Europe, is dissimilar from southern Italy, the *Mezzogiorno*, which is essentially Mediterranean in outlook, neither part of the peninsula houses any genuine fanaticism when it comes to relating politics with morality.[1]

Most northern Italians do not like to be identified with either the zealous reformer Savonarola or the much maligned amoral realist Machiavelli. They would prefer to be associated with the practical "middle way" political philosophy of Thomas Aquinas, who preached a rather commonsense social morality based on the avoidance of extremes. But if forced to choose between the two Florentines who lived a century or more after St. Thomas, one a self-appointed prophet-ruler and the other a would-be diplomatic counselor of princes, most would probably lean toward the latter. That would be even more the case in the south.

For a long time there has been a pronounced tendency in Italy to let the church be the church and the state be the state. That is the compromise which Pope Pius XI and Mussolini agreed to in the Lateran Accords of 1929, producing a *modus vivendi* between Italy and the Holy See on such issues as the international diplomatic status of the Holy See and Vatican City and the legal prerogatives of the Catholic church in Italy with regard to such matters as marriage, education, and the prohibition of a political role for priests.

Moreover, Italian politicians are the inheritors of a long tradition of politics and diplomacy in which foreign and defense policy questions have been considered the responsibility of the executive branch (king, duce, or president and prime minister in the Republic) rather than of the Parliament. Throughout the history of the Italian Republic since 1946, those questions have never figured prominently in election campaigns. These two tendencies, based on a delicate church-state understanding (which even the Communist party supports) and on Italy's constitutional tradition dating from, and even far beyond, the *Statuto Alberinti* of 1848, have powerfully reinforced each other with reference to the "peace" question in recent years. Up to now, therefore, the "peace movement" in Italy has enjoyed much more limited success than elsewhere. It would be too much to call it a "nonstarter." But like ungainly species of birds, it has, while running, not yet taken off.

The same major themes are found in the Italian as in other West European antinuclear movements: (1) strategic-political, (2) moral-ethical; (3) ecological; (4) the East-West versus the North-South focus; and (5) women's liberation. But relative emphasis, as one might expect, varies in accordance with the various personalities and groups that comprise the Italian movement.

The statements of Italian Communist party (PCI) leaders reveal a major focus on East-West relations and the overall strategic-military balance. Nevertheless the PCI has sought a position of equidistance from the Soviet Union and the United States, both of which they view as sharing the major obligation to pursue policies of disarmament. Such a stance accords with the strategy of the PCI to broaden its base of electoral support. For this purpose, the PCI seeks to portray itself as having a "responsible" and "autonomous" position with respect to the Soviet Union.

The pronouncements of the Italian Socialist party (PSI) also contain an emphasis on a strategic-political analysis of the "peace" issue. In sharp contrast to the PCI, however, the PSI leadership has been strongly influenced by a deeply rooted tradition within the party concerning the issue of peace and disarmament that may be traced back seventy-five years to the divisive debate within the Socialist party about Italy's entry into World War I as well as the long-term debates that have taken place concerning the party's proper relationship to the PCI. In addition, it is clear that PSI perspectives on the "peace" question reflect the party's concern about its domestic political standing. The PSI wishes to avoid the appearance of being subservient to the PCI in the pursuit of "peace."

Although the Christian Democratic party (DC) has embraced a strategic-political analysis, but from a quite different perspective, its views have been generally supportive of U.S. policy positions and highly critical of Soviet policy, in particular the SS-20s targeted against Western Europe. It is believed, however, that the left wing of the party is potentially susceptible to pacifist appeals, particularly those couched in moral-ethical-religious tones. Thus, were the church to become more active on the "peace" issue, at least a portion of the DC would mirror that ethical-moral-religious approach.

The Radical party (PR), before its leader, Marco Pannella, abandoned his preoccupation with world peace in favor of concentration on world hunger, approached the issue from both an ecological and a moral-ethical perspective, focusing on an exaggerated danger of a nuclear holocaust. Other political parties to the left of the PCI, the small Proletarian Democratic Unity party (PDUP) and the Proletarian Democracy (DP), for example, have reflected a mixture of themes. Predominant have been ethical-moral considerations with some emphasis on ecology and the North-South issue. Groups other than the various political parties emphasize a range of themes such as the ecological perspective in the case of the Associazione Ricreative Culturale Italiana (Italian Recreational and Cultural Association, ARCI), and the Ecological League. Women's branches in all but the more conservative segments of the party spectrum stress the connection between the "peace campaign" and feminine liberation from a male-dominated, social-cultural-political order.

A consideration of the position of the Italian Roman Catholic church on the "peace" issue reveals that the moral-ethical critique of nuclear weapons has not been actively promoted by the church hierarchy—a condition that contrasts sharply with the activism of the American Catholic Bishops in their Pastoral Letter on "The Challenge of Peace: God's Promise and Our Response." In Italy, the church has tempered support for efforts to promote disarmament with a recognition of the need to maintain an East-West balance. Thus, while supporting the cause of "peace," the church hierarchy has issued no calls for a renunciation of Italy's decision to deploy ground-launched cruise missiles at Comiso, Sicily. At the same time, however, there have been statements by individual priests and bishops in support of the protest movement. Finally, the small Protestant denominations have reflected a sympathy toward themes such as the North-South issue, women's liberation, and a danger of nuclear holocaust, which is often hysterically perceived as imminent.

What distinguishes Italy's "movement" is the lack of a unifying force or structure which could provide the leadership needed to make it a significant movement, a viable political entity. There exist structures which could conceivably serve as a catalyst — namely the church or one of the political parties, most probably either the PCI or the PSI — but, thus far, none has seen fit to assume this role. In the absence of such impetus, the Italian "peace movement" is unlikely to have great impact. Up to the present time, nuclear weapons issues have played no significant part in election politics.

THE ITALIAN PEACE MOVEMENT

Until the fall of 1981, Italy had been relatively untouched by the antinuclear demonstrations common elsewhere in Western Europe. Then, within a short time, demonstrations took place in Rome, Milan, Venice, Perugia, and other smaller cities, including Comiso in Sicily — the site for 112 of the ground-launched cruise missiles called for in the December 1979 NATO decision. Following initial demonstrations in late October and November 1981 — in the aftermath of those in Bonn and Amsterdam — not much was heard about an Italian peace movement. Even though the Italian manifestations of a peace movement have been minor or, at least, low-key in comparison to those in the Federal Republic of Germany, the Netherlands, and Britain, it would be erroneous to conclude that there is no active peace movement in Italy. One unique feature of the Italian peace movement is that its activities for the most part have been confined to Sicily and have drawn neither national nor international attention in the media comparable to its counterparts in other West European countries. Later we will examine why the groups involved have been unable to draw broader attention to their cause.

The United Committee for Peace and Disarmament (CUDIP) represents the original Sicilian peace group. Headed by Giacamo Cagnes, a Communist party member and a former mayor of Comiso, the CUDIP is thought to be linked to the Italian Communist party. To prove its autonomy from PCI, however, CUDIP points to another prominent member, Angelo Capitumino, a Christian Democrat who is a member of the Regional Assembly and a vice-president of the Sicilian Christian Association of Italian Workers (Associazioni Christiane Lavatori Italiani, ACLI). CUDIP has sponsored mass marches in Comiso, the first on October 24, 1981, when about 10,000 young people protested the plan to install ground-launched cruise missiles which allegedly would make a nuclear target for the Soviet Union. The second occurred on Easter Sunday 1982 when about

50,000 demonstrated in opposition to the cruise missile base. On both occasions, the PCI, as well as the Italian Federation of Labor, lent its support.

During the summer of 1982, CUDIP sponsored an International Camp that brought together West German Greens, representatives from Great Britain's protest movement at Greenham Common, and other Europeans. In September, 1982, the International Camp staged a demonstration that failed to attract substantial local support. Without the approval of CUDIP, the International Camp became the second autonomous peace group in Comiso. From twenty to forty or fifty of this group stayed during the winter months to become a rival of CUDIP. To CUDIP, the presence of the International Peace Camp has posed a continual problem: on the one hand, most people correctly regard CUDIP as a PCI-supported group. As such it must behave "responsibly" or Cagnes, as its leader, may endanger his chances to win re-election to local office. On the other hand, unless CUDIP supports or sponsors direct, nonviolent actions in support of peace, it risks the loss of its credibility as a *bona fide* peace movement.

Between November 22, 1982, and December 20, 1982, CUDIP sponsored a Milan-Comiso march which was significant because it provided the opportunity for those involved to publicize their objectives. Nine Milan intellectuals, including a Roman Catholic priest, issued the original call, and then several labor unions, as well as the Baptist, Methodist, and Waldensian churches of Italy supported the march. Two Italian bishops also joined in this effort, one from the Catholic Bishops Conference and the other from *Pax Christi*. Their objectives included the encouragement of public discussion of issues associated with disarmament, underdevelopment, and hunger; a consideration of peace initiatives, designed to raise public consciousness leading to the "suspension of all and every decision to install new missiles in Europe during the Geneva talks." The appeal also requested termination of the construction of the Comiso base as a positive contribution to the peace effort and specifically as a gesture toward the progressive reduction of nuclear arms in the West and the East until they have been eliminated.[2] In a letter supporting the Milan-Comiso march, Methodist Pastor Aurelion Sbaffi, president of the Federazione delle Chiese Evangeliche in Italia (Federation of Italian Protestant Churches, Italy's National Council of Churches, FCEI) called the effort an important contribution to promoting a "culture of peace." Only two dozen people actually completed the march, but they were joined in Comiso by a crowd of 8,000, including PCI members, the PDUP, and high school students. In addition, American, Japanese, and British peace groups as well as representatives of the Greek Communist party took part.[3]

The celebration of International Women's Day, March 9–11, 1983, illustrated the women's theme in the Sicilian peace campaign. Their activities included discussions among the women participants from several countries, especially British women from Greenham Common and some Americans, a demonstration against sexual violence and rape, and a sit-in at Magliocco Airport.[4] From their statements, it is apparent that the women in the Italian peace movement are interested in the "peace" issue as it supposedly affects the position of women in society. They have described themselves as women opposed to "all violence, oppression, and aggression — violence of rape, violence of arms, violence of the 'masters and the mighty.'"[5] They also linked their own efforts to those of women in other countries interested in the peace movement, especially in the United Kingdom from whom they have taken their models in addition to several American women.[6]

A Statement by Women of Sicily for Nuclear Disarmament, Catania Committee (Group for the Self-Determination of Women, Catania) provides evidence of the linkage made between the "peace" and the women's issue:

> let us make it clear that although we oppose war, we also fight against a false peace that ignores starvation and exploitation. We cannot accept a peace that benumbs consciences and builds up empires over women's labor. Women know that, being women, they are subjected in every society and in every social class to a specific exploitation: sexual work, mother work, housework, unprotected work, underpaid work. We also fight against that hypocritical peace that created the myth of the "Angel of the Home" when there is a need for women to stay at home to raise husbands and children for the Country and boosts the myth of emancipation when women are needed in factories and offices as cheap labor, or when, as it is nowadays, unemployment and militarization open to women the shining doors of military careers.
>
> Our NO to WAR coincides with the struggle for our liberation. Never have we seen so clearly as now the connection between nuclear escalation and the Culture of the Muscleman, between the violence of war and the violence of rape. Such is in fact the historical memory that women have of all wars, always and everywhere. . . .[7]

The statement goes on to demand an end to acceptance of the idea of war and unilateral disarmament now. Women's answer to nuclear death, as paradoxical as it might seem, could be a conscious refusal to give life. The statement contains an appeal for the conversion of military budgets into investments for a better quality of life. If this message from women is not heeded, the statement warns, "WE STOP MOTHERHOOD!"[8] This is Lysistrata's drastic remedy for the problem of war, modified for the age of the pill and abortion on demand, yet still quite radical for Italy. In order to emphasize their "humanity," these pacifist women have sought to demonstrate autonomy from men and the right to decide their own destiny. They have also sought to separate themselves from the political parties, which in their view have not addressed women's concerns but rather have tried to use women for their own ends. Thus, these feminist goals might be viewed as part of an Italian "counterculture."

An appeal issued by a Rome group of women calling itself Women Against Armaments (*Donne Contra gli Armamenti*) struck similar motifs in a December 1982 statement. In a document entitled "Manifesto: Appeal to All Women" the military economy was described as destroying the civilian economy; so "long as there are armaments and armies, there will be wars." Women, if they do nothing in opposition, are called accomplices in the death of those in underdeveloped societies who die of starvation or from war; in advanced countries arms are said to divert needed resources from social programs. An "unofficial" war continues "hidden, unavowed and unavowable," in a cult of militarism. The statement ends with an appeal to create a new cult of life among the upcoming generation. Among the steps for which this group calls is "immediate unilateral disarmament, as an essential prerequisite to world disarmament;" the statement claimed that it is untrue that "an armed 'peace' and negotiations based on the balance of military power can guarantee peace." Finally, they issued an appeal for the enforcement of the Italian Constitution, especially Article II in which Italy repudiates war as a means of resolving international controversies.[9] Statements that attack the alleged "militarism" of the two blocs and question the utility of the "balance of power" as an approach to maintaining stability reflect the professed neutralism of the Italian peace movement. But that brand of neutralism would result in Soviet hegemony in Europe, for the dissolution of the Warsaw Pact and NATO would lead to the formal decoupling of the U.S. security guarantee to Western Europe, while the Soviet Union would remain militarily the most powerful European state. Moreover, in advocating unilateral disarmament and asking that Italy take the first step by refusing to accept the missiles—a step that others could then follow—the women strike a theme similar to that of CND in Great Britain. Confrontations with police occurred, as in Britain and West Germany, when the women blockaded the main gate at the Comiso base as part of their activities for International Women's Day.[10]

Other groups have had an interest in the peace movement in Comiso. These have included ARCI, the PCI-recreational association, ACLI, the Catholic workers organization, and the minor parties, including PDUP, DP, and PR. Religious groups conducted a march on Good Friday in Comiso under the sponsorship of local Catholics and Sicilian sections of Catholic Action, ACLI, the Interconfessional Center for Peace, Catholic Boy Scouts, *Pax Christi*, the International Fellowship of Reconciliation and Grassroots Christian Communities. The organizers described themselves as Christians from different associations who had come to live in Comiso "in fraternal communion with the local parish communities" because of their conviction that "with the deployment of nuclear missiles, the atomic rearmament of Europe is beginning and a new exploitation of southern Italy is taking place . . "[11] The statement implies that there are similarities between the exploited "South" in world politics whose plight is supposedly exacerbated by East-West tensions and the "South" of Italy — the *Mezzogiorno* which still lags behind the Milan-dominated "North" in economic development.

Several conclusions emerge from this overview of the Sicilian campaign. First, the scope and impact of the various peace groups' activities in Sicily have thus far been strictly limited. Second, none of the institutions, including the church, the major political parties, especially the PCI and the PSI, which might lend credibility to the movement, have chosen to do so. This factor, in turn, combined with unimpressive turnouts, helps to explain a third important aspect of the Italian antinuclear movement, namely, the inattention of the mass media at the national and international levels to events in Sicily. The lack of an "official" endorsement or sponsorship by any one of these institutions has made the Sicilian campaign largely a "nonevent." Fourth, an examination of the Sicilian peace movement illustrates the important role played by outside groups from a diversity of sources — German, British, and American — which apparently realize that their holy cause is a nonstarter in Italy. Fifth, the efforts of the various groups have not elicited widespread public support comparable to that generated elsewhere in Western Europe. While many in the local population may express reservations about the possible negative effects on their social values of the new base at Comiso, the peace groups have not been able to convert this concern into active opposition to the base itself. The general political climate in Sicily has not been conducive to the success of the peace movement. The June 1983 election, for example, did bring about a shift of votes from the Christian Democratic party to the PSI, but the decline was less than the Christian Democrats suffered on the national level. The PCI position did not change. Thus, the election was viewed as a personal triumph for the socialist mayor and seemed to demonstrate that local issues were of greater importance to the voters than the cruise missile issue.

Finally, the events in Sicily illustrate that in Italy, no less than in other West European countries, some of the small and more extreme peace organizations have been willing to resort to extra-legal methods in the name of peace. Italian peace groups, like their counterparts in other countries, define "direct action" as "civil disobedience," such as the women's movement blockade of the Comiso base and the "invasion" of the base by the International Camp. The Italians, who historically contributed more than any other Continental people to the West's legal philosophy and fundamental concepts of law, are not today the most conscientious upholders of constitutionalism and legal practice; although they may be willing to ignore or by-pass the law now and then, they deeply abhor political violence, more than ever since the decade of terror by the Red Brigades. Thus far, a willingness to embrace outright civil disobedience has been restricted to the smaller peace groups. The political parties and most of those who actively oppose cruise deployment have sought to disassociate themselves from the use of violence.

THE PEACE MOVEMENT AND THE CHURCH

At the outset, one cannot but be impressed by the contrast between the Protestant churches in Northern Europe or the American Catholic church and the Italian Catholic church when it comes to concern over social issues. Pope John Paul II, on his visit to Nigeria in February 1982, sounded themes more likely to be echoed in other segments of the Italian peace movement than among the Italian hierarchy. In his address, the Pope declared that

> Economic and monetary superiority, the possession of material goods and resources or technological capabilities do not justify political or social superiority, the cultural or moral superiority of a people or a nation over another. This means, therefore, that any position which seeks to justify such superiority on an ideological or philosophical basis is not a valid position and must be rejected.[12]

Recalling his encyclical "Laborem Exercens" of September 4, 1982, the Pope expressed the view that

> Integral human development deserves special attention because it plays a very important role in the great cause of international peace. Peace throughout the world is possible only if there is peace within each country. Domestic peace will never be achieved unless each nation devotes the attention required for the promotion of just development to benefit all its citizens.[13]

The Pope was cautious, however, that the church not be interpreted as being opposed to the deployment of missiles in Comiso. This was evident during the Pope's meeting with Secretary of State Shultz early in 1983 and in discussions between American and European bishops concerning the text of the Pastoral Letter then being prepared by the American bishops. Indeed, Vatican reticence on the nuclear issue led one Italian bishop, Luigi Pignatiello of Naples, to protest the lack of clarity or direction in Vatican reports of these deliberations. Bishop Pignatiello went so far as to cite by way of contrast "the courage and clarity with which John Paul II faces the problems of Poland." This led him to "think that the problems that threaten the Western world could also be handled with equal clarity and without excessive prudence."[14]

The lack of a strong church position on peace questions has not prevented individual bishops or priests from adopting stances in support of the nuclear pacifists. Groups associated with the Catholic church have been quite active in the peace movement. The Pastoral Letter of the American bishops as well as statements by the bishops of East Germany have elicited reactions from Italian bishops and clergy. Two bishops have openly opposed the stationing of cruise missiles in Sicily and announced their support for the American bishops' position in condemning nuclear armaments. The Bishops, Dante Bernini of Segni, the president of the Justice and Peace Commission of the Italian Bishops' Conference, and Bishop Luigi Bettazzi of Ivrea, president of *Pax Christi*, the international Catholic peace movement, issued a statement in solidarity with the American bishops.[15] *Pax Christi* held a National Congress in Naples on November 5–7, 1982, at which members adopted an official resolution reaffirming their moral and political condemnation of the missile deployment at Comiso and reiterating their commitment to work with other groups to "make this country a symbol of the refusal to base security on an equilibrium of nuclear terror and a sign of united intent to foster international relations based upon trust."[16] Neither the ecclesiastical hierarchy nor the leaders of the political parties are at all anxious to see priests becoming actively involved in a politically controversial question.

In addition to *Pax Christi*, the Christian Association of Italian Workers (Associazioni Christiane Lavatori Italiani, ACLI) is another Catholic organization active in the peace movement. Founded in 1944 and claiming a membership of about 500,000, ACLI separated from the Christian Democratic party in 1969. Although a part of the "Catholic world," it plays an autonomous role in "reforming Italian civil society." It sponsored a little-publicized march from Palermo to Geneva on May 21–29, 1983, and issued a statement setting forth its objectives. First, ACLI appealed to the two nuclear superpowers to bring to a successful conclusion the negotiations on the Euromissiles at Geneva and to "determine new general conditions for a disarmament process" which is the only real guarantee for peace and development. The statement recognized that the diverse groups supporting the march held different stands on the question of the installation of new missile systems in Europe; all, however, wished to avoid any escalation. The ACLI statement contended that peace cannot be based on the principle of nuclear deterrence, especially when it is used to justify the deployment of additional nuclear weapons, and appealed for "permanent" negotiations in all fields of international relations. The statement demonstrated opposition to limited nuclear wars and opposition to the concept that the possibility of a successful first strike might exist. The two superpowers were charged with a special responsibility in the search for a reduction of international arms tensions. Still, the Geneva negotiations alone were considered insufficient for the achievement of peace. Negotiations for disarmament should encompass both nuclear and conventional arms in a comprehensive framework.[17] The statement called for the achievement of a balance of forces at the lowest possible level. Both superpowers should commit themselves to a "zero growth" in armaments while negotiations should move toward an effective "zero option." It was proposed that the SALT II Treaty should be viewed as a useful starting point in the search for arms reductions.

In the final part of its statement, ACLI attempted to draw linkage between the issue of the Euromissiles and the North-South problem.

> We stand among those who have not lost hope and want to work all the time to open new life and hope paths for mankind. We stand among those who believe it still possible, and therefore necessary, to work to shift from a war economy to a peace economy at a world level, i.e., to eliminate factors causing imbalance between North and South, with its dramatic consequences and to establish a political order in which violations of civil and human rights, which we still denounce in many parts of the world, are no longer allowed.

> Disarmament and reconversion to a peace economy for a new development are for us the elements of a more general peace culture, a culture considering peace as the condition under which justice, solidarity, democracy are achieved for a complete development of men and peoples.[18]

Beyond the Catholic organizations, sympathy toward the antinuclear movement has been expressed by some of the small Protestant denominations. For example, from December 26, 1981, to January 2, 1982, the Methodist retreat and reflection center, ECUMENE, held an "International Consultation on Peace and Nuclear Disarmament" attended by about 100 religious and lay people. Among those present were Laurens Hogebrink, representing the Dutch IKV, and several Americans, including a Methodist pastor. Among the Italians were Sergio Aguilante, the president of the Italian Methodist churches and a leader in interdenominational and secular peace initiatives since the 1950s, as well as Arrigo Bonnes, a Waldensian pastor and coordinator of a newly-created committee for peace and arms race of the Waldensian church and the Methodist church in Italy. In their concluding document, the participants called for collective action to prevent the building of the Comiso base and denounced the idea that the outcome of arms control negotiations in Geneva should be allowed to justify the emplacement of cruise missiles in Comiso. Specifically, the meeting recommended that Italy should withdraw "its consent to the NATO project for the European missiles and it underlines that contrary to what the NATO and U.S. government maintains, there is no military necessity to reinforce the nuclear arsenal nor to modernize it technologically."[19]

The Assembly went on to draw a close connection between peace and social justice. It called for the definition of a new role for Europe which would enable it to become politically and economically more autonomous of the two superpowers. Such a Europe, it was contended, should develop relationships with the Third World, particularly that of the Mediterranean, to eliminate "the inequality between North-South and to build a new international order based on justice, equality of the human person and the self-determination of the peoples."[20]

THE PEACE MOVEMENT AND THE ITALIAN POLITICAL PARTIES, POLITICS AND POLICY

The Christian Democratic Party

The strong support of the Christian Democratic party helped to build and to sustain consensus in Italy for the December 1979 NATO decision to modernize theater nuclear forces. From the outset, the DC has based its support on the need to redress the strategic imbalance in Europe created by the presence of Soviet SS-20 missiles aimed at Western Europe. Moreover, the DC has supported the negotiating positions of the United States at the Geneva negotiations. Especially vocal has been the DC Foreign Minister in the last Christian Democratic-led government, Emilio Colombo. Speaking at a Christian Democratic Party Congress on peace and security held in October 1981, Colombo commented on the imbalance of forces in favor of the Warsaw Pact. The Italian decision to install Euromissiles on its soil was defended as necessary to establish a new balance that might furnish the basis for negotiations leading to arms reductions. Commenting on the peace marches which had taken place shortly before in Comiso, Perugia, and Assisi, Colombo warned against confusing "an authentic culture of peace" with the "rhetoric of peace." In particular he suggested that young people who wished to demonstrate against missiles not yet installed should also take account of those already in place aimed against Western Europe.[21]

On other occasions Colombo spoke in support of President Reagan's zero-option proposal, finding unacceptable the terms of the Soviet counter-proposal to that offer, describing it as

> equivalent to a zero option for NATO and a limited reduction of the missiles already deployed in the USSR. This is an unacceptable position. In fact, it would mean the USSR's maintenance of the monopoly in missile weaponry. It is therefore a position of insecurity for Europe.[22]

At the same time, Colombo acknowledged the key role played by the Federal Republic of Germany in determining the fate of the missiles. In this interview before the March 6, 1983, German elections, Colombo observed:

> Of course, Germany's position is central to the missile issue, which involves the entire question of the defense of West Europe. A neutral Germany, or let

us say a Germany with a neutralist mentality while still remaining within the alliance, a Germany whose bonds with Europe were to be loosened would imply a substantial weakening of Europe and the West and would be a real victory for the Soviet Union, which would alter the world balance of forces to its own advantage. This would certainly not strengthen the balances that guarantee peace.[23]

In March 1983, Colombo reasserted the Italian government's commitment to the 1979 NATO decision and recognized the efforts of the Soviet Union to divide the West over the essential aspects of its defense.[24]

Colombo was firmly convinced that the Soviet Union retained a superiority in conventional and medium-range missiles which might tempt it to seek to expand its sphere of influence, and that it was, consequently the moral and political duty for Europe and the West to recreate a balance in Europe without prejudice to the security of Asia.

Speaking after the May 1983 summit of the leaders of the Western industrialized nations held in Williamsburg, the then-Christian Democratic Prime Minister Fanfani stressed that the joint statement on Euromissiles had been intended to ease rather than to complicate the Geneva negotiations. He also observed that it was in everyone's interest to reduce armaments so that more resources could be made available for the task of economic development and recovery. Fanfani noted that Japanese Premier Yasuhiro Nakasone had joined the United States and its West European allies in signing a communiqué calling for the dismantling of the Soviet SS-20 missiles because of Japanese concern about the deployment of SS-20 missiles targeted against Japan. Moreover, Fanfani defended the exclusion of the British and French missiles in the missile count. The Christian Democratic leader realized that the Andropov proposal to limit the number of Soviet missiles to that of the two West European nuclear submarine fleets (with no U.S. deployments) was an effort to divide NATO at its most sensitive point, since the British and French nuclear forces are purely national strategic deterrents; everyone knows that they do not protect West Germany or any other NATO allies.

Because of the endemic political instability which has characterized the Italian political scene, however, the DC approach to foreign policy issues has been more reactive than innovative. Moreover, for the Christian Democratic party, the contemplation of foreign policy or national defense issues is often painful because it can exacerbate tensions within the party. Most DC members probably support the statements of Colombo and Fanfani; some might even favor a broader Italian role within the Alliance. Generally, too, the DC has expressed support for what it has viewed as the more assertive foreign policy of President Reagan. Still, some reservations have been heard that this new vigor might be carried too far. In short, at one and the same time, Christian Democrats express contradictory fears:

that U.S. foreign policy might be too strong and that it might also be too weak. The DC wishes simultaneously to preserve the perceived benefits of detente and to prevent a further deterioration of East-West relations. These apparent contradictions may be explained in large measure by the endemic factionalism that exists in the broad-based Christian Democratic party. In addition, DC positions on foreign policy issues such as cruise missiles are affected by stances adopted by the other political parties, especially the Italian Communist party. In fact, it has been PCI criticism of Italian passivity within NATO and its alleged subordination to American policy that has led some DC members to advocate a stronger Italian policy within the Alliance. It has also increased Italian sensitivity to the need to be treated as a "first-class" member of the Alliance. For its part, the DC has tried to embarrass the PCI on the issue of Poland. In either case, the two parties seek to utilize these foreign policy issues to benefit their domestic positions.

While the DC has been steadfast in its support of the December 1979 NATO decision, there is some concern that the perennial factional strife within the party might lead it to compromise its position in order to retain its dominant position in governing coalitions, even when it does not fill the office of prime minister. The hopes that the DC might experience a reformist "renewal" with the accession of Ciriaco De Mita to DC party leadership suffered a setback with the party's defeat at the polls on June 26–27, 1983. Perhaps these concerns are overdrawn. Certainly, previous Christian Democratic-led governments maintained a strong position in support of NATO. Yet there remains an underlying concern that the DC leadership might "waffle" and make compromises on foreign policy issues in order to protect its own political position. That segment of the party which won out at the DC party congress in 1982 represents the "old" DC, traditionally less interested in foreign affairs and perhaps more willing to "deal" with the PCI if it were necessary in order to retain political power. Finally, the left wing of the DC empathizes with the moral-ethical concerns of the peace movement. It is difficult, however, to think of *Angst* in the Italian cultural context. In the meanwhile, the relative strength and shifting policies of the various political parties in the coalition government of Socialist Premier Craxi will be a key factor in determining the future positions of the DC toward defense and foreign policy issues.

The Italian Communist Party (PCI)

As a political party that enjoys the support of 30% of the electorate and with about 1.1 million members, the PCI has the potential to play a major role in the Italian antinuclear campaign. Except for its support of the October 24, 1981 demonstration and its sponsorship together with other leftist groups of a mass demonstration on June 5, 1982, the PCI has limited itself largely to a "rhetorical" position in opposition to the Comiso missiles and in support of the peace movement. Indeed, following the latter demonstration from which both the Italian Socialist party and the Radical party disassociated themselves, the PCI itself expressed some embarrassment at the anti-American tone of the march, which they blamed on the other participants.[25] Whether or not the PCI will revise its approach to the movement in the future will be a determining factor in the fortunes of that movement.

It is ironic that in a West European country with such a strong Communist party—similar to the French situation—forces of pacifism appear so weak. Throughout most of the 1970s, when the PCI pursued its strategy of gaining political power via an "historic compromise" with the Christian Democratic party (DC) in the hope that it might enter the government one day as a partner, it could be argued that the PCI had an interest in exercising restraint on the "peace" issue and sought to distance itself from the Soviet Union. However, now that the PCI has abandoned this course in favor of the "democratic alternative," it might have been anticipated that the PCI would shed its restraint in favor of a more confrontationist policy to try to "corner" the government on the missile issue and to monopolize the peace theme. Yet, this has not occurred. The reasons lie in the domestic strategy of the party. Its late leader, Enrico Berlinguer, led the PCI on a long-term course of action to convince the Italian electorate of the "respectability" of the PCI as a viable "alternative" to the ruling Christian Democratic party.

The major goal of the PCI remains to achieve political power whatever the strategy it adopts to accomplish this objective, "historic compromise" or the current ill-defined "democratic alternative." It is in the interest of the PCI to maintain its perceived autonomy from the Soviet Union. Thus, in recent years the PCI has appeared to be one of the most outspoken critics at times of Soviet actions, notably in Afghanistan and Poland. In attempting to determine whether the PCI might alter its attitude toward and support for Italian pacifism, one must bear in mind the likely impact of such a change on the credibility of its image as an autonomous political party which maintains its distance from the Soviet Union. Thus far Berlinguer's successor, Alessandro Natta, who was elected in June 1984, has shown no tendency to change the party's largely "rhetorical" support for the antinuclear movement. Still, there does exist within the party a small contingent opposed to the anti-Moscow orientation of the PCI. Moreover, if there were to be a groundswell of public opinion in favor of the peace movement, the PCI might decide to become more militant in support of it. The rhetoric of the PCI is in opposition to the missiles; in addition, the party has supported the Soviet proposal at Geneva to include the British and French nuclear forces as part of the Western deterrent. Thus far, however, the position of the PCI toward the peace question has been conditioned largely by its consideration of how that issue impinges upon its broader goal of achieving political power. The strategy of the "democratic alternative," if interpreted to mean that the PCI now intends to gain political power in opposition to the DC rather than in a coalition with it, may thus place a premium on the party's pursuit of policies which lend credibility to its claim to be a responsible political party. This, in turn, is likely to dictate a cautious course in regard to the Italian peace movement.

An examination of the statements of the PCI leaders provides evidence of the strategic-political perspective within which they view the peace movement. For example, during the summer and fall of 1981, PCI leaders continually stressed what they viewed as the increasingly deteriorating international scene, from which they concluded that peace constituted a central problem on Italy's agenda. Berlinguer disagreed with PSI Secretary Craxi's view that "peace is not endangered." In fact, the PCI secretary welcomed the emergence in Italy of a

> broad and composite movement defending peace; that this crucial question has found a prompt response from the party; that many other forces — in the parties and outside them — are starting to act together with us or on their own account; Catholic forces and organizations, which refer to the pope's appeals and exhortations, and socialist and secular forces, pacifist, ecologist, and other groups.[26]

Then PCI Secretariat member Alessandro Natta, at a Florence rally, spoke of the dangers of a nuclear holocaust. Natta alleged that

> Whatever the assessment of the balance of forces . . . the two major powers and the two blocs have a potential which, once unleashed could bring about nuclear destruction not once but seven times. . . . The level of war potential is such as to render scandalous yet another race to perfect new devices.

> This makes it even more outdated and unrealistic to think that peace can be guaranteed by the balance of terror, by the deterrence of mutual nuclear destruction, or by the possibility of "limiting" the nuclear clash to the European theater. This is the terrifying new idea behind the cruise and SS-20 missiles and the neutron bomb.[27]

According to Natta, the only way to provide security is to break the spiral of distrust and suspicion and to reduce armaments.

In a September 20, 1981 speech, Berlinguer described the August decision of the Italian government to proceed with the construction of the Comiso missile base as "an initiative which could lead to a future risk of nuclear reprisals against the island and the entire country."[28] Moreover, he contended that the threat of a nuclear conflict could be averted and "the people's masses can play a fundamental role in the indispensable and urgent action to safeguard peace."[29]

Reflecting the strategic-political perspective from which the PCI viewed the missile issue, Berlinguer and other PCI members have described the U.S.-Soviet rivalry as the primary cause of international tensions and have called for action by all those forces which could contribute to "moderation, detente, a brake on the arms race, negotiated solutions and building a new international economic order."[30] In particular, he mentioned the nonaligned movement, the Catholic and other churches, and the workers' movement as such forces. In praising the emergence of "a powerful movement of extraordinary breadth and vigor in favor of peace," he described it as a movement that transcends the confines of left-wing parties only.[31] Such statements, it is suggested, reflect PCI sensitivity to the perception that it alone is in favor of the protest movement. It prefers to legitimize its own interest and support by cloaking its efforts in a broader framework. Similarly, statements about the "autonomous" nature of the movement illustrate the concern of the PCI that it not be cast in the position of supporting the Soviet Union by its "peace" posture. Thus, in a report submitted to the Central Committee of the PCI before its sixteenth congress, Berlinguer called on the pacifist campaign to develop its autonomous character with respect to states, military blocs, and parties. Such autonomy implied, according to Berlinguer, that the separate components should retain their freedom to pursue their own initiatives within the struggle for peace. This would enhance the possibility that the peoples' desire for peace would be widely felt and influence governmental policy toward the goals of disarmament, detente, and peace. Thus, the PCI prefers to characterize the movement as a truly autonomous one which refuses to act as a tool of either bloc, even though it actually aids the Soviet side, which suppresses all peace demonstrations except those organized by the government against NATO arms.[32]

In a *L'Unità* interview, the questioner noted that on the issue of peace and international relations, the Communist party of the Soviet Union had been very critical of PCI stances for allegedly having underestimated the dangers of war and for seeking to balance responsibilities between the two blocs (i.e., absolving imperialism) and, most important, for abandoning a class view of the international struggle. Berlinguer, attempting to deny these charges, replied:

> We are so concerned about the international situation and the dangers of a nuclear conflict that we identify the aim of peace as the most decisive factor. . . .

> The class struggle remains an inescapable factor of the domestic and international situation, but in the nuclear era it, too, takes on partly different characteristics. It should be extended to include interests and needs (of liberation from underdevelopment, hunger and every form of oppression of nations) giving rise to conflicts and movements which cannot be confined to the logic of

military blocs. So today the relationship between the struggle for peace and the class struggle appears in terms different from those characteristic of the time prior to the nuclear era, which has also become the era of the explosion of the imbalance between the north and the south of the world. [33]

Berlinguer went on to chastise the CPSU, the party of peaceful coexistence, for failure to recognize this new situation. In these new circumstances, Berlinguer said, it is necessary to consider the security requirements of all states, whatever their size or class characteristics or domestic system. This requires that each state's foreign policies be judged separately to determine whether they promote peace or not. Distinguishing among the foreign policies of Reagan, Carter, Kennedy, and Johnson, Berlinguer declared that "the necessary presupposition for peaceful coexistence is the possibility that even states with a capitalist system can pursue or be induced to pursue a policy of peace." [34] To begin with a bias against the social system, Berlinguer contended, would be to deny "on principle that any real contribution to peace can come from the states of the capitalist area, and you end up by giving a sense of powerlessness and futility to peace movements, since everything is left to the balance of power between two systems, or rather between the two blocs." [35]

The PCI has endeavored to convince the public that the peace movement does not have an anti-American, anti-NATO bias. Evidence from polls conducted between 1976 and 1983 indicate, however, that the PCI has not convinced the public of "even-handedness" in its approach to foreign policy questions. In 1976, 35% of those polled found PCI views similar to those of the Soviet Union while 40% found them different and 25% didn't know. In 1979, before the Soviet invasion of Afghanistan, the comparable figures were 29%, 56%, and 14%. In March 1982, following events in Poland and Afghanistan, the figures were 29%, 57% and 14%. In the latest poll, conducted after the 1983 PCI Congress, the figures were 24%, 53% and 25%. In short, the impression often conveyed in the international press that the Italian public has been convinced of a PCI increasingly independent of Moscow is not borne out in the opinion polls.

In his address to the sixteenth party congress in March 1983, Gian Carlo Pajetta noted the party's support for "gradual disarmament, a balance and in the meantime an immediate 'moratorium.'" He maintained that even though the PCI had voted against the Italian government's decision to deploy missiles in Comiso, its position should not be interpreted as "unidirectional." He also sought to relate the problems of peace to the strategy of the "democratic alternative," calling for an active party role in issues of Italian foreign policy in order to examine all the needs and possibilities "on the road to peace, disarmament, and the elimination of blocs." [36] This reference to "the elimination of blocs" is of particular interest because it illustrates one of the continuing contradictions in PCI policies toward NATO.

On the one hand, it maintains support for Italian membership in NATO; on the other hand, it also supports the eventual dissolution of the blocs.[37] Those who understand Marxist dialectics, of course, are never troubled by such apparent contradictions.

At the Congress an effort was made to emphasize Italy's prominent international role, especially in the Mediterranean, where an appeal was issued for support of a concept of peace and security rejecting Italy's "reduction to a U.S. military offshoot" and the definition of "the Mediterranean as a sea of peace and a meeting point of civilizations." During the June 1983 election campaign, Berlinguer discussed the missile issue in the context of what he called the renewed cold war climate, placing the blame for the deterioration in U.S.-Soviet relations primarily on the doorstep of President Reagan. Berlinguer called for several steps to be taken: first, there should be a halt to the arms race. This required a worldwide "freezing" of nuclear weapons. Within this framework, negotiations should be conducted for as long as needed to reach a positive conclusion. Berlinguer cited three specific PCI proposals: (1) the rejection of the interpretation of the 1979 NATO decision for the automatic deployment of the missiles in the event of a failure of the Geneva negotiations along with a demand that the Italian parliament decide on the deployment and that work at Comiso be suspended in the meanwhile; (2) that at Geneva the negotiations should lead to a decision not to deploy either cruise or Pershing II missiles in Western Europe while the Soviet Union should be called upon for an adequate reduction and destruction of the USSR's SS-20 missiles; and (3) that a Geneva accord be implemented within a global framework for a comprehensive freeze on all nuclear weapons.[38]

Asked during an interview granted to *La Republica* on May 20, 1983, what the PCI, if elected, would do about the country's two major problems (i.e., the deployment of cruise missiles at Comiso and the reduction of the public deficit in 1984), Berlinguer stated:

> Our position is entirely analogous to that of several European socialist parties. We want the Geneva negotiations between the United States and the USSR to continue if an acceptable conclusion is not reached by the end of the year. Of course, in the event of the nondeployment of the U.S. missiles, we would request from the USSR a reduction and dismantling in line with the current level of Western missiles, including those of France and Britain.[39]

Finally, on Friday, June 24, the last day before all political campaigning had to stop, *L'Unità* carried a full-page advertisement by the PCI concerning the missiles. Written in red were the words: "There is no security in the shadow of the missiles." "For a future of peace, a vote for peace." Linking themselves with others interested in peace, the PCI said:

> The peace movement, in which communists, socialists, social-democrats, and Christians of all Europe and Americans want to put a halt to the missiles. The

Communist Party proposes: 1) the suspension of construction of the base at Comiso; 2) to extend the negotiations as long as necessary to reach an accord; 3) to reach in Geneva a treaty that stabilizes the reduction and destruction of Soviet missiles together with the renunciation of the Western Euromissiles; 4) to conclude the agreement as part of a global freeze of all the nuclear weapons in the world.[40]

In sum, the PCI's pursuit of political power—whether via the strategy of the "historic compromise" or the "democratic alternative" has constrained it to pursue a cautious course in regard to the Italian peace movement. Its credibility as a potential alternative party rests on its ability to convince the Italian electorate of its responsibility and autonomy in regard to foreign policy issues such as the missile question. Nevertheless, PCI statements indicate that the defense of peace remains a major party objective. The responsibility of the masses and the need for cooperation among progressive forces in promotion of the cause of peace is always stressed in the party's propaganda. The party also stresses the heavy responsibility borne by both the United States and the Soviet Union for the preservation of peace and the avoidance of nuclear war. Within this international context, it is the PCI's view that the peace movement constitutes an "autonomous" force that seeks to influence the policies of both blocs to promote disarmament and peace. It is important to the PCI, for domestic reasons, that its views and actions regarding the peace movement not be interpreted as having an anti-American, anti-NATO bias. Yet, as the statements of the party's leaders have indicated, there remains serious reason to suspect the party's loyalty either to NATO in general or to the Italian decision to deploy missiles at Comiso.

The Italian Socialist Party (PSI)

To understand contemporary attitudes within the PSI toward the Italian peace movement, an appreciation of the historical background against which they have been formed is essential. In this regard, events that occurred in Italy and Europe during and just before World War II shape current PSI attitudes. For example, in the mid-1930s, the Socialists were affected by the policies adopted by the Communist parties of Western Europe toward the Soviet Union. Italian Socialists saw international events within the context of an anti-fascist struggle and pursued a policy of "unity of action" with the Italian Communist party against fascism. A tradition of cooperation with the PCI was established, which has firm roots today within a segment of the party. Then, in 1947 and 1948 socialist ranks were split between the Nenni and Saragat factions over the question of what relationship the Socialists should have with the Soviet Union and the PCI. Even at the time of the debate over ratification of the North Atlantic

Treaty, there were distinct humanitarian and pacifist instincts within the PSI which could be traced back to Socialist opposition to Italy's entry into World War I.

By the mid-1950s, changes had occurred within the PSI in regard to perspectives on international affairs with the death of Stalin and revelations about his brutal role at the 20th Party Congress of the CPSU. These caused difficulties for Western socialist parties like the PSI which found it hard to adjust overnight to an anti-Stalin view.

In the PSI, Pietro Nenni had been the architect of the "unity of action" policy of the party under fascism. By 1955, it was acknowledged that the time had arrived to recognize that continued cooperation with the Communists was not an appropriate PSI strategy if the party was to have any prospect of governing. This lesson had been brought home to many in the party by the defeat of the "people's front," the joint electoral alliance between the Socialists and the Communists in the 1948 election. In short, the PSI recognized that Christian Democrats had to be treated as a permanent force. Events in France, as well, contributed to this changed perspective. Upon de Gaulle's return to politics and the formation of the Union for the New Republic (UNR), the Italian Socialists saw that it was possible for a Socialist party to attract voters who had traditionally voted Catholic. If de Gaulle was able to break religious party ranks, the PSI reasoned, it could also try to do so. Thus, at its 1955 Turin Congress, the PSI approved the "opening to the left." Another important ingredient to changed Socialist views was provided by Ricardo Lombardi, a member of the PSI left wing, who now acknowledged the "stabilization" of the East-West division in world politics. This permitted a recognition of NATO's contribution to peace and was viewed as an important proof of the increasingly Western orientation of the PSI. Socialists in Italy point out that, in contrast, the PCI did not recognize the contribution of NATO to stability until more than twenty years later. Yet another important milestone in the Westernization of the PSI occurred at its 1957 Venice Congress when the party split over the issue of cooperation with the PCI. Deciding not to cooperate with the PCI, the PSI shifted to the right. While the PSI supported the Atlantic Alliance, there remained some reservations because of the strong tradition of pacifism and neutralism in the party.

Within the PSI, there is constant tension between those who wish the party to emphasize a more Marxist image and those who believe that the party should have a noncommunist, social-democratic, pro-Western image. The party's present leader and Italy's Premier Bettino Craxi (only the second non-Christian Democratic premier, following his predecessor Spadolini) is supposed to represent aloofness from the Communists and the Soviet Union. As part of this approach, the PSI accepted the concept of NATO theater nuclear modernization. Some of Craxi's critics, both within and outside the party, attributed this move to Craxi's desire to gain respectability in the eyes of the American government — allegedly a prerequisite to his assumption of power as premier. Thus, Craxi allegedly was willing to abandon the traditional socialist commitment to pacifism in pursuit of political power.

Without Craxi and his supporters at the top of the party, there is concern that the party might swing "left." Craxi views Italy as a constructive member of NATO. It is often said that his position is a pragmatic one. What political price he would be willing to pay in support of his views is difficult to say. Certainly his views have not permeated the whole party. Craxi occupies a difficult position, therefore, in seeking both to support NATO and to placate strong pacifist and neutralist sentiment within the ranks of his own party.

In the peace marches, rallies, and debates called by the PSI on November 15, 1981 in cities throughout Italy, over 200,000 persons participated. Socialist leaders who spoke at these events supported President Reagan's "zero option." Both sides must return to zero, it was asserted, so that discussions could then be undertaken on further reductions of both nuclear and conventional weapons. Speaking at one of the rallies, Craxi mentioned the need to have full participation in the command and control of the new missiles and asserted the need for Italy and her European allies to participate in negotiations with the Soviet Union. "We cannot leave the keys to our security and to our very future in America's power. Everything must be the fruit of consultations."

Commenting on the earlier October demonstrations, in an interview conducted by *Lotta Continua*, Craxi was willing to grant the sincerity of the participants while not finding acceptable their aims. He charged that "there is a current which is manipulating these movements or is seeking to do so." Moreover, he stated that he did not share the view that a third world war was imminent. This does not mean, however, that one should be indifferent to the prospect of an uncontrolled arms race. In his view, too many resources were being wasted which could and should be used for more moral purposes.[41] Moreover, Craxi expressed the view that the balance of power is the principal guarantee of peace. Only a situation of balance could allow gradual disarmament to begin. "It is from a position of military supremacy that the threats to peace can derive."[42]

Following a 1983 visit to the United States, the then-Socialist Defense Minister Lelio Lagoria granted an interview in which he set forth what may be viewed as a socialist position regarding Italy's NATO role and its position as a Mediterranean power. Lagoria stated:

Italy has always argued that NATO is a defensive and geographically circumscribed alliance and that it therefore cannot be committed outside the area covered by the 1949 treaty. . . . But our countries, individually, have interests at stake even outside NATO territory. It is enough to consider the Middle East and the Horn of Africa. This is why I told Parliament when I presented the 1983 defense budget that the Atlantic pact does not completely guarantee the defense of Italian interests. New answers must be found to the new problems emerging from the new international situation . . . . The aim . . . is clear: a policy of stability and peace that will benefit international security.[43]

Despite the fact that Craxi and Defense Minister Lagorio have supported Italy's decision to accept the missiles at Comiso, such support does not extend throughout the ranks of the Italian Socialist party. In a debate on foreign policy held by the party's directorate in September 1981, Ricardo Lombardi expressed concern that Europe might become the battleground between the two superpowers in the event of a war. Contending that it was an impossibility to achieve a military balance between the two blocs, Lombardi called upon the PSI to raise its sights and propose the dissolution of the blocs again in new terms. Collective action by the European Socialists, promoted by Italian Socialists, should seek to free Europe from its position as a possible battlefield between the superpowers.[44] Events then unfolding in Poland gave Lombardi hope that the peoples of Eastern Europe could be won over to his approach. At the same time, the United States would have to be assured that this was a genuine process aimed at making Europe an area of "no danger to America or the USSR."[45] To begin this approach, Europe would have to disassociate itself from U.S. or Soviet world policy, to abandon requests for equal partnership in NATO, and to review the extent of its NATO commitments. Another PSI member urged the Directorate to conduct an initiative to have the government suspend the decision to install missiles in Italy, "reserving the right to implement the decision" only if the negotiations at Geneva were to fail. The Italian Socialists will share defense burdens only if NATO retains its defensive goals; this is very important to the party not only as a result of the nostalgia for pacifism but also because of the necessity to protect itself from charges by the Italian Communist party that it is militaristic.

In this context, the PSI reflected some ambivalence about the 1979 NATO decision to deploy Euromissiles. Although it was the Socialist Defense Minister Lagorio who took the decision, many PSI parliamentarians voted in support of the NATO modernization program more through party discipline than as a result of a strong belief in the need for the missiles. The predominant view within the party today is that, in the absence of an accord with the Soviet Union on INF, the PSI will continue to support deployment. Indeed, this fact distinguishes the Italian socialists from their counterparts in the other NATO countries where opposition in Socialist ranks has been much stronger. This support, however, is subject to change should significant opposition to the missiles develop elsewhere in Europe — especially in West Germany. Indeed, among many Italian Socialists there is a strong tendency to doubt the importance of a strategic-military need for the deployment of cruise missiles in Comiso. The major strategic reason for the missiles, according to this view, lay in Chancellor Schmidt's belief, stated in 1977 that the nuclear balance between East and West had been adversely affected by the deployment by the Soviet Union of the SS-20's. NATO had to redress the imbalance caused by their presence. In short, if West German security perceptions were to change, there might not be a need for the missiles any longer and Italy could then reverse its decision to accept them.

Other Political Parties and Groups in the Peace Movement

The small Radical Party (PR) was, initially, one of the original sponsors of the Italian peace movement. In addition, it had once been an advocate of women's rights before becoming a one issue party. Following a visit to Africa by its leader, Marco Pannella, the party had focused its attention exclusively on the problem of world hunger. Under the charismatic leadership of Pannella, it is possible that the PR could rediscover the peace issue. In particular, Pannella might draw lessons from the women's movement, which has emphasized the impact of the arms race on women in society and its relationship to the plight of the developing world which suffers from hunger and poverty, in order to draw attention to his own concern for the problem of world hunger.

Among the other organizations active in the peace movement is the Union of Scientists for Disarmament (*Unione degli Scieziati Per Il Disarmo*, USPID) which was founded in Rome in March 1983. Its goal is to promote and coordinate activities of scientists interested in contributing to the reduction of danger of war by increasing awareness of the risk of nuclear war and by developing analyses and furnishing information to the various peace organizations, and to parliament, about nuclear arms, the nuclear balance, and the evolution of strategic doctrines. Its principal objective is stated to be nuclear disarmament, although the organization recognizes that this problem cannot be isolated from the need to establish controls over other forms of armaments. USPID intends to cooperate with like-minded scientific organizations abroad in the pursuit of its goals.

Finally, in an effort to provide an umbrella organization to help coordinate the many local peace organizations found throughout Italy there is the Italian Recreational and Cultural Association (Associazione Ricreative Culturale Italiana — ARCI). According to its official statements, ARCI "fights for international detente, for peace and cooperation among all countries and all barriers, for the limitation of both nuclear and conventional weapons and the reduction of armies and for disarmament. ARCI fights at the side of the oppressed and of the peoples struggling for their liberation."

In its brochure, it describes itself as the main cultural association of the Left in Italy, "counting over 1,300,000 members and 14,000 clubs." Its membership consists of ecologists, cultural and theater operators, pacifists, sportsmen and sportswomen. ARCI supported the October 24, 1981 demonstration in Rome together with the PCI and other groups. It regarded this demonstration as particularly significant in the Italian peace movement because it represented the first occasion on which several of the groups cooperated in a joint venture. By bringing together several themes, ARCI has sought to encourage an appreciation of the linkages alleged to exist between the East-West conflict and the North-South conflict in world affairs. Among its recent activities have been the organization of a street-corner referendum throughout Italy asking whether or not the electorate favors the installation of nuclear missiles at Comiso and if public support exists for a national referendum on the question. In addition, it organized a one-week "University for Peace" in July in Umbria, attended by about 200 people, to discuss the various themes associated with the peace groups.[46]

THE WEAKNESS OF THE ITALIAN
PEACE MOVEMENT

The Italian peace movement has been unable to rally significant popular support. The overwhelming majority of the Italian people apparently believe that peace is made by the policies of governments, not by placards, slogans, and demonstrations. The inability of those groups involved in the peace campaign to mobilize antinuclear feelings among the public has meant that the political base of the Italian peace movement remains narrow. This small base, in turn, has constrained its ability to widen its support among the general public. In general, the antinuclear issue does not excite a public more concerned with the bread-and-butter issues of inflation and employment. Despite the fact that opinion polls appear to indicate widespread concern about the missiles at Comiso,[47] the public remains passive in its opposition. This passivity has been explained, in part, by the historical tendency of Italians to view foreign policy and defense issues as matters to be determined by their political leaders and not subject to public influence or scrutiny. To be sure, PCI officials have sought to change this perception among the public; indeed, some have asserted that the decision to deploy missiles in Europe will be the "last NATO decision." A changed political climate in Europe, the PCI contends, resulting from the peace movement efforts, will not permit future political leaders to make similar decisions without consultation with their populations. Thus, the PCI, while not itself playing an overly active role in the Italian pacifist campaign beyond lending rhetorical support, applauds the perceived changes in the political culture of Italy resulting from the movement's efforts. Thus far, however, PCI concern that too close an identification of the movement with the party might endanger its goal of proving its political legitimacy to the electorate has denied the Italian peace movement one of its natural leaders.

A second reason for the lack-luster performance of the Italian peace movement lies in the fact that, in contrast to the Federal Republic of Germany, where the ecologists played a major role in mobilizing antinuclear sentiment, in Italy the ecologists have been weak. There has never been in Italy a comparable antinuclear power movement to that found in the FRG. Thus, the antinuclear weapons movement did not have the base on which to develop as it did in the FRG. This lack of a viable Green movement in Italy has been explained by the lack of a tradition of grass-roots movements seeking to influence political decisions.

A third factor accounting for the weakness of the Italian peace movement is found in the unwillingness of the Roman Catholic church to assume a leading role on the peace issue. The relative silence of the church leadership has not meant that all Catholics have been immune to the appeals for peace and disarmament. But church influence in the peace movement has been limited primarily to the appeals and activities of a few individual bishops and priests at the parish level. The church in Italy simply has not played a role comparable to that of the Catholic bishops in the United States or of Protestant and, to a lesser extent, Catholic churches in other West European countries, where they have furnished the militant cadres of the antinuclear crusade with politically significant numbers.

Fourth, the failure of the Italian Socialist party to become a sponsor of the peace movement in Italy has also accounted for the weakness of the movement. Its evolution into a more moderate, Western party as well as the desire of its leader, Bettino Craxi, to prove his worthiness for government leadership, contributed to the cautiousness of the party toward the peace movement. Nevertheless there remain neutralist and pacifist elements within the party who are sympathetic to appeals for disarmament.

In sum, those groups which have constituted the bulk of the strength of the peace movement in the Federal Republic, the Netherlands, or Great Britain — whether they be ecologists, Socialists, Communists, or the churches — have not been willing to commit their fortunes, much less "go to the stake," for the antinuclear cause in Italy. When it came to the actual deployment of the missiles, the Italian government experienced less physical opposition and obstruction from antinuclear protesters than did the governments in Bonn and London. The installation was delayed for three months because of technical problems. During that time, Craxi — perhaps as a tactic for defusing the opposition — aroused Washington's ire by hinting at the advisability of a moratorium. Nevertheless, when the technical difficulties were overcome, the government proceeded with the installation.

In early April 1984, Defense Minister Giovanni Spadolini announced that the first 16 of the 112 cruise missiles allotted to Italy were in place at Comiso, Sicily. The next day, Craxi's government won a parliamentary vote of 317 to 25 in support of the missile deployment. The Communists abstained, after insisting that they wanted the question of the missile installation to be submitted to a national referendum. The Council of Ministers subsequently refused to permit a referendum on the issue.[48]

THE FUTURE PROSPECTS OF THE ITALIAN PEACE MOVEMENT

To many observers the fact that the Italian peace movement has not caught fire as it has in other North European countries has been somewhat surprising since Italy, as a potential recipient of nuclear missiles, presented to antinuclear opponents a natural target. Yet, as we have seen, they have failed to win the support of any of the major institutions which might enable them to transform Comiso into a rallying point for the cause. The themes sounded by participants in the Sicilian peace campaign have had limited appeal even in Sicily, much less throughout the rest of the peninsula. The inability of those involved in the movement to draw the attention of the mass media can perhaps be explained by the close linkage between the press and the respective political parties. Without the sponsorship of a major political party or the church, the peace movement in Italy has suffered from the lack of one of the vital ingredients which might, in other circumstances, have allowed it to increase in popularity and strength.

A key element determining the future of the Italian protest movement will be the role adopted by the PCI, which will be most likely to base its strategies on its perceptions of gains and/or losses that may be incurred from an increased involvement in the antinuclear campaign. The PCI might decide to use the issue to bolster its position with the youth among whom it has been losing support for several years. Its youth organizations today number about 50,000 in contrast to about 122,000 in 1976. In particular, with removal from the political scene of other leftist groups to attract youth (such as the Red Brigades or the Radical party), the PCI would seem to be in a favorable position to recruit new young members by mobilizing them around an issue such as war against the nuclear threat. Peace and disarmament, of course, hold strong attractions for the party faithful. One interpretation of the "democratic alternative" strategy of the PCI defines it as an effort to delineate the kinds of changes in society which the party wishes to encourage; society should be grouped around issues, such as peace and social welfare, and not around political parties. New alliances among "progressive forces" are to be formed outside the old party framework. In short, the strategy may be aimed not just at trying to change the old party alignments but also to encourage their breakdown. In light of the fact that the electorate evidently demonstrated its distaste for the "old party system" in the June 1983 election, this approach may work to the advantage of the PCI, which of all parties can maintain a disciplined structure.

Yet, the success of this strategy in regard to the peace issue will depend heavily upon the willingness of other interested groups to cooperate with the Communists. Thus far, both the small groups and the PSI have been reluctant to do so. The PSI refused to participate in the October 1981 demonstrations, asserting instead that "We do not march for Brezhnev." This attitude, in fact, can be found among other peace advocates who might otherwise be sympathetic to demonstrations against the missiles at Comiso.

Perhaps the most serious danger for the PCI in coopting the peace issue is the potential damage it might do to its image as an autonomous political party. Its ability to play a leadership role is constrained, therefore, by the reluctance of other interested groups to associate with them for fear of being instrumentalized by the PCI. Indeed, this concern is reciprocated by the PCI which, for its part, wants to be in control of events with which it is associated. The political complexion of peace demonstrations thus remains important to the PCI. Communists will not want to be isolated in their support of such demonstrations nor to have the peace movement seen as an extension solely of the PCI. If demonstrations appear to be dominated by a hard-core militant grouping, the PCI may be reluctant to lend its support. If, however, the demonstrations enjoy respectability from across the political spectrum, the likelihood of PCI support is greater. Moreover, the PCI also will be likely to look abroad for what might be termed the "external legitimization" of its support for the peace movement. Thus, demonstrations enjoying the support of a wide segment of the public in other European countries will provide the Italian Communists with a sense of the legitimacy of their own support for such endeavors. In short, although the PCI could play the role of leader or organizer in the Italian peace movement, the likelihood that it will do so appears small. Its domestic position means that it cannot afford to be branded as too pro-Soviet. As discussed above, public opinion polls conducted by Doxa indicate that the party has not been entirely successful in convincing the public of its autonomous position vis-à-vis the Soviet Union. The skepticism of the public evidenced in the polls cannot help but make the PCI leadership cautious in its support of peace movement activities.

Opposition to the missiles in Italy is counterbalanced by a fairly realistic appraisal of the Soviet threat. When respondents are questioned whether they want the missiles placed in Comiso as the only question, many express opposition. However, when the question is rephrased to take into account the presence of the Soviet SS-20 missiles aimed at Western Europe, respondents are more likely to support the emplacement of the missiles at Comiso.

In regard to the Geneva negotiations, at least two interpretations might be given as to their possible impact on the Italian scene. One view is that if the negotiations should resume and appear to have any chance of making progress toward an eventual accord, this will probably encourage contentions that additional deployment should be deferred to await the outcome of the Geneva talks. Another view, however, is that a failure to achieve positive results toward disarmament at Geneva might also encourage opponents to missile deployment, particularly if it is perceived that the United States is at fault. Not only will U. S. behavior at Geneva bear importantly, therefore, on the views and possible actions of those advocates of the Italian peace movement, but they are also likely to be affected by the Reagan administration's statements and behavior.

In short, the ability of the Reagan administration to handle adroitly the public opinion aspects of the missile and arms control questions confronting NATO will be a crucial determinant of the future actions and strength of the Italian peace movement. To the extent that there is growing opposition and dissension in the United States on such questions, it becomes easier for opponents of the missiles within the Italian peace movement to cloak their own opposition in a perception of lack of unity in the United States itself.

NOTES

1. For general background, see Luigi Barzini, *The Italians* (New York: Athenaeum, 1977); Dennis Mack Smith, ed., *Italy: A Modern History* (Ann Arbor, Michigan: University of Michigan Press, 1969); and P. A. Allum, *Italy—Republic Without Government* (New York: Norton, 1974).
2. *NTC News*, X, Nos. 1–2, January–February 1983, pp. 2–3.
3. Ibid. At its stop in Rome, Vinny McGee, chairman of the U.S. Friends of Comiso as well as the Fund for Peace and a former chairman of Amnesty International USA, was a representative of "the other America." In Comiso, the "other America" was represented by Marjorie Tuite, a Dominican nun and president of the National Assembly of Religious Women as well as Director of Ecumenical Citizen Action of Church Women United. The use of the phrase "the other America" is significant since it illustrates how the peace movement distinguishes between the "establishment" in the United States, which it sees as responsible for U.S. nuclear policy, while the "other America" is supposed to represent the "progressive," "peace-loving" America.
4. The official communique from CUDIP extended greetings to the marchers and pointed out its own nonparticipation and nonrecognition in some of the "militaristic" and "individualistic" forms of the struggle. It disassociated itself from responsibility for the encounter.
5. *The Bridge*, March–April 1983, p. 2. "A Statement of the Women of the International Peace Camp in Comiso and Women of Comiso entitled 'We Women in Comiso for an International 6th, 7th and 8th of March.'"

6. Ibid. Among American women participants were the Reverend Elizabeth Scott, a black woman from the Pittsburgh area and a Director of Justice for Women for the National Council of the Churches of Christ, U.S.A., whose theme was the need for peace with justice. She noted what she saw as the disproportionate effect of the reallocation of government spending on women. Another was Frances "Sissy" Farenthold, a former member of the Texas state legislature and a nominee for Democratic party vice presidency in 1980, who described the American nuclear freeze movement as a grass-roots effort in which women had played a prominent role. There was also a member of the Franciscan Peace Center in Las Vegas, Nevada, and a woman Presbyterian minister from Louisiana.

7. Excerpted from a statement by Women of Sicily for Nuclear Disarmament, Catania Committee (Group for the Self-Determination of Women, Catania), October 1981.

8. Ibid.

9. *The Bridge*, March–April 1983, pp. 12–13.

10. *The Bridge* reported that the same afternoon the Carabinieri invaded the International Peace Camp, confiscated tents and sleeping bags and burned other structures. In the evening, women from Comiso as well as women from the Women's Peace Camp at Greenham Common and members of the Comiso International Peace Camp held a silent vigil in protest against the alleged police brutality towards the women at the blockade and destruction in the International Peace Camp. Ibid., p. 11.

11. *The Bridge*, X, No. 5, May 1983, pp. 11–12. The women's group was reported to have bought about 4,000 square meters of land near the Magliocco Airport to be the site of a women's peace camp. To help pay for this purchase, Italian women's groups began a subscription whereby women symbolically would purchase one square meter for 5000 lire. Non-Italians were also solicited to contribute as an example of international solidarity.

12. "Pope Addressed Diplomats, Poles in Nigeria," ANSA, Rome, February 16, 1982. Foreign Broadcast Information Service (FBIS) — Western Europe, February 18, 1982.

13. Ibid.

14. *The Bridge*, May 1983, p. 14. The statement was found in the diocesan weekly *Nuova Stagione (New Season)*.

15. *Philadelphia Inquirer*, December 1, 1982.

16. *NTC News*, X, No. 1–2, January–February 1983, p. 7.

17. ACLI, "In Dialogo per la Pace," n.d.

18. Ibid.

19. For the text of the statement, see "Concluding Document of the International Peace Consultation at ECUMENE," in *Peace Efforts in Italy — Comiso*. Italian Ecumenical Center, Rome, February 11, 1982.

20. Ibid.

21. *The Bridge*, May 1983.

22. Interview with Colombo by Alberto Jacoviello, *La Repubblica*, February 13–14, 1983, p. 3.

23. Ibid.

24. *Corriere della Sera*, March 12, 1983, p. 4. Interview with Colombo by Andrea Purgatori on March 11, 1983, in Rome.

25. *La Repubblica*, June 3, 1982, p. 9. The march went by a route which took the demonstrators past both the Soviet and the American embassies on the eve of a visit by President Reagan.

26. "Peace, the Moral Question, the Democratic Alternative," *L'Unita*, September 13, 1981, pp. 1, 18.

27. *L'Unita*, August 29, 1981.

28, *L'Unita*, September 21, 1981.

29. Ibid.

30. *L'Unita*, November 9, 1981.

31. Ibid.
32. Text of PCI Secretary General Enrico Berlinguer 6 October Report to PCI Central Committee and Central Control Commission Session in Rome, *L'Unita*, October 7, 1982, pp. 10–11.
33. *L'Unita*, February 21, 1982, pp. 1–2.
34. Ibid.
35. Ibid.
36. *L'Unita*, March 6, 1983.
37. Ibid. Not only has the PCI challenged what they refer to as the "bloc logic," but they have opposed Spain's entry into NATO. In a 1981 report to the PCI Central Committee and Central Control Commission, the director of the PCI Foreign Policy Studies Center, Romano Ledda observed about NATO: "We have already heard certain objections and charges of abandoning the decisions taken regarding Italy's alliances. We confirm clearly that we do not intend to take any unilateral actions with regard to disarmament or our continued membership in the Atlantic pact. We believe that the existing politico-military blocs are still a delicate instrument of stability for both the Eastern and the Western blocs in the present acts that disrupt these balances — Spain's entry into NATO is one example — embody more dangers than advantages. We therefore have no neutralist temptations." But membership in one of the blocs, according to Ledda, did not mean that it is inappropriate to question the "bloc logic within one of the blocs" especially if, as he contended was the practice, the "bloc logic" required the subordination of the minor allies and "diametric opposition between the blocs." Ledda also remarked upon an emerging problem found in both blocs, i.e., their need to adopt to take account of diversified internal conditions. With regard to NATO, for example, Ledda argued against the extension of a NATO role beyond its present boundaries. In conclusion, Ledda contended that only the recognition of the transient nature of the politico-military blocs in world politics, the recognition of their internal diversification, and their "geographical delimitation and their defensive character can form the foundation for equal-based relations." *L'Unita*, October 6, 1981. In a joint PCI-PCE statement, Enrico Berlinguer and Santiago Carrillo said that Western Europe should play an essential role in promoting peace and progress of mankind "asserting its own autonomous policy for detente, for arms limitation and reduction, for the banning and destruction of nuclear weapons, . . . for the establishment of a new international economic order, . . . and for the elimination of bipolarism and of the split into opposing blocs. In this framework, Spain's entry into NATO would be a lamentable factor that would alter the existing balance, thus causing new tensions in the Mediterranean and Europe." "PCI-PCE Joint Statement," *L'Unita*, June 30, 1981, pp. 1, 13.
38. Ibid., March 5, 1983; *L'Unita*, May 1, 1983, pp. 1, 24. See also Berlinguer's report to PCI Central Committee session in Rome, "PCI Election Advance for Democratic Alternative," in *L'Unita*, May 12, 1983, pp. 16–17, for another statement on this issue.
39. *La Repubblica*, May 25, 1983, pp. 2–4.
40. *L'Unita*, June 24, 1983, p. 5.
41. Reprint of interview granted to *Lotta Continua* by Craxi: "Balance of Forces is Guarantee of Peace," in *Avanti*, November 8–9, 1981, p. 2.
42. Ibid.
43. *Avanti*, February 27–28, 1983, pp. 1, 24.
44. *Avanti*, October 1, 1981.
45. Ibid.
46. See *Pace in Movimento*, a periodical published by ARCI for a survey of its activities and a listing of local, affiliated groups. No. 0, 8 May 1983.
47. A clear majority (59%) in 1982 was unconditionally opposed to INF deployment — a percentage higher than in any other country surveyed. (In the Federal Republic of Germany, the figure was 42%, the Netherlands 42%, 41% in France and 39% in Great Britain).

Conditional acceptance, i.e., the willingness to accept INF deployment only in the event of failure of the arms talks with the USSR or "so long as there are arms control negotiations with the USSR at the same time," was found among 28% of those polled and unconditional acceptance only among 8%. An earlier survey conducted in November and December 1981 of Italian university graduates and students in Rome, Milan, and Naples found sharp differences in opinion among different age groups on such questions as their views of the United States, whether they favor NATO over neutrality, and their attitudes toward INF deployment in Italy. Present university students and recent graduates (a finding similar to that in earlier surveys conducted between 1977 and 1981. With 71% of the university students polled and 69% of those 34 and younger opposed to INF deployment, one might expect that the peace movement would be able to find willing recruits for its aims. That this source has not been mobilized can only be explained by factors unique to the Italian political scene.

48. "U.S. Missiles in Sicily Are Now Operational," *New York Times*, April 4, 1984; "Italian Premier Wins New Vote on Missiles," ibid., April 5, 1984.

Chapter 7

Pacifism and Antinuclearism in France: Perceptions of the Crises of Deterrence and Detente

James B. Foley

THE CRISIS OF DETERRENCE

One of the most remarkable features of the European-wide peace movement over the past few years has been the relative failure of pacifist and antinuclear sentiment to take hold among major segments of the French population. This has remained true in spite of three factors which might have been expected to produce a peace campaign in France comparable to those in the Federal Republic, Holland, and Great Britain. France is socially and politically similar in all essential aspects to her European neighbors, possesses a deep-rooted pacifist tradition, and for many years had been the strident champion of anti-American spirit in Europe.

Perhaps the most surprising development of all is that the Socialist-Communist government of François Mitterrand has consistently endeavored not only to thwart the spread of the peace movement onto French soil, but also to combat its influence and appeal elsewhere in Europe, and chiefly in the Federal Republic of Germany. Moreover, this effort has been marked by the virtually unprecedented public support of a French government in favor of the NATO double-track decision and the American position at the Eurostrategic negotiations in Geneva.

Indeed, if one were to compile a list of all the novel diplomatic initiatives of the Socialist government over the past three years, they would appear to constitute not only a radical departure from many of the policy tenets held by the *Parti Socialiste* in opposition, but also a significant modification in the form, if not always the substance, of the policies of the preceding governments of the Fifth Republic.

Among these initiatives, the following may be highlighted: the priority of modernizing France's nuclear deterrent strike force, sometimes justified publicly as permitting (though not guaranteeing) an extension of French deterrence beyond French borders; a desire to reinforce the strength and coherence of the NATO Alliance motivated by a fear that neutralist trends in Germany and unilateral/isolationist trends in the United States might be undermining the balance of power in Europe; and a commitment to strengthening Franco-German cooperation and planning in the security field. The latter ambition was made eloquently manifest in a speech Mitterrand delivered before the Bundestag on January 20, 1983. In the speech he exhorted the Germans, especially his fellow West German Socialists in the SPD, to remain faithful not only to the Atlantic Alliance, but more generally to the choice made by Konrad Adenauer to pursue German destiny wholly within, and not at the expense of, the West.[1] Franco-German military cooperation, it has been reported, aims at strengthening possible French participation in German defense by means of the new, longer-range tactical nuclear forces and the projected French rapid deployment force. The long-range goal of such a doctrinal and political evolution would be to create the famous "European pillar" within the Atlantic Alliance and ultimately to constitute the nucleus for a future independent European defense entity.

All of these policies undertaken over the course of the past two years betray a conception of peace and security that is fundamentally at odds with the positions of the *Parti Socialiste* (PS) of not many years ago. For it was only in 1978 that the PS went on record as favoring the retention of the *force de frappe*; before this, the party's conception of security policy was remarkably similar to that which today it resolutely combats. Previously, it considered disarmament, and French unilateral nuclear disarmament in particular, as the surest means of guaranteeing peace and security. Even after accepting the French deterrent in 1978, the PS continued to emphasize that it regarded disarmament as one of its highest priorities and suggested that a Socialist government would take immediate, concrete, and unilateral steps which, it was hoped, world encourage other nuclear powers to move in a similar direction.[2] Not until 1980 did the party express its support for continued modernization of French nuclear forces.

Parties are obliged to alter their positions when they assume governing responsibility. There was a need to take into account the general consensus among the French public in favor of France's deterrent force. The Communists, after all, had already embraced the *force de frappe* in 1977. What was equally important, however, was the evolution in Socialist thinking on the issue of disarmament as a transcendent goal in and of itself. The key element inducing a change in this area was the conviction that the balance of forces in Europe had dramatically shifted in the Soviets' favor with the introduction of the SS-20 missile. While all other major political parties (except for the PCF) agreed with this assessment, it was the PS which chose to make of it an issue in the 1981 presidential campaign, with Mitterrand chiding Giscard for not speaking out publicly on the issue.

The new reading of the European security equation led Mitterrand to reevaluate the priority he had earlier accorded to nuclear disarmament. The Soviet Union, after having reached a position of Eurostrategic superiority, was now advocating a peculiar form of disarmament, one that would prevent NATO from restoring the equilibrium broken by the installation of the SS-20s. This Soviet view was producing a dangerously loud echo among large sectors of the European public. Thus, disarmament became, in Mitterrand's mind, secondary to the reestablishment of a nuclear equilibrium, and this line of reasoning brought Mitterrand into direct conflict with the position of the European peace movement which, in a dramatically changed strategic context, resembled the former disarmament priority of the PS:

> If I condemn neutrality, it is because I believe that peace is linked to the balance of forces in the world. The installation of the Soviet SS-20s and Backfires breaks this equilibrium in Europe. I don't accept this and I admit that it is necessary to arm in order to recover the point of equilibrium. From there it will be necessary to negotiate.[3]

Although President Mitterrand and other governmental and party spokesmen have often reiterated their desire for disarmament, once a balance has been achieved, their efforts to counter the West European antinuclear movement have led them to play down the value of disarmament as a goal in itself and to deny that pacifism and disarmament are the best means at present to achieve peace and security. Instead, breaking with the PS's own disarmament tradition, they argue now that the best guarantee for peace lies in nuclear deterrence. The peace of France is guaranteed by its possession of an independent nuclear deterrent, and the peace of France's Alliance partners to the East is threatened by the very crisis of deterrence brought about by the deployment of the SS-20's combined with the popular movements which have sought to prevent a NATO counter-deployment.

In May of 1982, the PS officially adopted the new position in a document entitled "Peace, Security, and Disarmament," which it presented to the bureau of the Socialist International gathered at Helsinki. Here, profound divergences between the PS and her European sister parties in the International were brought to the fore on the issues of East-West relations, detente, and nuclear disarmament. Lionel Jospin, first secretary of the PS, opposed the point of view taken by the Finnish Prime Minister Kalevi Sorza, also shared by the Brandt faction in the SPD, according to which the Socialist parties must follow public opinion and unconditionally support the European peace movements or else risk alienating their natural constituency which consists of millions of "sincere pacifists."

The document presented by Mr. Jospin, on the other hand, begins with an unequivocal condemnation of pacifism: "Pacifism does not necessarily signify peace any more than speaking about disarmament guarantees security."[4] Secondly, the document asserts that security depends first of all on the respect for certain fundamental principles, including, "non-use of force, refusal of foreign occupations, the right of people to self-determination, the right of security for every people."[5] Finally, the PS unabashedly defends the utility of nuclear deterrence in maintaining the peace and security not only of France, but also of her European allies:

> In Europe, nuclear deterrence is the guarantee of armed peace, in waiting for the establishment of a system of regional security different from the logic of blocs. But this nuclear deterrence is in crisis and France must make her voice heard and contribute to the security of her European partners.[6]

Thus, in the view of the PS, the crisis of deterrence merits not the response proposed by the peace movement and encouraged by the Socialist International, for this would only consolidate the status quo in favor of the Soviet Union. Instead of this patently naive and idealistic approach, the PS proposes a classical *realpolitik* alternative based on the logic of the balance of power. Except for the notable aberration of the Napoleonic period which made the Corsican doubly illegitimate in the eyes of conservative statesmen, France in modern centuries has usually pursued a balance of power in Europe as a major foreign policy objective.

GISCARD AND THE CRISIS OF DETENTE

A second crisis, the crisis of detente, produced an equally remarkable evolution in the international diplomacy of the *Parti Socialiste*, one which paralleled the evolution of Socialist thinking on deterrence and disarmament.

The decisive event that provoked the apparent demise of detente and the consequent cooling of East-West relations was undoubtedly the Soviet invasion of Afghanistan in December 1979, culminating years of growing awareness in the West during the late 1970s of the dangers of the Soviet Union's unrelenting armament effort. Those years witnessed a ground swell of anti-detente, pro-rearmament sentiment which would carry Ronald Reagan to the presidency in 1980.

Reactions of an entirely different sort, however, were also being manifested in the West — reactions to the countermeasures the Western governments were preparing to take in response to the Soviet threat. The prospect of a new and intensified round of the arms race, especially one that would be characterized by the development of highly accurate and sophisticated first strike weaponry and nuclear war-fighting strategies, gave rise to fear and anxiety among the populations of the West, in spite of the fact that the Soviet Union had taken the lead in triggering such a race. The successful anti-"neutron bomb" campaign orchestrated several years earlier by Moscow served as a source of encouragement to all those who might wish to thwart the NATO effort to redress the imbalance in Eurostrategic forces.

The Soviet invasion of Afghanistan and the prospect of a renewed and intensified arms race — that is, the crisis of detente and the crisis of deterrence — mutually reinforced each other in such a way as to produce, especially in Western Europe, a war psychosis with debilitating effects on public opinion. But the invasion of Afghanistan was met in Western Europe not with a renewed commitment to stand up to the Soviet threat but with a desire to save detente unconditionally by opposing the measures advocated by the Carter administration. Thus emerged what Pierre Hassner has termed the "split detente." In sharp contrast to the past, when Soviet provocations or an increased tension in East-West relations could be expected to produce a closing of ranks in the West, the year 1980 saw the United States and Europe moving in different directions in reaction to events fundamentally affecting the security and vital interests of the entire West.

In France public opinion was similarly affected by the twin crises of detente and disarmament. A public opinion poll published in *Le Point* in June 1980 produced some startling results. Only 29% of those questioned hoped that the French president would even *threaten* to use the *force de frappe* if France were about to be invaded, and fully 64% agreed with the statement that, "war is too horrible, and must be sacrificed in favor of the maintenance of peace."[7]

President Giscard d'Estaing was evidently convinced that he had to take account of the growing fear of war and the widespread spirit of resignation which it produced in formulating his public diplomacy, and therefore deemed it prudent in the coming election year not to attempt to swim against the tide of public opinion in France. In this he was joined by Helmut Schmidt in West Germany. Both leaders recognized regretfully that public rhetoric calling attention to the dangers of Soviet behavior could only prove counterproductive, exacerbating fears and producing pacifist sentiment which would play further into Soviet hands. Consequently the two leaders endeavored to preserve what remained of detente and of a political dialogue with the Soviet Union. This brought them directly into conflict with Jimmy Carter's efforts to rally Western public opinion against the Soviet danger of which, he candidly admitted, following the Soviet invasion of Afghanistan, he had only just taken cognizance. They refused to accept Carter's implicit effort to draw an analogy between the current crisis and the dangers of appeasement à la 1939. Instead, as Schmidt suggested, the present situation bore a closer resemblance to that of 1914 with the attendant dangers of war by miscalculation or overreaction. Or, as Giscard put it, "the peace of the world depends on the ability of but a few men to keep their cool." Of course, implicit in this remark was the assumption that Giscard was, indeed, among this select company, whereas the American president perhaps was not.

Giscard failed to exploit what seems in retrospect to have been the leeway offered by the mood of French public opinion and for having gone so far in the direction of prudence as to weaken Western solidarity in the face of the Afghan crisis. His surprise, furtive visit in the Spring of 1980 to meet with Brezhnev in Warsaw represented a political blunder that was exploited against him in the presidential campaign by Gaullists and Socialists alike.

Did Giscard misread French public opinion? Perhaps it was not clear in 1980 that the French would manifest markedly different reactions to the emerging crisis from that of her neighbors, and that, in particular, the French people would remain relatively immune to the pacifist and antinuclear currents which were sweeping across Central Europe. In retrospect, it is possible to conclude that the signs of fear and defeatism revealed in the 1980 opinion poll were chiefly the result of the Afghanistan crisis (i.e., the realization that a decade of detente was coming to an end, and that the Soviet Union remained, as always, a power with hegemonial ambitions). In the light of developments since the election of Mitterrand in 1981, it now appears that the French were not suffering from the same fears of victimization and looming nuclear war which the crisis of deterrence was provoking in the FRG, Holland, and elsewhere. All major French political parties, including the Communists, support the national nuclear deterrent as the ultimate guarantee of France's independence. Certainly concern did exist among French elites and defense experts over the changing power balance in Europe; but even in these circles, the SS-20 was regarded as posing a threat principally to the NATO allies to the east who lack independent deterrents of their own.

There are several interrelated factors which help to explain why the French reaction has been different. Of principal importance was the fact that no American missiles were scheduled to be deployed on French soil. French leaders were therefore spared the thankless and often counter-productive task of having to justify this deployment before parliament, parties, and public by calling attention to the truly menacing nature of the Soviet threat.

Secondly, having refused earlier to modify their nuclear doctrine in the face of a changing strategic environment, instead of conforming to the shift in NATO doctrine from a strategy of massive retaliation to one of flexible response, the French had avoided a public debate that could have undermined the existing national consensus on the maintenance of the *force de frappe*. Whereas elsewhere in the West popular support for nuclear deterrence was being shaken by much-publicized debate over first-strike weapons and the prospect of limited nuclear war, the French, as the opinion poll revealed, were constantly being reassured by their leaders that nuclear weapons guaranteed both national independence and the prevention of war. One study of French attitudes towards nuclear weapons carried this conclusion:

> One may wonder whether the French have really understood the purpose of nuclear weapons. They have been told so much that these were non-usable weapons that they have finally come to believe that they were indeed destined never to be used. The French consensus is based perhaps on a misunderstanding.[8]

There is little doubt, nevertheless, that Giscard himself was fully aware of the growing threat which the modernization of Soviet nuclear and conventional forces posed especially to France's NATO partners and, by implication, to vital French interests. Throughout his presidency, Giscard sought to modify French strategic doctrine in a manner that would render French participation in the defense of her neighbors both more probable and more efficacious. This attempted modification was based on the frank acknowledgment that, even though the *force de frappe* might succeed in deterring Soviet aggression against French territory, the future of France's independence would be precarious indeed in the event that Soviet tanks were to reach the Rhine. But Giscard had to proceed with extreme caution in this direction for two reasons, one having to do with internal French politics, the other with France's long-term strategic interests.

In the first instance, Giscard had to guard against criticism from the jealous guardians of Gaullist doctrinal orthodoxy. These included powerful forces from all quarters of the political spectrum: The Gaullist Union for the New Republic (UNR) and the Communist party stood ready to oppose any efforts subject to interpretation as either harmful to the credibility of France's strictly national deterrent, or as leading France towards tacit reintegration into NATO, or both.

More importantly, Giscard apparently was quite concerned lest any move he might undertake towards a European defense system, a reinforcement of Franco-German defense cooperation, or a partial reintegration of French forces into NATO be construed by the Soviets as a provocation. Certain remarks he made in this regard following his summit meeting with Brezhnev at Rambouillet in 1975 have since become famous. He attributed his reluctance to open a discussion on European defense chiefly to

> . . . the fears—and I will say the understandable fears—for the Soviet Union of projects of organization of European defense in which the Soviet Union sees, at least in the short term, the risk of a certain threat or a certain European military pressure against herself.[9]

In February 1982, the former president revealed that, had he been re-elected, he had intended "examining with Helmut Schmidt the possibility of approaching a common reflection on the security problems of our two countries and of Europe."[10] In fact, the evolution of strategic doctrine begun under Giscard pointed towards movement in this direction and was duly condemned for this reason by alarmed Gaullists. In any event, Gisard's fear of provoking the Soviets was incontestable. His chief anxiety in this regard, apparently was that Moscow, if it liked, could work to undermine the credibility of the French deterrent force. Up to now, the Soviets had flattered and encouraged France's pretensions to national independence for the negative effects the French example continued to have on NATO coherence and solidarity. Possession of an independent nuclear deterrent seemingly precluded any possible French reintegration into NATO, which probably explains why it was accepted in 1977 by the French Communist Party (PCF). For Moscow, French Communist support for the *force de frappe* undoubtedly contributes to the maintenance of a neutralist French strategic doctrine, if not foreign policy.

However, if the Soviet Union ever saw that France was overtly moving away from its semi-neutralist, Gaullist orthodoxy in military policy, Giscard feared, it could respond by no longer playing the game of accepting what it undoubtedly regards as the "myth" of French national independence and by trying to undermine the national consensus on deterrence within France. To prevent this from happening, Giscard felt obliged to pursue a very subtle, delicate foreign and military policy, one which, to the untrained eye, appeared highly contradictory, manifesting an Atlanticism in intentions and deeds which often bordered on a seeming willingness to sacrifice French independence and a penchant in words for respecting Soviet sensibilities which could sometimes be interpreted as approaching appeasement.

In the final analysis, Giscard's complex and ambiguous policies wound up alienating many observers for often contradictory reasons. The Gaullists attacked him during the presidential campaign both for his allegedly Atlanticist military policies and for his failure to stand up forthrightly to the danger of Soviet arms and aggression. As to the latter charge, this was probably due to his anxiety over the strength and resolution of French public opinion and to his fears of provoking the Soviets. In this respect, one should not forget the tacit alliance which existed during the election campaign between Giscard and the PCF. It was no secret that Giscard was clearly Moscow's preferred choice for the presidency. The fact that this was generally known and exploited by the RPR and the PS throughout the campaign may perhaps indicate that Giscard had, after all, underestimated the depth of anti-Soviet sentiment within the country in the wake of the Afghanistan invasion and the crisis in East-West relations. He also underestimated, quite evidently, the extent to which such sentiment could produce a backlash against him in the election.

It is important to underline one last factor in Giscard's diplomacy during the "crisis" period leading up to the election. This was his unwillingness to come out publicly in favor of the installation of U.S. intermediate-range nuclear forces in Europe, in spite of the fact that he privately supported their deployment. François Mitterrand, on the other hand, made his support of the NATO double-track decision a theme of his campaign, and he openly criticized Giscard for having failed to express himself on this issue. What was at first thought to be perhaps nothing more than a mere opportunistic campaign tactic on the part of Mitterrand grew, under his presidency, into a full blown, energetic commitment in favor of NATO's effort to redress the Eurostrategic imbalance either by negotiations or, if need be, deployment of the U.S. systems on schedule.

MITTERRAND AND THE CRISES OF DETENTE AND DETERRENCE

The past two years have witnessed countless numbers of pro-NATO public pronouncements by PS party officials, such as Lionel Jospin and Jacques Huntzinger, leading military figures, and members of the government, including Pierre Mauroy, Claude Cheysson, Charles Hernu, and the president himself. It is apparent that two factors have motivated Mitterrand so deliberately to throw caution to the wind—a position which Giscard had guarded almost as a sacred article of faith. The first is that Mitterrand evidently felt he was domestically secure enough to permit himself to take what for Giscard would have been a step fraught with danger, given the Gaullist propensity to sound alarm bells whenever he made any Atlanticist moves. Gaullist orthodoxy held that the credibility of French deterrence required that France not involve herself in questions of Alliance strategic policy and diplomacy.

As for the second motivating factor in Mitterrand's pro-INF stance, the neo-Gaullist rhetoric on the inalienability of French independence ignored the fact that French security rested implicitly on the assumption that the Federal Republic would remain a strong and reliable member of the Atlantic Alliance, thus constituting a barrier to the advance of Soviet forces to the French borders. By the time Mitterrand assumed office, what may indeed have been essentially a politically motivated support for INF deployment became a matter dictated by overriding French national interests in the face of increasingly alarming trends in German public opinion. The prospect of a failure by NATO to deploy its missiles, the retention of the SS-20 force, and ultimately a neutralized West Germany was one which no French statesman could afford to ignore. Mitterrand's evident desire to reinforce NATO solidarity at this critical juncture could be likened to the concern expressed by President Pompidou when he voiced opposition to the potential withdrawal of American troops from Western Europe in 1970, when the Mansfield Resolution was being debated.

It should be remembered that, in developing an independent French nuclear force and in pulling France out of NATO's military wing, de Gaulle hoped to insure France against what he regarded as an inevitable weakening in the reliability of the American extended deterrent. Further, he foresaw that American nuclear "egoism" might one day lead the Federal Republic to seek its destiny by reverting to its traditional neutralist policy of balancing between East and West. To forestall such an eventuality so fraught with danger for French security and independence, de Gaulle moved to cement the Franco-German tie by means of the peace treaty he negotiated with Konrad Adenauer in 1963. This historic treaty contained a clause, which remained a dead letter until it was revived by Kohl and Mitterrand in October 1982, envisaging concrete defense cooperation and the elaboration in common of defense doctrines between France and the Federal Republic.

It is no secret that de Gaulle harbored great hopes for the Franco-German relationship, not the least of which was the ambition to use it as the foundation for a truly "European" Europe, one which would possess its own defense entity and would depend heavily upon French deterrent strength. It is likely that de Gaulle's would-be heirs, Gaullists who have consistently sought to reinforce France's own tendencies towards nuclear "egoism" and neutralism, understand neither de Gaulle's truly grandiose vision of the French role in Europe, nor his profound anxiety over the future security of a fragmented Western Europe in the face of growing Soviet power and a decline in the reliability and the credibility of the U.S. nuclear guarantee to its NATO allies.

It is fair to conclude, then, that Mitterrand's move to put an end to what one observer has termed the "national neutralism" of recent French security policy is entirely in keeping with General de Gaulle's conception of the role France ought to play as an independent, European nuclear power.[11] For de Gaulle, the object was to maximize France's security and freedom of maneuver by constantly shifting the weight of French power and influence in relation to the relative state of the balance of power, both worldwide and on the European continent. Thus, his decision to pull out of NATO and to try to woo Adenauer in this direction as well was a function of what de Gaulle then perceived to be an overwhelming military preponderance of the United States over the Soviet Union. In the early 1960s, therefore, it was a question in the short run of putting distance between France and the overbearing protector and, in the long run, of preparing the groundwork of a Franco-German-centered European defense system for the day when the Atlantic connection would begin to falter.

It has of course long been held in the United States that de Gaulle himself bears no small responsibility for lending impetus to a self-fulfilling prophecy, that is, for having precipitated the very crisis in trans-Atlantic relations which he claimed to be preparing himself against. In this respect, it is interesting to note that some French observers have remarked that France cannot entirely escape from responsibility for the neutralist drift in German politics. Writes Pierre Lellouche:

> If the former President [Giscard] had had the courage to take a position from the very beginning of the Euromissile affair five years ago, instead of feigning a shivering indifference, we undoubtedly could have checked — if not avoided totally — the neutralist drift of our neighbors. Without France, they and principally the FRG, had no choice but to fall back totally on the ever more incoherent leadership of the United States.[12]

Upon assuming office, Mitterrand apparently concluded that the alarming situation in Germany warranted France's shedding vestiges of the Gaullist "national-neutralist" legacy and forcefully bringing all her weight and stored-up influence to bear on behalf of a faltering NATO. There was reason to think that, in the short run at least, his unassailable domestic position would allow him to accomplish this change of course. There was thus a convergence between the urgency of the German problem and the freedom of maneuver which the overwhelming Socialist victory in the elections to the National Assembly conferred upon Mitterrand. All of the traditional guardians of anti-Atlanticist orthodoxy were temporarily silenced: the Communists, because they would be subject to governing coalition conformity; potential voices of dissent within the PS, because the president's hold over them was unchallengeable; and the two major parties of the Right, because they shared Mitterrand's anxiety over the course of events in Germany.

Furthermore, the rise of neutralist sentiment in West Germany and the prospect of what Egon Bahr calls "a security partnership" between the Federal Republic and the Soviet Union posed a direct threat to France's most vital interests. Thus, it is not necessarily a betrayal of de Gaulle's legacy for François Mitterrand to exhort the West Germans to be better allies of the United States. In terms of a strictly Gaullist, cold-blood assessment of the power balance in Europe, it simply was no longer realistic for Mitterrand, like de Gaulle, to demand that the FRG choose between France and the

United States. Rather, it was essential that every effort be made to reinforce both the German tie to the West in general and German confidence in nuclear deterrence. The two goals are related, for it is the crisis of deterrence that is undermining Germany's commitment to the West and luring it in the direction of neutralism.

General de Gaulle had foreseen this crisis, and understood that its origin had to do with the fact that the Europeans depended on the nuclear deterrent of a foreign power. He extricated France from this dilemma by providing her with an independent deterrent force, and it is because of this, more than any other factor, that France has thus far been spared the rise of antinuclear movements which are undermining the capacity of France's allies to resist the nuclear blackmail and intimidation of the Soviet Union. In his own time however, de Gaulle was never able to create anything approaching a credible French deterrent for Western Europe.

Like General de Gaulle twenty years earlier, but in a dramatically changed strategic environment, François Mitterrand is addressing himself to the manner in which France might contribute to West European security. The first and most immediate task is to prevent the decoupling of the security relationship between the United States and Western Europe, to counter rejectionist trends in West Germany which might in turn produce isolationist trends in the United States. Foreign Minister Claude Cheysson has remarked:

> The danger is to separate, if only in a demonstrative way, American defense and the defense of Europe. What would Western Europe be in the face of the gigantic conventional and medium-range nuclear arsenal of the East if there were no strategic nuclear forces? [13]

The second task is to demonstrate France's own willingness not to replace the American strategic guarantee, but to contribute concretely to German security. Finally, the last task is to open the possibility for an eventual movement towards a more united European defense effort. This France has done on several occasions within the Assembly of the Western European Union (WEU), which links France with Britain, West Germany, Italy, Belgium, Netherlands, and Luxembourg in a common defense treaty organization.

The object of this three-pronged offensive, highly symbolic in nature, is chiefly West German public opinion. In Mitterrand's view, what is involved above all in the current crisis of deterrence is a test of will. For France, it is relatively easy to meet this test because of her possession of a national deterrent force. Thus, what Mitterrand has attempted to do is to exploit fully the "healthy" state of French public opinion which it owes to its deterrent force, even if, as the opinion polls reveal, the French have no wish to use it should the bluff ever be called. But this is the point: What needs to be reinforced in West Germany is not so much the will to resist as the will to bluff. That bluff will appear all the more credible — to those *against* whom it is directed, and to those *for* whom it is proferred — by the concrete manifestation of France's Alliance and European solidarity.

It is quite plain that in unequivocally engaging himself in the struggle over Germany's and Europe's future, François Mitterrand has openly positioned himself as an obstacle in the path of the Soviet Union's grand design to separate the United States from the defense of Europe. Moreover, Mitterrand has raised the one specter which the Soviets have historically wished to avoid provoking as they seek to undermine Europe's Atlantic connection: a European defense system. In shedding all pretense of neo-Gaullist neutralism for the sake of a more fundamental Gaullist principle — preserving or restoring a balance of power in Europe — Mitterrand has openly provoked the Soviets in a manner which Giscard always sought to avoid.

Mitterrand's evolution in an anti-Soviet direction, however, was not only a product of the crisis of deterrence as a result of the changed military balance, or of the Soviet effort to wean the Federal Republic away from the West and send the Americans packing. The change can also be attributed to the evolution within the *Parti Socialiste* in reaction to the crisis of detente precipitated by the Soviet invasion of Afghanistan. Many attributed this transformation to electoral opportunism; the PCF, after all, had thoroughly discredited and isolated itself in French public opinion by supporting the Soviet invasion. Moreover, the Socialists, in tandem with the Gaullists, were able to exploit Giscard's seeming "softness" towards the Soviets in the wake of the Afghan crisis.

However, it is now clear that for some time the PS had been revising its traditional, knee-jerk interpretation of the Cold War and the value of detente. Whereas formerly the Socialists sanctimoniously denounced both superpowers for having divided Europe at Yalta and imposing their military bloc system in their respective spheres, now they were starting to qualify this judgment. The slogan, "get out of Yalta," formerly addressed to both superpowers, was beginning to sound more like a demand for the liberalization of the East bloc regimes. Jacques Huntzinger has even given this old slogan a new twist — "return to Yalta," implying a revival of the promise of freedom and democracy in Eastern Europe which Roosevelt and Churchill had sought to embody in the Yalta accords.[14]

A decisive event in this important shift in the Socialist perspective on detente was the rise of the independent trade union movement in Poland. For many among the rank and file of the PS, particularly the Socialist-leaning union, the CFDT, Solidarity embodied their own ideal of a *societe autogestionnaire* which they hoped to realize in France. The threat which the Soviet Union posed to Solidarity and to Polish independence made many in the PS realize that the prospects for a real long-term detente were linked integrally to the possibilities for social and political transformation in Eastern Europe.

This fundamental change in the Socialists' viewpoint on the nature of detente with the Soviet Union came about just as the other parties in the Socialist International, and chiefly the West German SPD, were beginning to accept the Soviet view of detente, that is, an unconditional one, just as they were embracing the Soviet positions on disarmament while the PS was moving in the opposite direction. Nowhere was the growing cleavage more apparent that in the divergent reactions of the SPD and the PS to the Jaruzelski coup of December 13, 1981. Helmut Schmidt said:

> The Western nations were called to Yalta in 1945 to divide Europe into spheres of influence, and any attempt to modify this balance could lead to war.[15]

Mitterrand's response was in sharp contrast:

> The Polish people know that they are still enduring the consequences of the Second World War and that they will not escape from this until the day when the division of Europe into two blocs *and the system which oppresses them* will have disappeared.[16]

The manifest desire of the Socialist government not to normalize political relations with the Soviet Union, at least at the highest levels, until progress has been made in both the Polish and Afghan crises, is in marked contrast with the accommodating attitude of the Giscard regime towards the Soviets. Thus the change in Socialist thinking was not opportunistic, but instead reflected a fundamental reinterpretation of the manner in which detente with the Soviet Union ought to be pursued. Mitterrand remarked at his press conference of June 9, 1982: "Would you like us to forget Afghanistan, Poland, the SS-20's? That's your affair. Not me, in any case, not me."[17]

The Socialist government's most dramatic break with Giscard's cautious diplomacy has been its decision to support wholeheartedly the American position on the controversy over intermediate-range nuclear forces in Europe. In doing so, François Mitterrand has brought himself into open conflict with both the Soviet Union and the European peace movements. By seeking to thwart their ambitions, he risks provoking their wrath and bringing the full force of their critical attention upon him at a time when his domestic authority is on the wane in France because of economic frustration.

The reason France, under Mitterrand, could assume such risks and maintain its nerve in the face of the Soviet threat is related principally to the fact that France has assumed responsibility for her own fate in the defense realm. For the allies, on the other hand, salvation has been sought in two ways, both of them, in the final analysis, irresponsible:

. . . (o)ne consists in relying on the great ally and on its nuclear force, hoping that it will continue to increase. The other consists in dreaming of a disarmament which will banish, as if by magic, the problems posed. These two temptations, in combination, lead to inertia in the area of national defense, and to an unconditional confidence in disarmament negotiations. This attitude leads to a lowering of one's guard without having resolved in a proper fashion the problems of European security. [18]

In the French view, therefore, the long-term guarantee of West European security will depend upon whether the Europeans choose to become responsible for their own security. This is a prospect which the Soviet Union would surely wish to foil. Moreover, it is one which, increasingly, the European protest movement is beginning to fear as an unwelcome by-product of its efforts. Writes one commentator:

The "French Euromissiles" appear to them [the peace movements] more and more as the beginning of a strictly European nuclear force which could be substituted for the NATO Euromissiles if the peace movements attained their objectives. [19]

In truth, Mitterrand views the current NATO missile plan as but a temporary, albeit crucial, solution to the problem of European security. The real long-term answer, which France's growing entente with the Federal Republic in the strategic field points towards, lies in the realm of a greater effort on the part of the Europeans to assure their own defense. Mitterrand's ostensible "Atlanticism" masks what is at bottom a truly European outlook on security questions.

However, this aggressively confident effort to reinforce Europe's will to preserve its independence placed Mitterrand on a collision course with the thinly-disguised Soviet campaign to cow Western Europe into lowering its guard and accepting *de facto* Soviet hegemony. Nowhere has this clash been more starkly exposed than in the successive interventions of Andrei Gromyko and François Mitterrand in the German election campaign. Mitterrand's speech before the Bundestag probably marked the definitive end of France's traditional role as an *interlocuteur privilegie* of Moscow. In fact, the whole thrust of Mitterrand's defense and military policies of the past thirty months can only mean that France has ceased to serve its useful purpose for the Soviets as a fetter on Western solidarity, as a destabilizing model of autonomy from NATO.

An indication of the possible consequences of this change can perhaps be gleaned from the reception given Foreign Minister Claude Cheysson during his February 1983 visit to Moscow. During their meeting, Yuri Andropov stuck firmly to his proposal of December 21, 1982, by which he justified the retention of SS-20s as a counter to the French and British nuclear deterrent forces. The cold encounter was a most humbling, if not humiliating, experience for Cheysson:

> He (Andropov) is not interested in the fact that we regard ourselves as independent.... He wants to take account of our forces not of our thinking.... But Mr. Andropov has no reply when he is told that by taking that action, the Soviet Union is in fact forcing us to rejoin NATO, which is surprising to say the least.[20]

If France under Mitterrand has chosen to emerge from its "national-neutralist" shell, then it must expect to pay a certain price for its pro-NATO, anti-Soviet policies. This price is the very one many French strategists warned about, and which Giscard had endeavored to forestall: the inclusion of French nuclear forces in the Eurostrategic balance. Raymond Aron absolves Mitterrand of blame for this, insisting that the Soviets would have inevitably taken this move sooner or later.[21] But the fact remains that the Soviets were bound to regard Mitterrand's European policy as a provocation, a threat to their own designs, and were thus likely to retaliate in some manner. Once the French acted upon the threat to their vital security interests in Germany posed by Soviet policy, openly abandoning the illusion of splendid national independence, the Soviets could no longer be expected to encourage such an illusion. Andropov's proposal to count British and French missiles, while opposing U.S. missiles in Europe, implies that the future nuclear balance in Europe is to be struck between the USSR and Western Europe.

It would appear that the Andropov move was designed in part to put Mitterrand on the defensive by undermining French support for his expansive and energetic foreign policy. Former Prime Minister Raymond Barre has criticized the president for having taken sides in the INF controversy. Secondly, the Soviets undoubtedly seek to keep Mitterrand on the defensive by turning the attention of European antinuclearists on France. Many in the peace movement have long held that their campaign can hardly succeed in the absence of a similar movement in France. At one point, leading figures of the Dutch peace movement announced their intention to try to spread the wave of antidefense and antinuclear sentiment to France.[22] Rarely did the convergence of interests between the Soviet Union and the European peace movement appear more obvious.

In this vein, the third object of Andropov's initiative against Mitterrand was to undermine the French national consensus that has existed around the *force de frappe*. Potential openings exist along the French political spectrum for the future growth of antinuclear and antidefense sentiment and the spread of pacifist contagion:

1. traditionally pacifist, pro-disarmament currents in the *Parti Socialiste* and among French Catholics;

2. factions among the PS (chiefly led by J. P. Chevenement) disaffected by the Atlanticist drift of the Socialist government; and
3. the French Communist party, whose adherence to the *force de frappe* could be subject to modification upon orders from Moscow.

Furthermore, growth of antinuclear sentiment among these three sectors might be stimulated by disaffection on the Left towards the rigorous economic austerity measures which the Socialist government decided upon in 1983. This possible sense of betrayal may be expressed in terms of opposition to Mitterrand's pro-NATO or pro-nuclear stances. The president, in turn, may be obliged to modify some of his positions, if only rhetorically, in order to compensate for the hard line on the economy.

One more danger, a particularly ominous one in respect to its long-term implications, may also lurk on the horizon. Andropov's linkage of the 162 SS-20s to French and British nuclear forces implied an eagerness to negotiate those remaining missiles away in exchange for a dismantling of the French and British deterrents. If ever the Soviets really wanted to provoke a serious debate in France over the *force de frappe*, they would have only to make such an offer. This would be the ultimate Soviet coup: first to use the SS-20 to decouple the United States from Europe, and then to achieve a complete denuclearization of the continent.

The Andropov offer thus permits us to take the full measure of the risks run by Mitterrand in engaging himself so openly on the current European crisis. It also warrants our tempering the overly optimistic analyses which have been made over the past several years concerning the apparent impermeability of French public opinion to pacifist and antinuclear sentiment. Jacques Huntzinger of the PS has declared:

> But can we be sure that, tomorrow, there will be no demonstrations if we begin work for the installation of mobile land missiles? Of this we know nothing. If, tomorrow, we took the decision to produce the neutron bomb, would there not be large campaigns? . . . One could say that there are, in France for tomorrow, possibilities of reaction which we must not underestimate.[23]

It has in fact been widely reported since the Fall of 1982 that the Socialist government indeed intends to proceed with production of the neutron weapon. Such a move, however, could be particularly risky in the context of intensified Soviet pressure and rising antinuclear sentiment in France. The 1982 PS document, "Peace, Security and Disarmament," sounded a troubled warning on this subject:

> There is no doubt that the support of public opinion for our policy of nuclear deterrence would be affected by a decision seeming to increase the probability of a nuclear war or of such a nature as to prevent the conclusion of a general agreement reducing conventional and tactical nuclear weapons in Europe.[24]

Many in the Socialist party, and not merely those opposed to it on doctrinal grounds, evidently fear that a decision to produce the neutron bomb would produce the very type of public debate over limited nuclear war and nuclear war-fighting scenarios which has had such debilitating effects on the defense policies of France's neighbors. Deployment of neutron weapons might have the paradoxical effect of bringing the enemy closer to home in the public consciousness and of raising the question of the efficacy of French nuclear forces in deterring war. Until now, it has been precisely the fact that France has distanced itself from the battlefield, both physically and conceptually, which has rendered French society immune to the crisis of deterrence and the contagion of antinuclear paralysis. It remains to be seen whether Mitterrand's effort to exploit the healthy state of French public opinion and make it work on behalf of European security in the face of Soviet intimidation and peace movement pressure will undermine this psychological distancing and weaken French resolve and support for nuclear deterrence. We should keep these risks in mind as we turn now to examine the current status of the peace movement in France and the prospects for its future evolution.

THE WEAKNESS OF THE FRENCH PEACE MOVEMENT

The peace movement as it has existed in France over the past three years has failed to rally significant popular support behind its positions, partly because of the nature of the political and social forces which constitute it.

The principal explanation for the extraordinary lack of strong pacifist and antinuclear currents of opinion in France has to do with the general popularity of the independent nuclear *force de dissuasion* begun by Guy Mollet and developed by General de Gaulle. With the acceptance of this force by the major parties of the Left, the PCF (in 1977) and the PS (in 1978), virtually no political space remained for the expression of opposition to French nuclear policy. Only the small, splinter-Left party, the *Parti Socialiste Unifie* (PSU) has maintained an unconditional rejection of nuclear weapons.

A second legacy of General de Gaulle, which has helped to spare France from the current crisis over nuclear deterrence, is the withdrawal from NATO's military wing, effected by de Gaulle in 1966. As a result, France was not affected directly by the NATO decision to deploy new intermediate-range American missiles on European soil.

Thus in France, peace activists have a singular difficulty in finding an issue that could arouse public fears and galvanize public interest in the dangers of the arms race. On the one hand, no major political figures or political parties are prepared to call into question French nuclear deterrent policy, a factor that severely hampers the credibility of the peace movement in France. On the other hand, the French people as a whole have apparently not felt themselves to be implicated in the U.S.-Soviet Euromissile crisis. The French terrain was therefore quite unfavorable to the development of the type of antinuclear and anti-American sentiment that has arisen in the other NATO countries, which have no deterrent force of their own and which are debating whether or not to accept new American missiles. Writes Pierre Hassner, it is thanks to the national consensus on the *force de frappe* "that politicians who are naturally anti-American—like Chevenement, for example—do not 'pass' over into pacifism."[25] So it is the Gaullist legacy of national nuclear deterrence and the semi-neutralist, even provincial, outlook this legacy has produced that accounts for the lack of urgency and panic characterizing French public opinion on the issue of nuclear weapons.

The extremely narrow political base of the peace movement in France constitutes its second major handicap. Elsewhere in Europe, particularly in Holland and the FRG, the strength of the movement owes itself to the fact that the antinuclear issue has virtually crossed all political boundaries; it has become an issue, in the eyes of its supporters, which transcends all political questions. In France, however, the antinuclear campaign has remained highly politicized, which accounts for its failure to attract an across-the-board audience. In particular, the organized movement has been confined to the margins of the political spectrum, to the increasingly narrow political space occupied by the French Communist Party. It has not achieved "critical mass."

Much has been made about Communist support and Soviet influence within the European-wide campaign, but most observers agree that the very appeal and success of the movement thus far has been due precisely to the fact that the Communists were quickly able to "drown" themselves, as it were, in a sea of millions of non-Communist pacifists and idealists united by an apolitical opposition to nuclear weapons. True, the European Communist parties, chiefly the German and the Dutch, were instrumental in instigating the antinuclear campaign, in getting it off the ground by preparing its themes and providing an infrastructure for popular mobilization. But, as Annie Kriegel has written in *Le Figaro*, success is measured by whether or not the movement is extended to wider segments of the population to the point where "the (communist) stamp begins to become indistinct and disappears behind a more respectable stamp . . ."[26]

This is precisely what has failed to happen in France. The original Communist-organized peace campaign, whose first public demonstration took place but eight days after the December 1979 NATO missile decision, has yet to extend itself to those elements which constitute the real strength and appeal of the movements elsewhere in Europe—the left wing of the

Socialists, traditionally pacifist-oriented Socialists, ecologists, and religious groups. These elements *do* exist in France, and the potential they embody for the emergence of a more powerful French peace and antinuclear campaign ought not to be underestimated. However, four factors have thus far prevented the coalescing of these elements into a movement that could mobilize their latent strength:

The Nature of the Official, Communist-Dominated Peace Movement

The *Mouvement de la Paix*, the French arm of the Soviet-led World Peace Council, is thoroughly dominated by the PCF. Although it is the most powerful peace organization in France, its appeal is severely limited by two handicaps imposed upon it by the PCF. First, it does not oppose unconditionally all nuclear weapons nor does it favor unilateral disarmament. Since 1977, when the PCF accepted the *force de frappe*, it abandoned its opposition to French nuclear weapons. Indeed, a reading of the voluminous literature of the *Mouvement de la Paix*, and an examination of press accounts of its activities and demonstrations, reveals *not a single* criticism of France's current nuclear force posture. This truly remarkable and glaring omission can only alienate the very audience which the PCF would like to attract—to wit, the idealist, leftist youth to whom all nuclear weapons, including French ones, are anathema, and for whom unilateral disarmament is an article of faith.

Secondly, the *Mouvement de la Paix* is, in spite of feeble efforts to appear somewhat evenhanded, not a politically neutral, unaligned movement. On the contrary, it is highly pro-Soviet and anti-American. Created in 1949, it cannot escape from the legacy of its Cold War parentage—i.e., the Stockholm Appeal "ban-the-bomb" ideology of the 1950s, with its vision of the world irrevocably divided into the aggressive, imperialist American camp and the Soviet camp, the "defenders of the peace."[27] This outlook is singularly unappealing to a French public which, on the Right and the Left, has taken cognizance of the reality of Soviet power and aggressive Soviet intentions, especially in the wake of the Afghanistan invasion. Moreover, the PCF thoroughly compromised itself before French public opinion when it came out in support of the Soviet invasion of Afghanistan.

Many observers expected that the Afghan crisis would undermine opposition in the West to NATO's rearmament plans, but it was only in France where this phenomenon occurred. Elsewhere, the reaction was precisely the opposite, for the Afghan crisis galvanized masses of people behind an effort to save detente and disarmament at any cost. In France, however, the blatant pro-Sovietism of the PCF undermined the credibility of its peace campaign, and alienated those forces which, in Germany, for example, were eager to support an honest, nonaligned effort to escape from the nuclear dilemma and the so-called logic of the blocs. Anyone in France who associated himself with the *Mouvement de la Paix*, the country's largest peace organization, could be easily discredited and found guilty by association with a pro-Soviet movement.

It is important to underline not simply the weak appeal which the *Mouvement de la Paix's* themes have exercised over the general public, but also its failure to mobilize those non-Communist elements of French society generally sympathetic to the cause of peace and disarmament. Not only has the *Mouvement* been completely silent on the question of French nuclear forces, it has also focused its attention in a one-sided, pro-Soviet manner on an issue—the INF controversy—that holds little interest for the French public. Finally, the limited appeal of the *Mouvement de la Paix* must be seen as another manifestation of the progressive political decline and marginalization of the French Communist party.

The Weakness of the French Ecology Movement

In Germany, the ecology party, the Greens, constitute what is perhaps the most influential element of the German peace movement. Their opposition to nuclear weapons was a direct consequence of their long campaign against the development of civil nuclear power. Moreover, the organizational strength, popular appeal, and political clout of their effective campaign against the German nuclear power program and on behalf of other environmental concerns (such as the extension of the Frankfurt airport) have been mobilized to the benefit of the equally formidable campaign against NATO's nuclear weapons deployment.

In France, a reverse phenomenon can be observed. The relative impotence of the French environmental movement has been matched by the failure of the movement to mobilize pro-ecology sentiment on behalf of a campaign against nuclear weapons. This is not to say that French society is coldly indifferent to environmental concerns, no more than it is to say that the French are untouched by pacifist and antinuclear sentiments. The problem, rather, is a historical one having to do with the traditional difficulties which grass-roots movements in France have encountered in trying to effect political change or penetrate the highly centralized, elitist, technocratic decision-making process.[28]

Throughout the 1970s, the French Green party achieved respectable results in both local and national elections. However, the French Greens have been consistently unable to thwart or modify France's almost unparalleled commitment to attain energy self-sufficiency via an aggressive development of civil nuclear power. Even the Socialist party, which was basically sympathetic to environmental concerns, has since coming to power continued almost unabated the policies of the preceding government on this issue. Moreover, the Socialists profess unabashedly their commitment to industrial growth and expansion, particularly of the high technology variety.

The Communist party has hoped to capitalize on the sense of disappointment and betrayal many environmentalists have felt in response to the Mitterrand government by enlisting them in its peace campaign. As we shall see, this effort is part and parcel of the PCF's plan to lay the groundwork for a future break with the PS and a mobilization of those elements of the French Left — both Communist and non-Communist — who will inevitably become disaffected by the compromises with reality that the Socialists are obliged to make while in power and which make participation in the Cabinet a source of increasing discomfort to Communists.

In fact, this issue points towards an even more fundamental difference between the French and German situations. This has to do with the plethora of extraparliamentary, autonomous social movements which emerged in Germany, particularly in the post-1968 period. What Pierre Hassner has referred to as the persistence of the romantic counterculture in Germany, with its rejection of industrial growth, technology, and existing political structures has no counterpart of significant influence in France. The difference between the two countries in this respect is due primarily to the diverging political fortunes of their two major Socialist parties, the SPD and the PS. The SPD, over the course of its thirteen-year rule, was obliged to follow a pragmatic line and remain close to the center of the German political spectrum. This, in turn, produced alienation on the part of many of its most leftist and youthful supporters, a feeling of betrayal and exclusion from the political process. In the final analysis, the pressure from the radical Left could not help but have a radicalizing effect on the SPD itself; and this leftward shift culminated in its fall from power and electoral setback of March 1983.

In France, the political trajectory of the PS over the last few years has been in a reverse direction, leading it towards greater pragmatism and moderation on both foreign and domestic issues. Disaffection may ultimately set in on the PS Left, but it is probably too early for that to happen yet. Before coming to power in 1981, the PS embodied at least some of the hopes of the romantic, idealistic Left; hence there was no great pressure for the formation of extraparliamentary, radical social movements. The party's platform included many of the libertarian concerns of the New Left, such as ecology, *autogestion*, and decentralization. Moreover, grassroots pressure groups faced more daunting structural obstacles in exerting political influence than did their counterparts in Germany. The prospect of an imminent Left victory at the polls throughout the 1970s tended to inspire optimism, rather than alienated pessimism, about the possibilities for social change in France.

The fact that the Socialists were so late in coming to power in France thus explains why they have been relatively untouched by the process of radicalization which has characterized their sister parties in the Socialist International. Moreover, their victory was greeted with expressions of joy; it was regarded as signalling the imminent realization of romantic hopes and dreams. The French Socialists were given enough breathing space after their victory to pursue their aggressively pro-nuclear power, pro-nuclear deterrence policies with little or no opposition from the Left in general. Even the PCF, coopted into the government, has had to remain circumspect.

Thus the French ecologists have found themselves confined to the political wilderness in recent years. They have been somewhat divided over the nuclear weapons issue with their leader, Brice Lalonde, having expressed qualified support for French deterrence policy.[29] Lastly, the Communists' attempt to coopt them into their own peace movement has been extremely problematic, given the PCF's commitment to both the civilian uses of nuclear power and the *force de frappe*.

The Weakness of Church Influence in the French Peace Movement

In Germany, in the United States, and above all in Holland, the organized, mostly Protestant churches have exercised a decisive influence in mobilizing mass support on behalf of the peace and antinuclear campaign. By questioning the morality not only of nuclear war but also of nuclear deterrence doctrines, they have helped to transform an issue that has traditionally been a province of the Left into one which cuts across all political and social boundaries. The almost irresistible appeal of the peace movement has perhaps been due to this joining of the debate over the morality of deterrence to the debate over the mechanics of deterrence.

In France, however, the churches have so far played an almost negligible role in the nuclear debate. There are perhaps sociological factors which account for this phenomenon; for example, the long anticlerical tradition and the precipitate decline in church attendance in France in the postwar era. Perhaps the most important factor is that French Catholicism, in Hassner's words, is "more cynical than puritanical"—that is, it is more accepting of the logic of *raison d'état*, less inclined to demand of the state an adherence to a Weberian ethic of absolute ends, than are its Protestant counterparts.[30] Moreover, the Catholic church in France refuses to divorce the debate over morality of nuclear weapons from the question of responsibility in facing up to the totalitarian threat. A statement on peace and disarmament, issued by the French bishops in November 1983, carried the following passages:

Nobody wants war. . . . Yet some countries are bent on reaping the benefits of warfare without paying the price of war: By brandishing its threat, they make permanent use of blackmail. While former democracies are kept by force within the Soviet bloc, the Western democracies are subject to constant pressure to neutralize them and to bring them, if possible, into the sphere of influence of Marxist-Leninist ideology. The latter, convinced that it holds the secret to the total liberation of mankind and of nations, thinks itself mandated to impose upon all what it believes to be the greatest good.

There is no question here of cultivating a Manichaean view of the world—all the evil on one side, all the good on the other. The West is also ailing. Materialism—whether theoretical, as in communist societies, or practical, as in the West—is a deadly disease of humanity. And Marxist-Leninist states do not hold a monopoly on imperialism. Sometimes they gain a following even within the systems that oppose them most strenuously. But it would be unfair to simply state and accept the conflict of ideologies while closing one's eyes to the domineering and aggressive character of Marxism-Leninism, which holds that everything, even a nation's hopes for peace, must be used as a tool for world conquest.

Given those conditions, should there be no absolute condemnation of all warfare but not peace-loving nations at the mercy of those animated by an ideology of domination? In their efforts to avoid war, peaceful nations could fall prey to other forms of violence and injustice: colonization, alienation, deprivation of freedom and identity. Pushed to its ultimate consequences, peace at any price leads a nation to all sorts of capitulations. Unilateral disarmament could even encourage aggressive behavior on the part of neighbors by presenting them with the temptation of an easy prey.[31]

This does not mean that French Catholics are indifferent to the nuclear debate. On the contrary, the Catholic peace organization, *Pax Christi de France*, has argued, much like the American Bishops, that the church has both a right and a duty to speak out on the nuclear issue. Like the American Bishops, the French hierarchy condemns the use of nuclear weapons against population centers. It even points out the contradiction between the prodisarmament rhetoric of the Socialist government and its actual program for the modernization of French nuclear forces:

the Churches would like to emphasize the dangers which exist for the future of democracy in France of too great a difference between the language employed by her leaders and the reality of the policy they pursue.[32]

Nevertheless, in terms of concrete proposals, the French Catholic church does not go nearly as far as its American and Dutch sister churches. It argues for disarmament, but it insists that the disarmament be "general, reciprocal, and controlled."[33] This prudent recommendation flows from the following premise:

> . . . the security of Europe is founded on a balance of forces which it would be dangerous to modify unilaterally. Finally, and with profound anguish and a certain sense of scandal, [the French Churches] recognize that nuclear weapons play a decisive role in organizing the defense of the Northern Hemisphere and that, in France, nuclear deterrence, sometimes challenged in particular by numerous Christians, is the object of a majoritarian con

While urging the Mitterrand government to assume an a   in promoting world disarmament, the French bishops do not expect rapid progress in that direction under prevailing international conditions. For the present, they support the moral right of a state to pursue a policy of nuclear deterrence. Since they clearly disagree with what seems to be the teaching of the U.S. bishops — namely that it is immoral to threaten to do that which it is immoral to do in fact — their statement warrants quoting at length:

> The central question thus becomes the following: Given the context of the current geopolitical situation, does a country that is threatened in its existence, its liberty or its identity have a moral right to meet the threat with an effective counterthreat, even if that counterthreat is nuclear?

> Until now, while stressing the possible consequences of such a parry and the terrible risks it entails, the Catholic Church has not felt the necessity to condemn it. Such logic, of course, is the logic of distress, and its weakness is obvious. Of course, it is to avoid having to wage war that one wants to show oneself capable of waging it. One does serve the cause of peace in deterring an aggressor by inspiring in him, through fear, a minimum of wisdom. The threat of violence does not constitute violence. That is the basis of dissuasion, and it is something we often forget when we attribute the same moral status to the threat as to the use of violence.

> Nevertheless the dangers of the logic of dissuasion are obvious. To leave the potential aggressor no doubt as to the credibility of one's defense, one must show oneself to be firm in one's resolve to resort to action if dissuasion fails. Moreover, the moral legitimacy of resorting to action is more than unclear — especially in France, where our deterrence is that of the weak facing the powerful, a "poor man's deterrence" which relies on a wholesale threat: for lack of means, it is compelled to threaten cities; and that is a strategy the council condemns, clearly and finally. . . .

> Yet the threat does not constitute use. Does the immorality of use entail the immorality of the threat? Not necessarily. For according to the council, "We cannot set aside the complexities of the situation as it stands." Given the state of violence and sin in which the world exists, it is the duty of politicians and

military officials to defuse the blackmail to which the nation could be subjected.[35]

The Absence of the *Parti Socialiste*

The evolution of PS thinking on detente and disarmament which brought the party into open conflict with the European peace movement and led it to eschew participation in the French antinuclear campaign accounts, more than any other factor, for the signal failure of the French peace movement to reach the type of mass audience enjoyed by its European counterparts. Elsewhere in Europe, the Social Democratic parties have become over the past three years Moscow's preferred partners on security issues. Whereas Willy Brandt returned from Moscow to exclaim that Brezhnev "trembled for peace," François Mitterrand has refused to allow a full normalization of Franco-Soviet relations in the absence of progress on the Afghan, Polish, and SS-20 issues. Why, then, the uniqueness of the *Parti Socialiste Français*?

The first explanation must be searched for in the history of the Left in France. There are, in effect, several competing traditions on the issues of defense, patriotism, and pacifism. The French workers' movement has traditionally manifested an internationalist, pacifist outlook which dates back to the period of the Commune. Until the outbreak of WWI, in particular, the French Socialists regarded war as strictly a capitalist phenomenon, contrary to the interests of the working class.

However, the French Left can point to another tradition, one in which the interests of the Left are equated with defense of *la patrie*. This tradition goes all the way back to the aggressive patriotism of the Revolutionary period, and it tends to legitimize an unabashed commitment to the defense of France. "Defendre la Revolution," "defendre le socialisme": These two slogans demonstrate the emotional power which the appeal to past traditions can have in mobilizing support among the Left's electorate for a strong defense effort. Such an appeal to the memory of the Revolution and to the memory of Jean Jaures can be particularly powerful when the Left is in power.

The long experience that the Left has had in power at successive intervals in French history has tended to produce a somewhat cynical attitude toward the requirements of statecraft which helps to temper the native idealism of the Left. Perhaps this cynicism also has something to do with a sense of responsibility toward remaining faithful to France's status as a great power, to its traditional role on the stage of world politics. This constitutes a great contrast with Germany for, as Michael Bosquet argues, "the Germans (quite differently from the French, notably) have never experienced a world-wide vocation. We have forgotten that they are, in many respects, less Western than the Poles or the Czechs."[36] Thus the desire to maintain the role of France as a great power, common to governments of the Right and the Left, leads the Socialists to subordinate their disarmament rhetoric to the interests of balance of power politics. The German Social Democrats, on the other hand, feel they have much less at stake, much less to lose, in coming to an "arrangement" with the great power to the East, which holds the key to a possible reunification of the German nation. Remarks German peace activist, Rudolf Bahro, "Why should we object to a 'Finlandization' of Europe?"[37] For the French Socialists, however, such a prospect would have catastrophic consequences for the future of both the Socialist experiment in France and for national independence. This prospect produces a Socialist *realpolitik* and an appeal to the tradition of a militant Jacobin patriotism.

Many intellectuals on the German Left have lashed out at the PS for its self-interested criticism of the German peace movement, for its cynical support of the Kohl government, and for its alleged betrayal of Socialist ideals. While there is indeed a healthy measure of national egoism in forming the PS's opposition to the peace and antinuclear campaign, there exist, nevertheless, profound philosophical differences between the PS and the SPD over their respective evaluations of the nature of the Soviet regime. In other words, the German desire to reach an accommodation with the Soviet Union which might alienate the FRG's sovereignty can not be explained merely as a function of German indifference towards enjoying the status of a great power, but also as a manifestation of fundamental ignorance of the totalitarian phenomenon.

In France, on the other hand, the evolution of the PS in an anti-Communist direction was one of the most significant developments on the French political scene of the past decade. This change was first produced in reaction to the great and tumultuous events of May 1968 when, at what appeared to be a revolutionary moment in French history, the Communist party revealed itself to be deeply conservative, a force of order opposed to radical change. With the creation of the PS in 1971, many of the libertarian, anti-Leninist ideals of the post–May 1968 period were taken up by the new party. The vision of a socialism at once radical and libertarian, with its ideals of decentralization and *autogestion*, helped the PS to attract voters on the Left from the PCF to the point where, by the end of the 1970s, it had supplanted the PCF as France's major Leftist party. Moreover, the PS's new anti-Leninist ideology was more than reinforced by the party's decade-long alliance with the PCF, especially when the latter deliberately torpedoed the Left's election hopes in the 1978 campaign. François Mitterrand undoubtedly learned much from his often bitter alliance with a party that takes its orders from Moscow. His goal—largely already realized and a major historical achievement—was, in Mitterrand's own words, "to create the conditions such that the Communist party itself be put in a situation where it cannot do what it wants to do, but it will do what it can do."[38]

The second major factor influencing the PS's movement towards anti-communism is what Pierre Hassner has termed, the "Solzenhitsyn effect" — that is, the irresistible influence of the testimony of Soviet and East-bloc dissidents on the true, totalitarian nature of the Soviet regime.[39] Their testimony, in fact, dealt perhaps a definitive blow to the illusions of all those on the French Left, outside the PCF, who still looked somewhat fondly on the "homeland of the Revolution." The emergence on the French scene of the Soviet dissidents in the early to mid 1970s, the phenomenon of the "New Philosophers" in 1977–1978, and the Soviet Afghanistan invasion of 1979 all helped to cement a new view of the Soviet Union as a totalitarian and predatory regime just as the PS was nearing the conquest of power in France. At the PS's party congress in Valence in October 1981, the Soviet delegation led by Boris Ponomarev was roundly booed![40]

This changed view of the Soviet Union has contributed directly towards the wariness and outright hostility of the PS towards the European peace movement. Writes Hassner, "most of our intellectuals with antinuclear sympathies . . . remain vigilant in their anti-totalitarian struggle.[41] This points to a startling contrast between the positions of the PS and those of the SPD's left wing on the issue of the link between disarmament in the West and liberalization in the East. In Germany, hundreds of thousands demonstrated against the visit to Berlin of Alexander Haig, but only tens of thousands demonstrated against Brezhnev's visit, and an equally paltry number took to the streets against Jaruzelski's coup. In France, the numbers have been reversed: great demonstrations on behalf of Solidarity, less significant ones against NATO.[42]

The left wing of the SPD opts for the priority of disarmament over armed vigilance in facing the Soviet threat and in overcoming Soviet domination of Eastern Europe. Rudolf Bahro has declared that,

> In the event we were to take our distance from America and if Western Europe would be ready to accept its own denuclearization, would it be unthinkable that the USSR would consent, in exchange, to liberate the Eastern countries from their present limited sovereignty?[43]

Such a declaration runs completely contrary to the point of view of the *Parti Socialiste*. For the French Socialists, Soviet domination of Eastern Europe is a product not of security paranoia, but of the inner logic of a totalitarian system which cannot abide the existence of an independent, democratic, socially autonomous neighbor which would undermine the legitimacy of Communist rule throughout the Soviet Empire. In a polemic with Bahro, the French Socialist intellectual, Andre Gorz, retorted:

Do not the lords of Soviet imperialism perhaps feel more threatened by the example of an independent trade union movement or of independent intellectuals (e.g., in Prague), who demand basic rights, than by our pig-headed military apparatus so alienating our peoples?[44]

In the final analysis, both the concern for jealously protecting French independence and the sense of duty towards dissidents and liberalization efforts in Eastern Europe have led the French Socialists to opposite conclusions on how to deal with the Soviet Union from those of the German Social Democrats. Further, the PS is engaged in an open effort to thwart Soviet designs on Europe, and thus it is unthinkable that the party should lend its support to a movement which, unwittingly or not, tends to serve Soviet interests. And in the case of the PCF-dominated French peace movement, the servility, of course has not been so unwitting.

The very elements which constitute the strength of the peace movements elsewhere in Europe — ecologists, churches, and socialists of every variety — that is, those elements which submerge Communist participation and help to create a broad-based appeal, are those whose participation is weakest in France. Until now, these elements have been discouraged from participating in a movement dominated by the Communists and frowned upon by the Socialist hierarchy, which remarkably fails to address the issue of French nuclear weapons. Nevertheless, the "army" of idealistic peace marchers does exist at the grass-roots level. A public opinion poll in November 1981 demonstrated that fully 50% of the French declare their solidarity with the pacifist movement.[45] The real question to be answered, now that the European peace movement has targeted France for special attention, is whether or not the *Parti Socialiste* will be able to keep the lid on the pacifist and antinuclear sentiment which exists within its own rank and file.

FUTURE PROSPECTS OF THE FRENCH PEACE MOVEMENT

The PCF, with uncanny foresight, had ordered the revival of the *Mouvement de la Paix* as early as 1978.[46] The goal of the movement was twofold: first, to mobilize French public opinion against NATO's missile deployment and second, to appropriate the peace issue to the benefit of the PCF during the presidential campaign, thereby isolating François Mitterrand. The peace issue was thus one among others which the PCF would attempt to exploit throughout the campaign in an effort to depict Mitterrand as a fraudulent leftist. At the December 20, 1979 peace rally, Mitterrand was denounced as an "accomplice to NATO."[47]

Once François Mitterrand was firmly established at the Elysee Palace, however, and once Communist ministers were included in the new government, the PCF was obliged to interpret the Socialist triumph as indeed a victory of the Left. Governmental solidarity also demanded a silencing of public criticism. Nevertheless, the campaign of the *Mouvement de la Paix*, with its pronounced anti-NATO bias, constituted an implicit critique of Mitterrand's forceful support of the NATO position in the Euromissile crisis. Moreover, the Communists broke ranks with Mitterrand's party during 1983 by supporting Andropov's call for including French and British nuclear weapons in the INF negotiations.

After Mitterrand's victory, then, the PCF was forced to tone down the public rhetoric of its peace campaign without, however, modifying its two principal aims: to use the movement to promote Soviet negotiating positions and to advance the political interests of the PCF at a tactical level. In terms of the latter goal, the aim has first been to exploit the peace issue in an innocuous manner in order to demonstrate the party's continued ability to mobilize its own rank and file. This it has more or less accomplished with the two major demonstrations it has organized since the 1981 elections. On October 25, 1981, between 30,000 and 50,000 demonstrated in a Paris peace march, and on June 20, 1982, a march designed to coincide with the UN special session on disarmament attracted over 200,000 supporters.

Nevertheless, the PCF has thus far failed to make significant progress towards achieving its longer-range goal, one which, incidentally, coincides with Soviet ambitions. That is to give the movement the type of broad-based social dimension its counterparts have enjoyed elsewhere in Europe. The party has been hampered in this effort by its continued participation in the Socialist government. But the groundwork must be prepared for this eventuality, and it is significant to note in this respect that the only theme consistently—in fact, repeatedly—sounded by the *Mouvement de la Paix* that could have a concrete bearing on the French situation is an unconditional opposition to the enhanced radiation warhead, often misnamed the "neutron bomb." One other interesting possibility is suggested by the fact that a principal leader of the *Mouvement de la Paix*, Pierre-Luc Seguillon, is a member of the PS and, in particular, its extreme left-wing faction, the C.E.R.E.S. This faction favors the retention of the *force de frappe*, but it advocates a strictly neutralist, nonaligned, anti-American foreign policy for France. With the recent departure from the government of Jean-Pierre Chevenement, the leader of the C.E.R.E.S., the possibility opens up—for the day when the PCF will return into opposition—of a Communist-left wing Socialist alliance which could hope to mobilize the Left against Mitterrand's pro-NATO policies. A decision by the government to produce the neutron warhead could be particularly explosive in this context.

There is no doubt that the PCF has proven itself to be woefully inadequate to the realization of its long-range task. Now that both Moscow and the European antinuclear campaigns have begun to cast a watchful eye on the French situation, the French peace movement can be expected to concentrate its fire, either directly or indirectly, on Francois Mitterrand, his support of NATO's negotiating position, and his refusal to consider the inclusion of French nuclear forces in the Eurostrategic negotiations.

The first step taken towards the constitution of a more credible and influential peace movement in France came with the decision by the European movements to bypass the *Mouvement de la Paix* and recognize a federation of peace groups, *Comités pour le desarmament nucleaire en Europe* (CODENE) as their only true and legitimate counterparts in France.[48] What is common to the more than twenty organizations gathered under the CODENE banner is the fact that they are nonaligned or neutralist, and that they reject all forms of nuclear weapons. As their name indicates, they aspire towards a complete denuclearization of Europe. This puts them in direct opposition to the pronuclear stance of both the PS and the PCF, and it also constitutes a rejection of both the *Mouvement de la Paix's* pro-Sovietism, and the pro-NATO stance of the Mitterrand government.

Two organizations in particular regrouped under the CODENE banner demonstrate the type of audience which the independent French peace movements will seek to influence in the mid-1980s, namely those elements of the Left and counter-Left which are traditionally attracted by pacifist and antinuclear appeals, and who may feel themselves to have been somewhat betrayed by the defense policies of the Socialist government. The new approach thus constitutes an attempt to undermine the authority of the Mitterrand government by appealing over the heads of the Socialist hierarchy to the party's own constituency, to ecological groups, and to the non-Communist forces to the left of the PS. Moreover, this attempt has been aided and abetted by Yuri Andropov's effort to pressure France into bringing her nuclear forces to the negotiating table.

The *Parti Socialiste Unifie* (PSU) is the only major party of the Left not to have embraced the French nuclear deterrent force. As such, the party stands to gain much in the event of a dramatic increase in antinuclear sentiment in France. The PSU's positions are remarkably close to some of the old discarded themes of the PS itself. It condemns the imperialist bloc-policy of both superpowers and argues for a neutralist France to be "aligned" only with the nonaligned Third World. Finally, the PSU favors unilateral French nuclear disarmament and wants especially to prevent the formation of a Franco-German bloc centered on a French nuclear guarantee.[49]

The other group of especial interest within the ranks of the CODENE is the *Mouvement pour une alternative nonviolente* (MAN). MAN is an avowedly antipacifist organization; it believes in France's right to legitimate self-defense but opposes the Fifth Republic's reliance on nuclear deterrence. It does so first of all on the grounds that French deterrence will not work because it is based on a bluff which the adversary knows is not credible.[50]

Secondly, MAN opposes French deterrence policy on ideological grounds, and it is here that the group's ideas may strike the PS in a vulnerable area. It argues, in particular, that nuclear weapons help to maintain an elitist, technocratic, and militarized society, which by definition must be undemocratic and unsocialist. Instead, MAN proposes a defense policy in harmony with the Socialists' goals of social transformation, one which, unlike nuclear defense, does not lead to a demobilization of the people, but rather calls upon the people to participate in their own defense. MAN urges that France move gradually, through a process called *transarmement*, to "another defense . . . which would substitute for false nuclear deterrence a deterrent based on the determination of the people to defend itself against a potential aggressor."[51] MAN points to several historical examples, such as the Swiss and Yugoslav models, to demonstrate the feasibility of "popular defense." It is worth noting that Defense Minister Charles Hernu, before coming into office, espoused similar ideas, without, however, advocating the abandonment of the *force de frappe*.

CONCLUSION

What are the prospects in the coming year for the French "peace movement" to break out of its lethargy and emerge as a legitimate equivalent of the comparable movements in the FRG, Holland, Great Britain, and the United States? Will it, as the European peace movements and the Soviets desire, be able to force France to accept that her nuclear forces be counted at the Geneva Eurostrategic negotiations? Will it be able to arrest the development of Franco-German military cooperation? Will it be able to undermine the French national consensus on nuclear deterrence? In short, will it be able to roll back the defense policies of François Mitterrand, and those of his predecessor governments under the Fifth Republic?

The answers to these questions can only be highly tentative and speculative in nature. Much depends on the political, diplomatic, and economic developments of the coming year. The least that can be said with certainty is that President Mitterrand will surely be subject to a type of domestic and international pressure which his predecessors never knew.

A key element in these developments is the new political path chosen by the French Communist party in July 1984, when the four PCF ministers resigned from the government in a dispute over the Socialists' steel industry restructuring plan, forcing Mitterrand to resort to a referendum in September 1984 for a strengthened mandate. This choice depended on several factors, including Mitterrand's economic policies, pressure from Moscow, and tactical considerations. Most observers had long expected the Communists to leave the government sooner or later, simply because Marchais' party had been steadily losing popularity for being tied to Mitterrand, who was sounding less and less like a Socialist. Their freedom of radical maneuver has been greatly enhanced.

However, the most important variable continues to be the Socialist party itself, both within the hierarchy and among the rank and file. An ominous note was struck with the departure of Research and Industry Minister J. P. Chevenement from the government. If bickering and dissension break out at the top of the PS, as it began to do even prior to the 1983 elections, they are bound to have a disquieting effect on the fidelity and enthusiasm shown toward Mitterrand's policies throughout the base. It is in this manner that the dikes could be eroded which until now have resisted the expression of the genuine pacifist and antinuclear sentiments held by a large percentage of the Socialist electorate.

Lastly, the future of the peace movement in France will depend upon the policies and political fortune of François Mitterrand. Certainly he will not be able to avoid provoking some dismay and disappointment as he grapples with France's severe economic woes. However, he displayed a remarkable degree of political astuteness in retaining Pierre Mauroy as prime minister and in keeping the PCF as long as he did in the role of a decidedly junior partner. He has managed up to mid-1984 to cover his vulnerable left flank all the while steering his economic course in the opposite direction. Henceforth that task will be more difficult.

Mitterrand's message to the Western allies during the missile deployment crisis has been a consistently firm one. In his January 1983 address to the Bundestag in Bonn, referred to earlier, he said: "Whoever gambles on the decoupling of the European continent from the American continent would call into question the maintenance of equilibrium and . . . of peace."[52] The French president's words from the podium of the Parliament were interpreted as a warning that Europe "must not be deprived of means to answer the nuclear weapons specifically directed against her," and that West Germany had become the weak point in the struggle that was shaping up over the future of Europe because so many Germans were tempted to pursue a pacifist, neutralist course in the hope of achieving reunification. Mitterrand's principal fear appeared to be that West Germany, which in the past had sometimes been thought by French observers to be too subservient to the United States and too rigidly pro-NATO, might now disturb the balance of power in Europe by tilting too far toward an accommodation with the East — one that would pose dangers to French security if it led to a diminution of the U.S. strategic commitment to the Continent. Inasmuch as the SPD, along with the Greens, wanted French nuclear forces taken into account in the Geneva negotiations, Mitterrand found himself closer to Chancellor Helmut Kohl and the CDU than to the West German Socialists.[53]

At the summit meeting of the leaders of the world's seven principal industrial democracies, held at Williamsburg, Virginia in May 1983, Mitterrand had reservations about the idea of converting an economic conference into a super-NATO for the purpose of reiterating the Western position on Euromissile deployment and arms control negotiations.[54] Perhaps some of his reservations were intended as bargaining counters on economic policies, but others were due to a reluctance to be seen as too closely associated with the NATO powers, for which he was under severe criticism from his Communist coalition partners. The French delegation at Williamsburg contributed to drafting a statement somewhat more conciliatory in its approach to the Soviet Union than other recent alliance communiqués. Mitterrand finally subscribed to a text in which the seven declared their intention to "maintain sufficient military strength to deter any attack, to counter any threat and to ensure the peace." Western arms, vowed the leaders, will never be used except in response to aggression. They urged the USSR to cooperate toward meaningful, equal, and verifiable arms reductions and warned that Soviet efforts "to divide the West by proposing inclusion of the deterrent forces of third countries, such as those of France and the United Kingdom, will fail," because "consideration of these systems has no place in the INF negotiations."[55]

The seven reaffirmed their openness to negotiating a balanced INF agreement. At a press conference, Mitterrand said that it was useful to go back to the basic premises concerning the balance of forces in Europe, and not to add new elements that would complicate further the approach to negotiations. With regard to the Summit Communiqué assertion that the level of missile deployment would be determined by the negotiations and that, in the absence of an agreement the allies would proceed with the planned deployments, Mitterrand noted that this was exactly what he had said in his Bundestag address.[56]

Later, when the campaign against the installation of the NATO missiles neared its hysterical climax, the French president urged the Western allies to remain firm and to keep stating their position clearly. Speaking in Brussels in October 1983, he said: "I'm against the Euromissiles. But I notice two terribly simple things about the current debate: Pacifism is in the West and the Euromissiles are in the East. I consider that an unequal relationship."[57] A month later, he described the trial of strength through which the East and the West were passing as the most serious international crisis of the last two decades. He predicted that the Soviet Union would walk out of the Geneva INF talks when the deployment of Pershing II and cruise missiles began, but he also expressed the opinion that the rupture would not be permanent.[58]

Once NATO had demonstrated its ability to carry out its decision, Mitterrand began to play the role of conciliator, calling on both superpowers to return to the bargaining table. He displayed his even-handedness by cautioning the West against offering special inducements to Moscow to resume negotiations, while advising the United States not to create "new causes of dissension" in East-West relations just when the new Chernenko government might be reassessing the advantages of renewing talks with the West on arms control and other issues.[59] During his visit to Moscow in June 1984, Mitterrand showed no signs of softening his tough stand on the USSR. He publicly toasted Andrei Sakharov, criticized his hosts for failing to live up to the Helsinki Accords of 1975 on human rights, and made needling remarks about Poland, Afghanistan, and Vietnam which were not reported by *Pravda*.

Now that the Communists have left the government, the *Parti Socialiste* may come under mounting pressure to tilt leftward. But Mitterrand has at his disposal certain weapons which he might use to parry Communist leverage. To Soviet threats and blandishments he can respond with an appeal to patriotism and national independence. To charges of pro-Americanism and subordination to NATO, he can respond with a higher-profile socialist diplomacy in the Third World. Another major factor which is entirely under Mitterrand's control is the decision whether or not to produce the neutron warhead. Since many observers assume that a favorable decision has already all but been made, the real question may be over whether to announce it now, in the present context. Such a decision could precipitate a major, debilitating debate on French nuclear policy at a most unpropitious moment — a moment in which the French peace movement is still searching for an issue around which it can mobilize public support.

The last, and perhaps all-important, variable is the state of the French economy. Both Mitterrand's personal authority and his ability to govern after the referendum of September 1984 will depend upon a restoration of the economy's health. Without a change for the better, the unity of the PS at the top will begin to come apart, thus removing what has thus far been the most powerful bulwark against the rise of pacifist and antinuclear sentiment from below. Moreover, a robust economy is, after all, the *sine qua non* of a continued and vigorous French effort in the fields of national defense and security. If French economic troubles mount to the breaking point, the present French consensus on nuclear deterrence may collapse, popular opposition to defense spending may rise, and antinuclear pacifism may well become more fashionable than it has hitherto been. Should this happen, an important source of political support for NATO's "two-track" approach to modernization and arms control negotiations will begin to dissolve.

NOTES

1. Michael Binyon, "Mitterrand tells Bonn to stand firm with NATO," *The Times*, January 21, 1983; Bernard Brigouleix, "Les socialistes allemands se démarquent des thèses de M. Mitterrand sur la sécurite européenne," *Le Monde*, 24 Janvier, 1982, p. 1.
2. "Convention Nationale sur la Défense," *Le Point et la Rose* (Paris: Organe du Parti Socialiste, Juin 1979) pp. 30–31.

3. *Stern*, July 9, 1981, in *Défense Nationale*, Octobre 1981, p. 175.
4. *Le Monde*, 28 Mai 1982, p. 8.
5. *Le Monde*, 4 Juin 1982, p. 3.
6. *Agence France Presse*, 26 Mai 1982.
7. *Le Point*, 403 (9 Juin 1980), pp. 51–52.
8. "Les Débats," *Défense Nationale*, Décembre 1982, p. 92.
9. *Le Monde*, 12 Février 1982, p. 28.
10. Ibid.
11. Pierre Lellouche, "Réplique à . . . Gabriel Robin," in *Le Monde*, 26 Janvier 1983, p. 2.
12. Ibid.
13. Cheysson before the National Assembly, November 19, 1981, in *Défense Nationale*, Janvier 1982, p. 179.
14. Jacques Huntzinger, "La Politique Extérieure du Parti Socialiste," *Politique Étrangère*, No. 1, Mars 1982, p. 37.
15. *New York Times*, January 3, 1982.
16. French television, January 30, 1982, in *Défense Nationale*, Mars 1982, p. 182. Emphasis added.
17. *Le Monde*, 10 Juin 1982, p. 11.
18. PS document on "La Paix, la Sécurité, et le Désarmament," in *Le Monde*, 4 Juin 1982, p. 3.
19. Christian Mellon, "Le nouveau mouvement de la paix européenne," in *Projet*, 167, Juillet–Août 1982, p. 841.
20. Jacques Almaric, "Andropov as Viewed by Cheysson: A Cold and Tough Negotiator," *Le Monde*, 23 February 1983, in *Foreign Broadcast Information Service*, 23 February 1983, pp. K3–K4.
21. Raymond Aron, "Paris et Bonn face aux SS-20," *L'Express* 1647, 4 Février 1983, p. 39.
22. *Boston Globe*, March 9, 1983, p. 12.
23. Jacques Huntzinger, "L'Esprit de Défense en France," in *Défense Nationale*, Décembre 1982, p. 40.
24. *Le Monde*, 4 Juin 1982, p. 3.
25. Interview in *Le Nouvel Observateur*, 26 June 1982, p. 38.
26. Annie Kriegel, "Le P.C.F. et le Mouvement de la Paix," *Le Figaro*, 24–25 Octobre 1981.
27. Patrick Jarreau, "Le Mouvement de la paix et les autres," *Le Monde*, 24 Octobre 1981.
28. Dorothy Welkin and Michael Pollak, *The Atom Besieged* (Cambridge: MIT Press, 1982), p. 121.
29. Mellon, p. 840.
30. Pierre Hassner, *Arms Control and the Politics of Pacifism in Protestant Europe*, International Security Studies Program, Working Paper Number 31, Woodrow Wilson International Center for Scholars, October 1981, p. 35.
31. Excerpts from the document "Win the Peace" in "French Bishops Face Up to Nuclear Peril," *Wall Street Journal*, November 25, 1983.
32. *Le Désarmement*. Point de vue d'Églises chrétiennes de France, 2 Juillet 1982, p. 2.
33. *Le Journal de la Paix*, January 1982, p. 4.
34. *Le Désarmement*, p. 2.
35. "Win the Peace," *Wall Street Journal*, November 25, 1983.
36. Michel Bosquet, "La 'Finlandisation' de l'Europe?" in *Le Nouvel Observateur*, 26 June 1982, p. 36.
37. Rudolf Bahro, "Pour un refus de toute force de dissuasion nucléaire," in *Le Nouvel Observateur*, 26 June 1982, p. 37.
38. François Mitterrand, *Politique 2*, quoted in René Rémond, "Politique 2 de François Mitterrand," *Le Monde*, 21 Janvier 1982, p. 10.
39. Interview in *Le Nouvel Observateur*, 26 June 1982, p. 38.

40. Richard Eder, "Pacifism Sans France," *New York Times*, November 12, 1981, p. 10.
41. Interview in *Le Nouvel Observateur*, 26 June 1982, p. 38.
42. Pierre Hassner, "L'Eurogauche Entre les Euromissiles et la Pologne," *Politique Etrangère*, no. 1, Mars 1982, p. 102.
43. Bahro, *Le Nouvel Observateur*, 26 June 1982, p. 37.
44. Andre Gorz, "What, Then, Is Freedom? Reply to Bahro," in *Telos*, 51 (Spring 1982), p. 127.
45. Mellon, p. 840.
46. *Le Point*, 475 (26 Octobre 1981), p. 85.
47. Branto Lazitch, "Pandemic Pacifism," *L'Express*, 31 July–6 August 1981, pp. 46–48, *Foreign Broadcast Information Service*, 10 September 1981, p. 3.
48. Mellon, p. 841.
49. *Pour Une France Non-Alignée*, Les Propositions du P.S.U. (Paris: Syros, 1981), p. 22.
50. "Défense: le nucleaire contre le socialisme," Supplément à *Non-Violence Politique*, no. 53 (Montargis: 1982), p. 2.
51. Ibid., p. 4.
52. Quoted in "Playing Nuclear Poker," Special Report, *Time*, January 31, 1983.
53. John Vinocur, "Missile Debate Widens," *New York Times*, January 24, 1983; William Drozdisk, "Mitterrand Gives Boost to Kohl in Speech on Arms," *Washington Post*, January 21, 1983.
54. Maurice Delarue, "Declaration de Williamsburg sur la sécurité suscite de serieuses reserves de la part de M. Mitterrand," *Le Monde*, May 31, 1983.
55. "Text of Summit Arms Control Statement," *Washington Post*, May 30, 1983.
56. Maurice Delarue, "M. Mitterrand demand que la negociation reste ouverte," *Le Monde*, June 1, 1983.
57. John Vinocur, "Mitterrand Presses NATO to Be Firm," *New York Times*, October 15, 1983.
58. Michael Dobbs, "Mitterrand Tells West: Maintain Missiles Resolve," *Washington Post*, November 17, 1983.
59. Richard Bernstein, "Mitterrand Bids U.S. Not Rile Moscow," *New York Times*, March 24, 1984.

Chapter 8

European Antinuclear Movements and the NATO "Double-Track" Decision: Implications for Future Alliance Strategy and Force Posture

Jacquelyn K. Davis

Although it was a unanimous decision of the Ministerial Council of the North Atlantic Treaty Organization, the intention to deploy in Western Europe 572 new generation intermediate nuclear weapons, in the absence of agreement at the Geneva arms control negotiations to dismantle the Soviet SS-20s deployed since 1977, provoked controversy among NATO members and deeply polarized public opinion throughout Western Europe. In spite of the fact that the NATO decision itself was taken as a result of European concern over a perceived and growing imbalance between NATO and Warsaw Pact strategic-nuclear forces based upon the deployment by the Soviet Union of the SS-20 IRBM, the Backfire bomber, the modern SU-25 (Frogfoot) aircraft, and development of a new generation of shorter-range "battlefield" nuclear weapons to replace the older FROG, Scud, and Scaleboard systems, the Alliance decision of December 12, 1979 brought to light deepening differences of opinion within Western Europe over national defense and NATO force modernization issues and priorities. More than this, however, as a result of a carefully crafted political campaign against NATO deployment plans, fundamental questions were raised about the management by the West of relationships with the East, and in particular with the Soviet Union, as well as the future of the transatlantic security relationship that has sustained peace and stability on the Continent since the years following World War II.

A variety of groups, including established political parties as in the case of the SPD in the Federal Republic of Germany and the Labour party, first under Michael Foot and later under Neil Kinnock, in Great Britain (a party which, when in office, had supported the modernization of NATO defense-deterrence capabilities); religious organizations, especially the Protestant churches; and environmental coalitions, such as the Greens of West Germany and older groups including the European ecological movement — all sought to shatter the consensus in support of the Alliance deterrent posture. Although each adopted its own agenda with regard to specific national and/or European-oriented objectives — with, for example, the Dutch IKV seeking to disavow the Netherlands' role in NATO nuclear policies, the Greens and SPD seeking West Germany's withdrawal from NATO, and the British Labour party desiring to impede Britain's planned modernization of its national nuclear force — all had in common one immediate objective, to overturn the NATO decision of 1979 and to reduce sharply, if not eliminate altogether, Western nuclear forces. A longer-term objective of most of the antinuclear groups in Western Europe was the establishment of a European nuclear-free zone extending to the Soviet Union, although it was generally conceded that this is a long-term goal, not easily achieved.

However vocal and well-orchestrated the opposition, it failed. In November 1983, in the absence of real and substantive progress at the Geneva arms control negotiations, NATO began its INF deployment and the anticipated "Hot Autumn" of mass European protests failed to materialize, at least in the numbers and to the extent that had been feared by Alliance and European government officials. For many Europeans, the reaction of the Soviet Union to the initial NATO deployments, first by walking out of the arms talks and later by escalating its arms build-up in Eastern Europe, was poorly received and judged to be indicative of Moscow's lack of interest in regional stability. For others, the NATO deployment represented a *fait accompli* against which little or nothing could be done. While vowing to fight on, the disparate coalition of European antinuclear groups began to erode as the one objective upon which they all agreed seemed no longer within reach. Each determined to develop its own agenda, with, for example, the Greens seeking to strengthen and consolidate their political power in West Germany, while the SPD emphasized the development of new frameworks for relations with the East. Elsewhere in Western Europe, but particularly in the northern Protestant nations, the groups of the European antinuclear coalition undertook to regroup, focusing on a variety of social and domestic issues, including but not limited to relations with the United States and the future of the Atlantic Alliance.

On the one hand, in hindsight the INF deployment could be viewed as a victory for the Atlantic Alliance, as a demonstration that NATO had surmounted a crisis that threatened its unity and its very existence. But in reality, the fact remains that the INF controversy was and is indicative of a widening gap within West European countries on defense issues. It also bespeaks a fundamental difference in perspective between the United States and its European allies with respect to the management of relations with the Soviet Union.

Thus, the significance of the INF controversy for the future of Alliance relations extends well beyond the immediate deployment issue. By exacerbating popular fears of nuclear war, especially the prospect of a limited nuclear war in Europe, opponents of the INF decision were able to exploit the latent and widespread European uncertainty about the reliability of the United States as an ally. Employing their considerable organizational skills to develop networks throughout Western Europe, antinuclear protesters succeeded in uniting a broad coalition of groups in their cause, ranging from those concerned with ecology to women's rights. As a result, the INF issue became embroiled in domestic political squabbles, altering the terms of debate from a question of military-deterrence policy to a political test of leadership for European NATO governments. In so doing, the precedent is set for public debate on subsequent alliance decisions concerning weapons deployments and programs for modernization. What is not yet clear, however, is whether or not antinuclear groups in Western Europe can preserve their coalition and, to what extent, in the context of West European domestic politics, they will succeed in further polarizing public opinion and generating opposition to other alliance decisions.

In considering the potential of European antinuclear movements for influencing NATO policies as well as the future of the Alliance itself, there can be no uniform assessment since their strengths vary from country to country. Each of the West European antinuclear groups is imbued with its own peculiar domestic perspectives, born out of a specific historical-cultural context. Thus, despite considerable efforts to develop a transnational, institutional network, the European antinuclear movement remains devoid of an international dimension. Notwithstanding antinuclear activists who can be counted on to participate in "pacifist events" outside their national borders, the movement is relatively small and its credibility within the various national settings has often been challenged, especially when such meetings have resulted in ardent criticism of Western (i.e., the United States and NATO) policies without mention of the Soviet arms build-up, the invasion of Afghanistan, or human rights violations in the USSR. When, on occasion, members of the European antinuclear coalition have come together to discuss a future agenda, the outcome has tended to be disarray, in part because of the varying priorities of each of the groups and because of the disregard shown by the East for the group's objectives when they conflicted with Soviet policy initiatives. The repression by Warsaw Pact governments of independent "peace movements" in Eastern Europe has presented to Western antinuclear groups a moral dilemma, creating tensions not only between different nationally-based groups, but also within the antinuclear coalitions themselves.[1]

Nevertheless, little comfort can be taken from the fact that West European antinuclear groups have not been able to develop closer organizational links. By focusing on specific, short-term issues, such groups can continue to erode the defense consensus upon which the West has relied for more than a generation. The plethora of antinuclear movements in Western Europe today, in the words of one West German analyst, has "a great deal more to do with the spiritual conditions of our time than fear of a nuclear confrontation."[2]

If the contemporary European antinuclear movement can be characterized as social-psychological in its basic dimension, its manifestations in West European countries must be assessed with reference to each nation's attitudes, values, and historical conditions. In the Netherlands, where neutrality has long been an acknowledged tradition, born of Holland's reliance on mercantile pragmatism and Calvinistic moralism, contemporary antinuclear activists focus their efforts on nuclear issues, believing that such weapons represent an ultimate form of immorality. A pragmatic people, Dutch antinuclear activists have no desire to oversee the dissolution of NATO, or even to support a Dutch withdrawal from the Alliance. Neither do they seek unilateral disarmament of the West, although they support "unilateral initiatives leading to multilateral disarmament."[3] What Dutch antinuclear activists continue to seek is the denuclearization of Holland and the withdrawal of the Netherlands from all of its nuclear tasks in NATO. In the face of popular pressure, the Dutch government continued to postpone a decision on whether to allow deployment of the forty-eight cruise missiles allotted to Holland as part of the NATO decision. Consistently the Dutch government has opted to put off deployment in the hope that an arms control agreement would be negotiated that would obviate the need for action by The Hague.

In the absence of a Dutch deployment decision, or if the government loses an eventual vote on the issue, Alliance cohesion will, at worst, be marginally affected inasmuch as deployment is already proceeding in the pivotal countries of the Federal Republic, Italy, and Great Britain. Politically, however, a continued postponement of the deployment decision by the Netherlands and Belgium, which, too, has sought to finesse its initial acquiescence in the 1979 NATO decision, may have far greater significance in Washington where members of the U.S. Congress, reflecting constituent disenchantment, increasingly are prone to doubt the willingness of U.S. allies to shoulder a proportionate burden of the common defense.

Notwithstanding the Dutch tendency toward more parochial issues, the conglomerate of religious and secular groups which opposes the deployment of ground-launched cruise missiles in the Netherlands could readily form the nucleus of a broader-based European protest movement directed against further changes in NATO force posture and Alliance strategy. One notable potential target could be the adoption by the NATO Defense Council of the Follow-On Forces Attack concept (FOFA). The Rodgers Plan, as it is commonly called, is a tactical concept designed to revitalize NATO's theater strategy in the face of changes that have been detected in Soviet/ Warsaw Pact theater doctrine and force posture. While not a radical departure from current NATO planning, which emphasizes the primacy of forward defense, FOFA provides for the simultaneous interdiction of enemy, follow-on, second and third echelon forces or Operational Maneuver Groups (OMGs), which are assessed as being central to Soviet/Warsaw Pact theater tactics. The campaign against FOFA and the newly adopted U.S. Army AirLand Battle doctrine, which includes counteroffensive options within the defensive framework of U.S. and NATO strategy, is already being orchestrated by antinuclear groups in Europe.

As in the Netherlands, a highly organized antinuclear coalition, which includes the opposition Green and Social Democratic parties in the Federal Republic of Germany, is attempting to generate popular support against changes in U.S. and NATO planning as a means of bringing the issue of membership in the Atlantic Alliance itself into the forefront of the national defense debates in Western Europe. With Federal elections scheduled for February 1987, the prospect looms of an opposition coalition based on participation of the Greens and the SPD, with the Free Democratic Party (FDP) having lost its momentum and its electoral support from the center-left which opposes the domestic economic policies of the ruling CDU. If such a scenario were to evolve, with the SPD leadership moving increasingly to the left of center, a Green-SPD coalition would be positioned to challenge the present orientation of West German foreign policy, including Alliance membership.

To regard the Greens and the rise in West German neutralist/pacifist sentiment as representing more than a transient phenomenon, one must assume that traditional Western values, as embodied in the principles of the Atlantic Alliance, no longer hold validity for a new generation of West

Germans, many of whom have no memory of World War II or of the post-war struggle for Europe. Youthful rebellion and alienation from the relative affluence of the postwar era may be the price that advanced industrial societies must pay as the socialization process fails to keep pace with changes demanded by progress and prosperity. The United States experienced its period of agitation and rebellion during the upheaval of the so-called Vietnam era. European youth may now be expressing some of the same concerns as their American counterparts, only a decade later. Unlike the U.S. case, however, the Europeans have no Vietnam of recent vintage against which to vent their frustrations. Their dissatisfaction with the relentless demands of technological advance, together with waning job prospects, has contributed to a loss of faith in established political institutions. To some Europeans the Atlantic Alliance has come to symbolize their dependence on the United States. For the West Germans, in particular, the Atlantic Alliance is viewed by many as representing the major stumbling bloc to reunification. While not dismissed, the Soviet hold over the German Democratic Republic (DDR) does not loom large as a factor in the nationalist aspirations of much of the German Left since there is little that can be done to influence Soviet policies. As a pluralistic society, however, the United States is subject to great influence from within and from outside. The United States and Western institutions like NATO, quite simply, can be influenced more readily than can a totalitarian Communist state such as the USSR.

This accounts in part for the bias of Western antinuclear groups against U.S. policies and the effort to justify, as in the case of Soviet SS-20 deployments, Moscow's actions as strictly defensive responses to Western attempts "to encircle" militarily and politically the Soviet Union. In this context it is hardly surprising that, in addition to criticisms of U.S. and NATO tactical planning innovations, West European antinuclear groups are seeking to oppose the American Strategic Defense Initiative (SDI), on the basis that: (1) it is supposedly destabilizing and will generate a new arms race in outer space; (2) it will undermine the foundation of the East-West deterrence relationship; (3) it will lead to the abrogation of the SALT I ABM Treaty, which is widely perceived in Europe as the most successful of all U.S.-Soviet arms control agreements; and (4) it will codify the strategic decoupling of the United States from the defense of Western Europe, because it is incorrectly supposed that the United States would be defended by the SDI but Europe would be vulnerable to the threat of political blackmail or an actual Soviet attack.[4] In Britain and France, the two countries which also deploy nuclear forces, opposition to the U.S. SDI is not limited to antinuclear groups but is more widespread because of its potentially profound implications for British and French national deterrent capabilities. The British Labour party—like its SPD and Green counterparts in the Federal Republic—along with the Committee for Nuclear Disarmament (CND), is prominently involved in the attack against the SDI; and it is also opposed to the deployment by Britain of a national nuclear force. Indeed, the most recent Labour party platform calls for the elimination of British deterrent forces and the renunciation of the "first-use" concept as a part of NATO's Flexible Response strategy.

Paradoxically, the Mitterrand government opposes the SDI not as a result of any great national antinuclear fervor, but principally on the basis of its potential implications for the national deterrent force. Unique in this respect in Western Europe today, France enjoys a remarkable defense consensus based upon widespread popular support for the French independent national nuclear force. Although by no means uniform (there does exist in France an antinuclear coalition based on elements of the French Communist party, the left wing of the Socialist party, and other radical groups such as the MRG), the French defense consensus has its origins in an emphasis on autonomous action and independent, often chauvinistic, thinking. As both a Mediterranean and a predominately Catholic country, comparable in this respect to Italy where the antinuclear movement has failed to generate substantial popular support, France has thus far been spared a divisive national debate on defense/national security issues. Unlike Italy, which participates in the integrated military command structure of NATO, France since 1967 has been unencumbered by Alliance decisions on strategy and weapons modernization and thus was not subjected to a parliamentary debate regarding NATO Pershing-2 or cruise missile deployments. Surprisingly, at least to many in the West who failed to understand François Mitterrand's views, the Socialist president of France strongly endorsed the NATO double-track decision as a means of re-establishing equilibrium in the Eurostrategic balance of forces. Beyond this, Mitterrand criticized neighboring European publics for their lack of support for deployment, likening European antinuclear protesters to a "fifth column."[5]

Reflecting the national consensus on French nuclear forces and support for civilian nuclear power generation in France, the French Catholic bishops, in their "Letter" entitled *Waging the Peace*, stood in sharp contrast to their American counterparts. The Catholic bishops of France stated that the concept of nuclear deterrence is morally justified as long as nuclear weapons exist. Holding to the tradition of Catholic thought, which sets forth the theory of just war, the French bishops emphasize that societies which value human rights, freedoms, and dignity must possess the means by which to deter aggression and to defend against a potential enemy. Democracies have never converted dictatorships simply by the power of example or by unilateral disarmament. Disarmed states have not converted their militarily armed neighbors to pacifism. Based on such premises, the

French government is continuing to modernize its nuclear force capabilities. In the current four-year *Programme Loi*, France has given priority to the modernization of its strategic and "prestrategic" (tactical) nuclear forces, some would say to the detriment of French conventional capabilities. This trend in French military modernization stands in sharp contrast to NATO efforts to raise the nuclear threshold by upgrading alliance conventional force capabilities.

The French emphasis on autonomy and national independence explains, too, the general support for civilian nuclear power, although there is less approval for nuclear power technology than for the national deterrent force. In fact, in France, the contemporary antinuclear coalition grew out of the civilian nuclear power protest movement which played upon popular fears of a "Three-Mile Island" type incident. Still, the strength of the civilian protest movement, in recent years, has waned amid a growing recognition of the need to develop alternative sources of energy.

In the Federal Republic of Germany protests against civilian power generation have been organized by environmentalist groups like the Greens and the left wing of the SPD. In a potentially important development, the Greens of Hesse left their coalition with the SPD as a result of a bitter dispute over the future of two civilian nuclear power plants located at Hanau, near Frankfurt.[6] Under former Chancellor Helmut Schmidt, the West German Social Democratic party had been an ardent supporter of the development in West Germany of civilian nuclear power technologies. While the post-Schmidt SPD is less supportive of nuclear energy, there remain elements in the state parties which strongly support its economic potential for the FRG. In Hesse, the erosion of the so-called "Red-Green" alliance means that the Social Democrats, while the single most popular party in the state, has lost its absolute majority and may be unable to govern effectively until a new election is scheduled. More importantly, however, the failure of the SPD-Green alliance casts a shadow over the possibility of other "Red-Green" alliances, including one at the national level.

The emphasis on environmental issues that is fundamental to the Greens' agenda, then, could diminish the potential effectiveness of a concomitant campaign, in the Federal Republic and elsewhere, against the Atlantic Alliance. To the extent that the Greens and the Social Democratic Party (SPD) are in competition for the same broad segment of the West German population, the split over further development of civilian nuclear power could play a critical role in determining whether the SPD will seek to move even further to the left and adopt a more radical defense policy than that which emerged from their 1984 Congress.

In May 1984, the Social Democratic party affirmed its commitment to the Atlantic Alliance, while advocating the adoption by NATO of a military strategy based upon the concept of "no-first-use of nuclear weapons" and a build-up of the Alliance's conventional forces to preserve the East-West deterrence relationship. However, the party failed to support the increases in defense spending that would be necessary to attain this policy objective.[7] More controversial is the concept of a joint East-West security arrangement that was advanced by the SPD at its Party Congress, according to which,

> security is only obtainable — in this age of weapons of mass destruction and mutually assured destruction — *with* the potential enemy and not against him. The common threat to the participants in the East-West conflict is an undeniable fact. The states in the two alliances must live in joint security or else they will jointly perish. What we need is a security partnership which opens up prospects of overcoming the madness of pursuing the arms race . . . . The joint efforts to reach a security partnership do not signify any blurring of the differing power interests among the various blocs or of their differing sets of values. Nevertheless, our beliefs and our values as well as our socio-political objectives can only be translated into reality if we have peace. There no longer exists anything which makes warfare worthwhile or justifiable.[8]

Explicit in the SPD concept is the rejection of military power as an instrument of policy in the nuclear age. This is a prevalent theme in the literature of the European antinuclear movements, as it is, incidentally, in that of the U.S. nuclear freeze coalition. The subjective nature of the European antinuclear campaigns, with their prejudice against rational analysis of the dynamics of the global security environment gives rise to the false presumption that the Soviet Union shares Western values and strategic conceptions. By their attempt to inject a particular conception of morality into Western decision making or on security issues, European antinuclear activists have been able to shift the context of the debate away from the legitimate concerns of defense and national security policies toward more emotive concepts of war and peace.

The anti-American slant of the European antinuclear movements has been shaped by a political expediency which emphasizes "Europe for the Europeans" and the dissolution of "blocs" in Europe. Relying on a broadly based "peace offensive," which has received direct Soviet support through "front organizations" such as the World Peace Council, locally based antinuclear groups blossomed into well-organized national movements whose express intention was to undermine the NATO INF deployment but whose larger purpose was the neutralization of Western Europe by means of the dissolution of NATO. These goals also coincide with the aims of those within the European antinuclear coalition who are linked to Communist party organizations. While it would be incorrect to suggest that the European antinuclear movement is the stepchild of Moscow, its objectives are fostered by the Soviet Union, which has long sought to "decouple" Western Europe from the United States and to expand its influence over the Continent.

However, overt attempts by the Soviet Union to co-opt European antinuclear sentiment against the United States seem, by and large, to have failed, given the rise in support among Western groups for their counterparts in Eastern Europe. Many European analysts concede that the erosion of Moscow's influence over various groups within the Western antinuclear coalition came about as early as 1982, in the wake of the imposition of martial law in Poland. Further contributing to the diminution of Soviet influence over the movement has been Moscow's reaction to the rise of antinuclear groups in Eastern Europe, but particularly East Germany, as well as the harsh response of the Soviet leadership to likeminded Western criticism against the continued build-up and modernization of the strategic, theater-oriented nuclear and conventional military forces of the Soviet Union. For the West German Greens, in particular, Soviet influence over the West European antinuclear movement has proven politically embarrassing, as its one-time ally, the West German Communist party, continues to make statements attempting to link the Greens to its initiatives. Within the Greens, there has emerged a split over political strategy and electoral tactics between those who emphasize "ideological purity" at the expense, perhaps, of electoral success and those who wish to attract the votes of the center-left in West Germany. With more pragmatic party members seeking to attain political respectability, an alliance with the West German Communist party, real or perceived, may be counterproductive to the Greens' electoral aspirations.

The relationships among European antinuclear groups, the Soviet Union, and the more pro-Soviet Communist parties of Western Europe vary, with some parties the object of contention in the national-political debate, as in France. The pro-Soviet Communist party of the Netherlands played a major role in that country's campaign against deployment of the Enhanced Radiation Weapon — commonly referred to, as a result of a slick propaganda campaign, as the neutron bomb. So it was natural that, after 1979, the Communist Party of the Netherlands (CPN) emerged as a major actor in the Dutch antinuclear movement. Together with leaders of the World Peace Council and the Dutch Interchurch Peace Council, the CPN championed the antinuclear cause against NATO modernization. However, with the Soviet invasion of Afghanistan and the declaration of martial law in Poland, the CPN began to distance itself from Moscow, even abandoning its Marxist-Leninist rigidity in favor of greater political flexibility and greater emphasis on domestic and social issues.

In Britain and France, too, alliances between the national pro-Soviet communist parties and the Campaign for Nuclear Disarmament (CND) and the *Mouvement de la Paix*, respectively, have not redounded to the interests of either of the antinuclear coalitions. By refusing to denounce the Soviet arms build-up while continuing to attack the defense modernization programs of the United States, the CND has alienated some who otherwise might have served as staunch supporters. To a lesser extent, this is true, too, of the British Labour party under the leadership of Neil Kinnock. The 1984 Labour party manifesto renouncing Britain's deterrent force; Mr. Kinnock's subsequent trip to Moscow where he apparently pledged to make a fundamental change in Britain's strategic posture if (or when) Labour returns to office; and Labour's support for the 1984–1985 coal miner's strike (its "Communist element is so overt, even triumphalist, that the Labour party and its Leadership has been cowed into following the Communist lead. . . .")[9] — all have generally worked against Labour's efforts to broaden its public support. The opposite has been true among workers who increasingly perceive the Conservative government to be "partisan" in the miner's strike. However, the approaches by Arthur Scargill and Neil Kinnock to Libyan and Soviet authorities for financial support for Britain's striking coal miners seem to have been intolerable for most Britons, even those who tend to support the workers' objectives, raising the fundamental issue of Labour's future agenda for Britain. It is too early to speculate on the electoral prospects of the Labour party or the third-party Social Democrats whose leadership is composed principally of dissident members of the Labour party. Nevertheless, it is clear that a broad public perception of a close relationship between Labour and the British Communist party will not be conducive to electoral success for Britain's Left.

In France, the Communist party is closely identified with both the Soviet Union and the *Mouvement de la Paix* which has been given new life in France as a result of the Euro-missiles controversy.[10] The prominent differences between the French Communist party and the mainstream of France's Socialist party, including President Mitterrand's support of the NATO double-track decision, have contributed to an open split among the parties of the Left, culminating last summer in the decision of the PCF to withdraw from the Mitterrand-Mauroy government.[11] So long as the PCF adheres to its staunchly pro-Soviet stance, French political analysts speculate that the party will "fall into irreversible decline," if, in fact, the process has not already begun.[12] The Communist party has been steadily losing support in France, to the point where it received a mere 11% of the votes cast (half the level of five years earlier) in the European parliamentary elections held in June 1984. Many within the PCF attribute much of the blame for the party's decline to its current leader, Georges Marchais, whose support within the PCF has plummeted to 44%.[13] As long as the French believe that "the [French] Communist Party equals the U.S.S.R. equals the Gulag," its prospects for engendering greater public support either for the

Mouvement de la Paix or other coalitions directed against French defense policies are limited.[14] If, in February 1985, at the seventy-fifth triennial conference of the PCF, Marchais is retained as party leader, as most analysts predict, it is likely that the CPF will continue its decline into a small, impotent, and militant party like the British Communist party.[15] Alternatively, it could split, as did the Spanish Communist party, into militant and pragmatic "Eurocommunist" wings, each of whose influence would likely be considerably diminished from that of today's party. Or, if Marchais is deposed as leader, it could evolve into an Italian-style Eurocommunist party which would offer greater prospects for influence on the French political scene; at this time, however, this seems to be the least likely option for the PCF.

The decline in popular support for the PCF enhances the strength of the French Socialist party, although for a variety of reasons, principally having to do with domestic economic problems, the opposition right-wing RPR and the centrist UDF are generally expected to erode the Socialist party's parliamentary majority. This stands in contrast to the situation in Italy, where the Communist party has, over the last year, increased its electoral strength, due, in part, perhaps, to a "sympathy vote" following the death in June 1984 of its popular leader Enrico Berlinguer. More significant, however, has been the factor of popular discontent with government domestic policies and charges of corruption against the Christian Democratic party. In the June 1984 European parliamentary elections the Communist party, for the first time, garnered a greater popular vote than did the Christian Democratic party. Nevertheless, the influence of the PCI is said to have dropped perceptibly in Italian life, with most Italians explaining the large Communist parliamentary vote on the basis of its symbolic, protest nature. The European Parliament is generally assessed to be a weak institution, having virtually no control over national policies. Moreover, Prime Minister Bettino Craxi and his Socialist party have emerged as fiercely anti-Soviet and pro-Western, both popular stances among the majority of the Italian people. Even Italy's Communist party holds to the position that, "it [is] right for Italy to belong to NATO."[16] In addition, the government's attempts at economic reform, based upon Craxi's strong support for a free-market economy, have attracted the growing support of the Italian people.

As demonstrated by the evolution of the Socialist-led government's economic program, Italian politics are extremely sensitive to public opinion, more so probably than in other West European nations. Having said this, however, it is also important to realize that in the Italian political context, security policy and strategic issues have had, since World War II, little influence on public policy debates. Thus, it was hardly surprising to close observers of the Italian scene that the 1979 announcement of the NATO double track decision, followed on August 7, 1981, by the Italian government's decision to base Italy's allotment of NATO cruise missiles at Comiso, Sicily, generated but a mild public reaction. The decision, coming just after local elections and just prior to the summer "vacation exodus," would probably have gone unnoticed altogether by Italian antinuclear activists except for the unfortunate timing, a day later on August 8, 1981, of President Reagan's announcement of the continued development of the Enhanced Radiation Weapon (ERW). The coincidence of the two announcements heightened public awareness of security issues and played upon Italian fears—as it did elsewhere in Western Europe—of nuclear war. As in other European nations, local protests merged into a national campaign which attracted, to varying degrees, support in all of Italy's political parties. The Italian Communist party—not, however, without some difficulty, given its desire to sustain the perception of an independent stance from the Soviet Union—was the first Italian political party to oppose the deployment of NATO cruise missiles in Italy. Aside from the PCI, the Proletarian Unity Party (which has since merged with the PCI), and the Radical Party, which boasts the support of about 3.5% of the Italian electorate, the institutional basis of the Italian antinuclear movement is embryonic, and its activities are restricted largely to reactions to specific issues as they arise.

Neither is there in the Italian antinuclear movement any single, unifying body. Antinuclear protests, marches, and rallies have been carried out by a proliferation of local groups, sometimes dominated by a particular political party, but often by ad hoc religious or pacifist groups. In Italy, as has been the case elsewhere in Europe, antinuclear activities have been heavily supported by groups outside the country, bespeaking the tendency of the European movements to emphasize and develop transnational links. Comiso "support-groups" have been developed in the Netherlands, the Federal Republic of Germany, and, more recently, in Britain.

In each of the countries under study, the national antinuclear coalitions have been successful, to varying degrees, in focusing public debate on the specific issue of NATO's double-track decision. But, at the same time, they have been singularly unsuccessful in disrupting the deployment process, with the exception of the Low Countries whose governments are seeking yet another delay with regard to their respective deployment decisions. More than this, they have been unable to attract broader support for the underlying objective, held by most within the European antinuclear coalition, of Western theater nuclear disarmament. Consequently, in their postdeployment debates on the future direction and tactics of the movement, West European antinuclear activists are seeking to identify new, limited objectives which seem politically within reach and which potentially hold appeal for those in the center and center-left of the European political spectrum. Already, the Greens of West Germany, like their Dutch counterparts, have targeted the U.S. AirLand Battle strategy, NATO's Follow-On Forces Attack concept, and the U.S. Strategic Defense Initiative as the focus of opposition in 1985 and beyond.[17] During the December 1984 visit of Soviet Politburo Member Mikhail Gorbachev to Britain, Neil Kinnock observed that, "the American 'Star Wars' project poses a greater threat to NATO than any external pressure from the Soviet Union."[18] Similar themes have been expounded in recent months throughout Western Europe at meetings of antinuclear groups.

If West European antinuclear activists have been able to agree on specific issues to be targeted, they have been unable to develop a consensus on tactics, on the best means of attaining their objectives, either in the short or long term. In their December 1984 Congress, the West German Greens narrowly avoided a formal split between so-called fundamentalists and reformers by leaving open the issue of a Red-Green alliance. While most of the 800 delegates to the meeting favored the fundamentalist approach, outright rejection of an alliance with the SPD failed to be adopted because delegate attention was directed to a controversial speech delivered by Rudolf Bahro who compared the evolution of the Green party to the Nazi movement.[19] While fundamental differences remain between those who view the Greens as a "protest movement" that belongs "on the streets" and those who desire political power, the Greens' Congress pointed up a growing phenomenon in the European antinuclear movement: the decision to offer support for, and work more directly with, other groups to attain national political power.

If the antinuclear groups of Western Europe succeed in organizing and agreeing on a European agenda, their chances for influencing NATO priorities will be considerably enhanced. With respect to the broader objective of nuclear disarmament, far more unites West European antinuclear activists than divides them. Thus, emphasizing their European links, the ecology parties of Britain and Italy have decided to change their name to the Greens and to place themselves on the ballot in the May 1985 local elections.[20] On the national level, however, the prospects for such groups to attain political power will remain limited unless and until they develop a broader agenda to include issues of practical, domestic concern, such as those pertaining to the economy.

It is clear that the rise of the antinuclear movement in Western Europe is not a transient phenomenon. Despite their inability to block the NATO INF deployment, European antinuclear activists will continue to attempt to chip away at the defense consensus that for so long served Western interests so well. They will likely emphasize short-term, specific targets like AirLand Battle and SDI as a means of attracting greater popular support for their longer-term objective of Western disarmament. Against such a concerted, well-organized political campaign, responsible Western statesmen and leaders outside government will have to mount an extensive effort aimed at educating Western publics regarding the consequences if the European antinuclear movement succeeds. Above all, these would be the attainment by the Soviet Union of strategic-military superiority over the Continent, with the attendant prospect of the neutralization of Western Europe and the dissolution of NATO.

NOTES

1. See, for example, Henry Kamm, "Soviet Group Is Jeered at Disarmament Rally," *New York Times*, July 20, 1984; and Mario Modiano, "Meeting of Peace Groups Breaks Up in Disarray," *The Daily Telegraph*, February 10, 1984.
2. Hans Ruehle, "The Peace Movement in Historical Perspective," draft chapter in forthcoming book to be published by the Konrad-Adenauer-Stiftung, Saint Augustin, Federal Republic of Germany, 1985 (English edition).
3. Charles Hargrove, "Holland and the Bomb: 1, Their Ideal Is Neither Red nor Dead," *The Times* (London), August 2, 1982.
4. In general, European understanding of the SDI is poor. According to the U.S. conceptualization, Allied security, especially that of NATO Europe, is fundamental to the SDI concept. Moreover, many Europeans fail to appreciate the extent to which the Soviet Union itself is *already* engaged in its own strategic defense program. In addition to the fact that Moscow today deploys the world's only active ABM network, the Soviet Union already is spending more than the United States on research and development of strategic defensive technologies.
5. For a comprehensive view of François Mitterrand's view of the European antinuclear movements, see his remarks at the l'Hotel de Ville, Brussels, reprinted in, "La France face à Pacifisme," *Le Monde*, October 14, 1983, where Mitterrand stated that "The West has pacifists while the East has Euromissiles."
6. Rupert Cornwell, "Greens Quit Alliance with SPD," *Financial Times*, November 21, 1984; and "Hesse Alliance Collapses Over A-Power," *The Times* (London), November 21, 1984.
7. See Joseph Rovan, "Le 'non' à Marx des Socialistes Allemands," *Le Monde*, November 19, 1984; James M. Markham, "Bonn Opposition Affirms NATO Tie," *New York Times*, May 20, 1984; and "The Opposition's Role in Bonn," *Financial Times*, May 21, 1984.
8. Quoted from the English translation of *Report Submitted to the SPD Executive Committee by the Working Group on 'New Strategies.'* (Chairman—Egon Bahr; Members—Hans Apel, Count Wolf von Baudissin, Wilhelm Bruns, Andreas von Bulow, Horst Ehmke, Katrin Fuchs, Erwin Horn, Gerhard Hermann, Christian Krause, Oskar Lafontaine, Ulrich Mackinsen, Alfons Parvelczyk, Hermann Scheer, Klaus von Schubert, and Karsten Voight), dated July 1983, pp. 5–6, 6–7.
9. "We Have Been Warned," *The Times* (London), Editorial, November 29, 1984.
10. In France the *Mouvement de la Paix* has been in existence for over fifty years. Organized around local and national institutions and having ties internationally, in its contemporary incarnation the *Mouvement* is composed of a broad coalition of groups—feminists, ecologists, ecclesiastics, political parties, Trotskyists, and anarchists. Also prominent in the *Mouvement* is the Communist-controlled French General Confederation of Labor or CGT.
11. Pierre Mauroy has since been replaced as prime minister by Laurent Fabius.

12. See Diana Geddes, "French Communist Hardliners Challenged by Militants," *The Times* (London), December 4, 1984; and Diana Geddes, "Marchais Under Fire as Communist Dissidents Refuse to Toe Party Line," *The Times* (London), October 30, 1984.

13. Geddes, "Marchais Under Fire. . . .," op. cit.

14. Quoted from John Vinocur, "The Same Communists, Only Weaker," *New York Times*, July 29, 1984.

15. In December 1984, the British Communist party formally split into "Eurocommunist" and pro-Soviet wings, further diminishing its electoral influence in Britain. Politically, however, the split could be extremely significant for British politics. The split, which was caused by domestic-economic and not foreign policy issues, raises the possibility that the "moderate" Eurocommunist wing of the CPB will forge a coalition of "anti-Thatcher voters" with the British Labour party, creating the equivalent of "an historic British Compromise." Already some of the positions of Kinnock's Labour party, i.e., "the call for more local cooperatives, local authority enterprise and industrial democracy (as against the Labour left's traditional commitment to nationalisation)" echoes many of the Eurocommunists' positions. According to one observer of the British scene, "Nine months of the miner's strike have reawakened faith in traditional class politics on the left, particularly among Labour's demoralized activists. The strength and politicisation of the striking miners had led many left-wingers to conclude that trade unionism need not be as high bound as they had supposed. And the conflict between the National Union of Mineworkers and its pickets and the police and the courts has given credence to the 'hard left' view of the state as partisan." Seumas Milne, "It's the Fall-Out That Matters," *The Guardian*, December 18, 1984.

16. Remarks of Alessandro Natta, the new leader of the PCI, quoted in "Communist Party Urged to Toe the Moscow Line," *Financial Times*, September 7, 1984.

17. See "Les Manifestations pacifistes contre les manoeuvres de l'otan ont eu peu de succes," *Le Monde*, September 27, 1984.

18. Quoted in Anthony Bevins, "Star Wars Fear Raised by Kinnock," *The Times* (London), December 20, 1984.

19. Michael Binyon, "Uproar but Greens Compromise," *The Times* (London), December 10, 1984.

20. "Les Ecologistes se lancent dans l'arène politique," *Le Monde*, December 11, 1984.

Chapter 9

West European Antinuclearism and the Alliance: A Retrospective Assessment

Robert L. Pfaltzgraff, Jr.

Opposition to the allocation of resources, human and material, to the common defense is based upon a deeply-rooted desire to find an alternative to warfare for the resolution of disputes among nations and a mistaken tendency to equate disarmament with peace. The assumption that armaments competition leads inevitably to war and that the reduction of weapons will produce peace represents important elements of the antinuclear protest movements surveyed in previous chapters. The present opposition represents the most recent manifestation of sentiment that can be traced not only to the unilateral disarmament efforts of the middle years of this century — the Campaign for Unilateral Disarmament in Britain, the Stockholm Peace Appeal, and "peace" marches elsewhere in Europe — but also to the numerous attempts between the two World Wars to develop norms and international frameworks to replace resort to armed conflict as a means of settling international disputes. Neither the League of Nations nor the Kellogg-Briand Pact outlawing war as an instrument of national policy was sufficient to prevent the outbreak of World War II just a generation after World War I — the war that was considered to be the "war to end all wars."

Although there has been evidence of opposition within the Soviet Union to the amassing of even larger numbers of sophisticated weapons by the Soviet state, it is within the pluralistic societies of the West that such debate has flourished unfettered by the stifling controls of political repression practiced in totalitarian societies. Although the rise of protest against weapons coincided with the increasing lethality of the means of destruction, the principal characteristic of the present international security environment is the unprecedented capabilities available to the Soviet Union. The atomic monopoly which once afforded the United States clear escalation dominance as a deterrent to a land thrust across Europe by superior Soviet conventional forces gave way first to superpower nuclear parity and subsequently to the preponderance of the Soviet Union in nearly all of the indicators of nuclear weaponry. The deployment of the Soviet SS-20 force of intermediate-range nuclear missiles, which began in 1977, was preceded by the rise of the present antinuclear protest movements in Western Europe in the early 1980s, in the years just before the beginning of deployment of the Pershing II and ground-launched cruise missiles by the United States, undertaken in accordance with the NATO "double track" decision that had been approved unanimously by the NATO Ministerial Council in December 1979. Aside from the destructive potential of modern weapons, the reasons for the growth of antinuclearism in Western Europe are numerous and complex. There has always been an uneasy coexistence, within the respective security perspectives of West European allies, between the hope that the threat to escalate to the nuclear level would be sufficient to deter, or prevent, the outbreak of another devastating war on European soil and the apprehension that, in the event of the failure of nuclear deterrence, a future war would be fought on European soil to the exclusion of the territory of the superpowers and that Europe would bear the brunt of the consequences of the failure of deterrence. The rise of such fear in Western Europe was symptomatic of a decline in the political trust upon which the Atlantic Alliance had been based at the outset as well as the heightened vulnerability of the United States to Soviet nuclear missiles, a condition that might lead to the "decoupling" of an American security guarantee from NATO-Europe. If the protests that erupted in the cities of most West European countries had as their immediate goal the prevention of the deployment of INF forces under American control, they bespoke the fundamental problem facing the United States and its West European allies, resulting from the erosion of the security consensus that had shaped NATO in its early years. Without being willing, or able, to replace the security guarantee provided by the United States in the Atlantic Alliance with a defense capability or an alternative security arrangement in strictly European hands, substantial segments of West European populations, if not the governments themselves, viewed with alarm the prospect that their security depended upon decisions over which they had little if any control. Perhaps it is less than coincidental that the antinuclear protest movement remained weakest in France, which had built a national nuclear force fully under French control and based upon technology produced largely in France. In contrast, the largest of the

West European protest movements arose in the Federal Republic of Germany, which was not only the place of deployment for the largest part of the INF force, but also the point of greatest concentration of NATO ground forces. Any war that broke out in NATO-Europe was likely to include at the outset the territory of the Federal Republic of Germany. No forward defense of NATO Europe could be mounted without the Federal Republic of Germany; by the same token the *sine qua non* for West German participation in the Atlantic Alliance understandably had always been the firm commitment of its members to the defense of Western Europe as close to the inner German border as possible. By the early 1980s, the Atlantic Alliance faced the dilemma inherent in a forward defense of the Federal Republic of Germany under the conditions produced by the changing superpower strategic-military balance exacerbated by a deterioration in the political relationship between Washington and Moscow. Among the fears expressed by the more articulate of the antinuclear protesters was the prospect that, in the event of war in Europe, the United States might escalate to the use of INF forces against Soviet targets, while no such capabilities would be launched from American territory. Such was the spector of "decoupling" that had long haunted the Atlantic Alliance but which became a premise of the antinuclear movement's opposition to INF deployment.

It is not possible to study the antinuclear protest movements of Western Europe without noting the presence of at least a slight anti-American orientation. The unprecedented dependence of the states of Western Europe, once the shaper of international events, upon the United States as the indispensable part of a counterpoise against the Soviet Union, under even the best of circumstances would have produced frictions among allies sharing common values and goals. If the United States periodically questioned the need to retain in Western Europe large-scale ground forces nearly two generations after the end of World War II, within Western Europe the fear existed that the American security commitment, especially in the form of reduced ground forces, might be altered unilaterally by the United States in ways detrimental to European security. Frustrated at their inability to influence the policy of the Soviet Union on the deployment of the SS-20, the protest movements focused on the United States which furnished an inviting target because of the proximity of its military capabilities stationed on West European territory and the ease with which the protesters could gain instantaneous access to the printed and electronic media of pluralistic societies. Despite, or perhaps as a result of, their inability to penetrate the closed, obdurate leadership of the Soviet Union, with its censored, tightly state-controlled media, the protesters directed their attention to the only targets of opportunity available to them. If they could not establish campsites or stage protest demonstrations at Soviet missile installations, they could nevertheless undertake systematic political activities designed to undercut Western defense policies at such widely separate geographic locations as Greenham Common in Britain and Comiso in Sicily. Soviet propaganda alternated between the blandishment of peace that would result from the nondeployment of Pershing II and cruise missile capabilities and the threat of heightened tensions that would be the supposed consequence of the actual stationing of such systems in Western Europe. Such Soviet pronouncements attracted far less attention than the few offhand statements from American policy makers speculating about hypothetical conditions under which "limited" nuclear war might be fought in Western Europe. West European criticism was directed against the United States for suggesting, even in highly tentative terms, a contingency in which nuclear weapons might be used, while planning to deploy in Western Europe nuclear forces in response to the already formidable, and growing, Soviet SS-20 capabilities. The United States did not begin deployment of the Pershing II or the ground-launched cruise missiles until November 1983. Nevertheless, the onus for rising East-West tensions was usually placed equally on Washington and Moscow, or in some cases even more fully on the United States than the Soviet Union. Although the antinuclear protest movement was the object of attempted Soviet manipulation (by the admission of some of its members) and its basic goals of a disarmed Western Europe and weakened NATO coincided in this respect with those of the Soviet Union, its social and political dynamics, as well as the political values that it embodied and the tactics for the most part that its members employed, had their origins in the pluralistic societies of the West, for they would not have been tolerated in the Soviet Union or in other totalitarian societies.

Within each of the protest movements there were distinctive features that could be traced to unique national historic circumstances. The West German protest movement had conceptual links to the "German Question," which could not hope to be resolved without the reduction of the political influence and military presence of the superpowers in Europe. The reunification of Germany would remain a distant and unrealizable goal as long as the Federal Republic of Germany was integrated within the Atlantic Alliance as the bulwark of a NATO forward defense. Reunification and NATO membership were mutually exclusive conditions, with the attainment of the former dependent on the renunciation of the latter. If the German Question was deeply embedded in the past, it was equally possible to find the origins of other dimensions of the West German antinuclear protest movement in earlier generations and, in particular, in a quest for the allegedly bucolic virtues of the preindustrial age embodied in the German romanticism of the early nineteenth century. Although much of the environmental pollution problem of the Federal Republic of Germany is traceable to the German

Democratic Republic, which imposes far fewer restrictions upon such activity than the "post-industrial" West, one of the original objects of the protest movement in the Federal Republic of Germany had been the environment. Even before focusing on the nuclear weapons issue, the protesters had waged campaigns against the development of nuclear power plants, together with other efforts to correct what they saw as the encroachments of advanced technology upon the ecological balance.

In sharp contrast to Germany, the protest movement in the Netherlands was built on a legacy of neutralism that had kept Holland out of World War I but failed conspicuously to do so in World War II, despite the extensive efforts made by the Dutch government at the time to avoid any pretext for Nazi invasion. Although the Netherlands, together with other Benelux countries, had played an important role in the formation of the Atlantic Alliance, antinuclearism by the 1970s had found fertile ground both in the traditional framework of neutrality and in theological pacifism in the churches in several West European countries. Although Protestantism, as an organized religion, does not attract a widespread following in the secularized societies of contemporary Western Europe (judging by sparse church attendance), the antinuclear movements were stronger in countries with nominally Protestant populations than in predominantly Catholic states. While endorsing steps toward arms reduction and attempting to relate the contemporary strategic setting to traditional church "just war" doctrines based upon the idea of proportionality between the use of force and the goal on whose behalf it was to be employed, West European Catholicism acknowledged the need for nuclear weapons as the basis for deterring their employment by the Soviet Union. Nowhere was the national consensus that encompassed the governing and opposition parties, as well as the church, more apparent than in the French Catholic Bishops' Pastoral Letter that endorsed the national nuclear program of the French Socialist Mitterrand government. By contrast, the British antinuclear movement represented a sharp divergence from the policies of the Thatcher government, which was committed not only to the deployment of cruise missiles but also to the acquisition of a new generation national British nuclear force even at the expense of conventional defense capabilities. The British Labour party, which had split in the years after its defeat at the hands of Mrs. Thatcher's Conservatives in 1979, and again in 1983, embraced within its ranks strong elements of radical "nonconformist" Protestantism, elements of organized religion that had once formed a vibrant alternative to the Anglican church. In this respect akin to continental European Catholicism, the Anglican church stopped short of embracing the tenets of unilateral disarmament more characteristic of Protestant political activism in Europe, as well as in the United States. Thus religion provides one frame of reference for comparing and contrasting antinuclear protest movements within Europe.

Catholicism was not as deeply rooted as Protestantism in Northern Europe, the setting for the most vocal of the opposition to nuclear weapons. This included not only the Federal Republic of Germany, the Netherlands, and the United Kingdom, but also Denmark and Norway, with the latter two countries, for reasons that transcend those of religion, having long had a strict prohibition against the deployment of any nuclear weapons on their territory. In Italy, with its long, but not always untroubled, relationship with the Vatican and perhaps as a result of the historical role of Catholicism in Italian political life, the antinuclear protest movement remained weak.

It is self-evident that, in pluralistic societies, political movements, to have effect upon policy, must ultimately find expression within one or more of the political parties. A political system from which such movements were totally excluded would cease to reflect the spectrum of public opinion and thus would no longer be representative of the various constituencies that comprise the state. It is precisely this distinction that separates the Soviet Union and other totalitarian societies from the political systems of the democracies of the North Atlantic area. Unlike the Soviet Union, the defense policies of NATO countries depend upon the preservation of a national consensus sufficiently durable to sustain adequate strategies and capabilities. The emergence of antinuclear protest movements both reflects and perhaps reinforces the dissensus on national security policy in Western Europe that sharply distinguishes the 1980s from the previous history of the transatlantic relationship. Such movements found expression principally within the political parties of the left-of-center, in particular in the Federal Republic of Germany and Great Britain after such parties had left office. Even a cursory examination of the characteristics of the British Labour party and the Social Democratic party in the Federal Republic of Germany recalls the extent to which they have altered their orientation in defense policy to accommodate the antinuclear protest movements. Having formed a central element of a broadly-based security consensus that included the principal right-of-center party then in opposition, the British Labour party and the Social Democratic party in Germany, out of office, have repudiated policies for which they once stood. In Britain one of the effects of the leftward lurch of the Labour party has been the formation of a British Social Democratic-Liberal party alliance that purports to stand as a "centrist" alternative to both the Labour and Conservative parties. In the Federal Republic of Germany, however, among the effects of the antinuclear protest movement has been the formation of the Greens as a movement *qua* party that has gained representation at the local, state, and federal levels in West Germany and in the European Parliament as well. Conceivably, the German Social Democrats, if they fail to absorb the constituency represented by the Greens, will move back toward the center of the political spectrum, thus becoming a more credible contender as an alternative to the Christian Democrats, as happened in the years after the SPD joined the mainstream of West German politics at the end of the decade of the 1950s. For most of the history of the Federal Republic of Germany, the small Free Democratic party has cast its support to the Christian Democrats or to the Social Democrats to form a governing coalition. Beset with internal schisms, fading leadership, and declining electoral support, the future of the Free Democrats had become uncertain in the early years of the 1980s. The rise of the Greens as the party able to perform the past role of the FDP, holding the balance between the two major parties in the West German political system, would have ominous implications for defense policies in the Federal Republic of Germany. It would open the prospect for a coalition between the Greens and the SPD unless the Christian Democrats were able to broaden their own electoral base sufficiently to command an absolute majority (exceeding the combined total of the SPD and the Greens).

An examination of the security debate within Western Europe reveals a large number of widely held theories related to the fear of nuclear war allegedly resulting from armaments set within a context of pessimism about the future; concern that conflicts in the Third World will somehow spill over to involve Europe; and the conviction that, if only by power of example, by the unilateral reduction of armaments, Western Europe can somehow help to defuse conflicts between the superpowers. Apprehension about nuclear war leads to advocacy of programs whose effect would be the unilateral disarmament of the Atlantic Alliance or, at the least, demands that the United States show maximum flexibility in arms control negotiations with the Soviet Union. To dissect the perspectives of the antinuclear protest movement is to yield essentially the following summation: (1) INF forces should not be deployed in Western Europe because, since they can strike targets in the Soviet Union, they are provocative to Moscow and therefore destabilizing for Western Europe. Even though the Soviet Union continues to deploy SS-20 missiles targeted against Western Europe, such Soviet systems are said to be essentially for "defensive" purposes; (2) NATO should not deploy weapons or develop military strategies that provide for the targeting of Soviet-Warsaw Pact forces and the conduct of operations far behind the front lines of enemy forces in the event of war because such concepts in themselves are provocative. They represent supposedly an offensive strategy, even though NATO would be *responding* to a Soviet-Warsaw Pact attack against its territory; and (3) the conduct of military operations on NATO territory cannot be contemplated because of the vast devastation that would be inflicted upon combatants and civilians alike in Western Europe. Of course, the purpose of NATO strategy and force levels, from the beginning of the Alliance, has been to deter conflict by maintaining at least some of the capabilities that would be necessary to confront an adversary with unacceptable damage at each of these levels—from the battlefield to the territory of the Soviet Union.

If the deterrence posture of the Atlantic Alliance has sufficed to furnish the security environment within which Western Europe has enjoyed a period of peace unparalleled in the 20th century, the projection of such trends is fraught with risk because the future is seldom simply an extrapolation of the past. Although the lessons of history are not self-evident, it is nevertheless instructive to attempt to assess the implications of one era for another point in time. The armaments competition that preceded the outbreak of World War I coincided with the rise of political tensions among the major powers. The destruction resulting from World War I produced broadly based opposition in the Western democracies to armaments that made difficult the development of adequate defense capabilities until several years after the expansionism of Hitler's Third Reich became apparent. As Britain's Chancellor of the Exchequer before becoming prime minister in 1937, Neville Chamberlain had argued consistently for greater economies in defense spending, holding in 1933 that "today financial and economic risk are by far the most serious and urgent that the country has to face, and that other risks have to be run until the country has had time and opportunity to recuperate and our financial situation to improve."[1] Less than two years before the outbreak of World War II, the Chamberlain Cabinet was engaged in protracted debate over the priority to be given to defense preparedness and domestic social programs. The burden in peacetime of greater defense was impossible to contemplate because it was necessary to preserve the financial strength of the country. Closely related to the economic case against rearmament was the theme that Britain, as Chamberlain stated it, must avoid increases in the defense program which would lead to a new arms race and thus impede the prospect for an improved political relationship with Hitler. Because of the destructiveness of modern weapons, the British governments of the day, with widespread public support, especially in the first half of the decade of the 1930s, called for rapid and comprehensive disarmament as a means of averting the danger of another war. In 1932, Winston Churchill wrote: "There is such a horror of war in the great nations who passed through Armageddon (World War I) that any declaration or public speech against armaments, although it consisted only of platitudes and unrealities, has always been applauded, and any speech or assertion which set forth the blunt truths has been incontinently relegated to the category of 'war mongering'."[2] The twin themes of prohibitive cost and an arms race supposedly leading inevitably to war, popular in the 1930s, found resonance in the antinuclear protest movements in Western Europe in the 1980s.

Basic to the political perspectives of such groups is the assumption that the present reality can be transformed into a new society—domestic and global—in which old approaches and ways of thinking will give way to new relationships among individuals and groups. Unilateral disarmament, the "demilitarization" of societies, and the development of a global community, are said to represent the alternative to armaments competition within the power balances that have usually characterized international political relationships. Although the national circumstances of antinuclear protest movements differ and there are numerous variations in their prescriptions, the belief that the present world can be changed in some significant fashion lies at the core of their program. The substitution of a form of utopia, whether in this world or the next, forms an indispensable part of much of the philosophical-religious tradition of the Western world, from the humanism of antiquity to the Enlightenment and, above all, encompassing the Judaic-Christian religions. Nevertheless, deeply embedded in the philosophical-religious tradition of the West are the contending forces of good and evil, the clash between the flaws that place severe limits on the ability of humankind to progress to a higher stage of civilization and the belief that whatever may be its present deficiencies, they may be altered, whether by religious awakening, education, leadership, or political institutions, to bring about a new order of relationships, sharply different and infinitely better than those of the past. The greater the perceived limits upon the malleability of the human spirit from sin to a form of righteousness, the greater has been the tendency among political philosophers to seek a modicum of stability, harmony, and peace within a framework that balances one group against another. Presumably, a world consisting entirely of persons with shared values that eschewed the resort to violence in any form for the attainment of goals—a world furthermore in which political differences had either vanished or had been contained within agreed institutional frameworks—would have little or no use for armaments which therefore could be drastically reduced or abolished with or without an arms control agreement. In the absence of such a set of patterned relationships, and if the prospect for their attainment is thought to lie beyond the human capacity in the near term if not in a longer time period, the solution to the problem of security is to be found in the preservation of the means for defense. In this perspective, the burden is heavy upon those who would seek to abolish the capabilities for defense of the society within which they exist without simultaneously achieving similar changes in the political system against which such military means are directed as a result of major political differences. Unilateralism represents an act of faith undertaken in the hope that it will elicit a form of reciprocity on the part of an erstwhile adversary. Although the Soviet Union, in keeping with Marxist-Leninist precepts enjoining against "adventurism," has shown prudence in the use of force, there have been no expressions of altruism emanating from Moscow in the form of weapons deployment restraint in return for unilateral decisions taken in the United States and Western Europe either to cancel or to delay the deployment of new weapons systems. Notwithstanding the courageous actions of the oppressed dissidents in the Soviet Union, or the activities of East German "peace" groups, it is obvious that the perspectives of the antinuclear protest movements will not induce the Soviet leadership to beat its swords into plowshares, despite the endemic agricultural problems facing the Soviet Union, even though it possesses some of the world's most fertile lands. Instead, the Soviet Union will continue to amass armaments as a manifestation of tensions and as the means for the attainment of political goals, including the control of populations and territories within its direct or peripheral sphere of influence, and the capability for the projection of power into remote regions extending from Central America to Southeast Asia. In the turbulent world of the late twentieth century, as in earlier years, numerous groups and individuals have been prepared to employ military means to achieve their goals. In the revulsion against the carnage of World War I, the belief emerged that, as a result of war's excesses, there was no goal for which force could be used rationally. If such sentiments accorded with the prevailing tide of opinion in the victors, the vanquished had other ideas. In order to change the undesired status quo it would be appropriate to employ whatever means might be needed. There existed political goals, including territorial expansion and a quest for international hegemony, on whose behalf force was to be employed. Appeasement did not produce reciprocity; instead, the dismemberment of Czechoslovakia furnished what Churchill termed, after the Munich accords, "the first foretaste of a bitter cup which will be proffered to us year by year."[3] It is symptomatic of the abundant political differences of the late 20th century that force has been used at the state and subnational levels on behalf of a large number of causes since the end of World War II, and for the most part in the Third World which has replaced Europe as the principal arena for armed conflict.

The unilateral disarmament advocated by antinuclear protest movements would leave the disarmed hostage to the will and intentions of those who remained armed. No society can be expected to risk its survival in the fragile and unsubstantiated hope that such an act of faith will have its intended redemptive effect upon an opponent. No act of self-abnegation, even if it represented the collective will of Western Europe and the United States, could confidently be expected to lead to reciprocity on the part of the Soviet Union. It might indeed have the reverse effect of encouraging the Soviet Union, together with other hostile actors, to use force in support of their goals against those who had disarmed. The profound differences about the relationship between peace and armaments, between deterrence and defense, between armaments and stability, symbolized by the antinuclear protest movements and their critique of present defense policies, are likely to influence the national security debate in Western Europe and the United States in the years ahead and to sharpen differences within a broad political spectrum in at least several countries. To an unprecedented extent, the defense of members of the Atlantic Alliance will rest upon uncertain domestic foundations unless the means can be found to establish within pluralistic societies the basis for a security policy sufficient to meet the threats and challenges of a politically divided continent and the world beyond Europe.

NOTES

1. Quoted in Martin Gilbert, *Winston S. Churchill: Profit of Truth 1922-1939* (Boston: Houghton Mifflin, 1977), p. 455.
2. Quoted from article by Winston Churchill in *The Daily Mail* (London, May 26, 1932); Martin Gilbert reference, p. 845.
3. Quoted in Martin Gilbert, *Winston S. Churchill*, Volume 5, 1922-1939 (London: Heinemann, 1976) p. 1001.

Name Index

Subject Index

Afghanistan, Soviet invasion of, 39, 43, 134, 155, 157, 164
Airland Battle concept, 92, 193, 202
Alternatives, 66–67, 75, 79–80
Anabaptists, 83
Anarchism, 23, 65
Anglican church, 47–50, 209
Angst, 19, 23, 28, 62–64, 81, 83, 84, 88, 92
Anti-Americanism, 18, 44, 46, 70–71, 91, 104, 106, 139, 194, 197, 207
Anti-Atomtod Movement, 6, 84
Anti-Ballistic Missile (ABM) Treaty, 194
Anticapitalism, 19–31
Anti-consumerism, 22, 66, 70
Anti-modernism, 19–24, 27–31, 65
Antinuclearism
  in Britain, 35, 50–56
  in Federal Republic, 71, 84–92
  in Italy, 121, 146
  in Netherlands, 101–116, 192
  in Western Europe, 2, 3, 6–7, 194, 197, 205–215
Antiparliamentarianism, 24, 63, 70, 197
Antirationalism, 19–20, 22–24, 27–31
Arms control negotiations, 1, 15, 90, 109–114, 138, 142, 148, 166–168, 185, 190
  See also Disarmament, Double-Track, and Zero option

Balance of power, 132, 137, 141, 143, 153–155, 161, 178
BAOR, *See* British Army of the Rhine
Belgium, 113, 115
Bensberger Circle, 87
Britain, 32–58, 192, 194, 198, 205, 208, 212

British Army of the Rhine, 55
British Labour party, 35–36, 41, 50–58
British nuclear forces, 39, 41, 50–54, 56, 134, 166–168, 185, 194, 209

Calvinism, 98–99, 100, 102
Campaign for Nuclear Disarmament (CND), 6, 34–41, 46–47, 49–54, 195, 198–199
CPGB, *See* Communist parties
Catholic bishops
  American, 122, 128
  French, 175–177, 195, 209
  Italian, 124, 128, 145
Catholics
  in Britain, 33
  in the Federal Republic, 81–88
  in France, 174–177
  in Italy, 124, 126, 145
  in the Netherlands, 98, 101–102
  in Western Europe, 12–13, 209–210
Christian Association of Italian Workers (ACLI), 129
Christian Democratic parties
  Christian Democracy (CD) of Italy, 122, 127, 131, 133
  Christian Democratic Appeal (CDA) of the Netherlands, 98, 109–114
  Christian Democratic Union/Christian Social Union (CDU/CSU) of the Federal Republic, 92
Christian pacifism, 12–13, 33–36, 46–50, 76, 81–88, 101–107
Church and the Bomb, The, 47–50
Comiso, 123–124, 128, 130, 134, 138–139, 144, 146–147, 201, 208
Committee for Abolition of Nuclear Weapons Tests, 35

220

ABOUT THE EDITORS AND CONTRIBUTORS

James E. Dougherty is a Senior Staff Member of the Institute for Foreign Policy Analysis, and Professor of Politics at Saint Joseph's University. He is the author, co-author, or co-editor of more than a dozen books and nearly 50 articles on arms control and strategic affairs. His latest book is *The Bishops and Nuclear Weapons* (1984). Since 1981 he has been the United States member of the United Nations Advisory Board on Disarmament Studies.

Robert L. Pfaltzgraff, Jr., is President of the Institute for Foreign Policy Analysis, and the Shelby Cullom Davis Professor of International Security Studies at The Fletcher School of Law and Diplomacy, Tufts University. His recent publications include *National Security Policy: The Decision-Making Process* (1984), *International Security Dimensions of Space* (1983), and *The Atlantic Alliance and U.S. Global Strategy* (1983).

Clay Clemens received his M.A.L.D. from The Fletcher School of Law and Diplomacy, Tufts University, where he is writing his doctoral dissertation on the *Ostpolitik* of Chancellor Helmut Kohl's government. As a member of the research staff of the Institute for Foreign Policy Analysis, he co-authored a study on the policies of the Green party in West Germany and prepared the two chapters included in this volume.

Thomas M. Cynkin received his M.A.L.D. and Ph.D. degrees from The Fletcher School of Law and Diplomacy, Tufts University. As a member of the research staff of the Institute for Foreign Policy Analysis, he contributed to studies dealing with the U.S.-Soviet strategic-military-political relationship as well as the Atlantic Alliance, prior to joining the United States Foreign Service in 1984.

Jacquelyn K. Davis is Executive Vice-President and Senior Staff Member of the Institute for Foreign Policy Analysis. A specialist in U.S.-Soviet and NATO affairs, she has lectured widely in the United States and abroad. Dr. Davis is the author and co-author of numerous books and monographs, including *The Cruise Missile: Defense Bargain or Bargaining Chip?* (1977) and *The Atlantic Alliance and U.S. Global Strategy* (1983). She is currently co-editing a book on the future of the Atlantic Alliance.

James B. Foley received his M.A.L.D. from The Fletcher School of Law and Diplomacy, Tufts University. As a member of the research staff of the

Institute for Foreign Policy Analysis, he specialized in the philosophical background of the West European antinuclear movement in France. He is presently a member of the United States Foreign Service.

Diane K. Pfaltzgraff is Associate Professor of Political Science at the Philadelphia College of Textiles and Science. For more than a decade she has observed Italian political affairs, on which she has contributed articles, monographs, and a chapter to the Institute book, *Atlantic Community in Crisis* (Pergamon, 1979).